The Consultant

SUCCESS IN MEDICINE SERIES

The Consultant Interview

WRITTEN BY

Dr Sara Louise Watkin, MD MBChB FRCPCH
Medical Director, Medicology Ltd
Consultant Neonatologist, Elizabeth Garrett Anderson Wing,
University College London Hospitals NHS Foundation Trust

Mr Andrew Vincent, DipM MCIM
Chief Executive, Medicology Ltd

OXFORD
UNIVERSITY PRESS

OXFORD
UNIVERSITY PRESS

Great Clarendon Street, Oxford, OX2 6DP,
United Kingdom

Oxford University Press is a department of the University of Oxford.
It furthers the University's objective of excellence in research, scholarship,
and education by publishing worldwide. Oxford is a registered trade mark of
Oxford University Press in the UK and in certain other countries

© Oxford University Press 2012

The moral rights of the authors have been asserted

First Edition published in 2012

All rights reserved. No part of this publication may be reproduced, stored in
a retrieval system, or transmitted, in any form or by any means, without the
prior permission in writing of Oxford University Press, or as expressly permitted
by law, by licence or under terms agreed with the appropriate reprographics
rights organization. Enquiries concerning reproduction outside the scope of the
above should be sent to the Rights Department, Oxford University Press, at the
address above

You must not circulate this work in any other form
and you must impose this same condition on any acquirer

Published in the United States of America by Oxford University Press
198 Madison Avenue, New York, NY 10016, United States of America

British Library Cataloguing in Publication Data

Data available

Library of Congress Cataloging in Publication Data

Data available

ISBN 978-0-19-959480-1

Oxford University Press makes no representation, express or implied, that the
drug dosages in this book are correct. Readers must therefore always check
the product information and clinical procedures with the most up-to-date
published product information and data sheets provided by the manufacturers
and the most recent codes of conduct and safety regulations. The authors and
the publishers do not accept responsibility or legal liability for any errors in the
text or for the misuse or misapplication of material in this work. Except where
otherwise stated, drug dosages and recommendations are for the non-pregnant
adult who is not breast-feeding

This book is dedicated to our children, Kate and Oliver, who put up with holidays of mum and dad writing and hotly debating stuff that should never be debated on a family holiday!

Acknowledgements

There are always many to thank and it's difficult to know where to start. However, start we must and so we'd like to say a big thank you to the consultants who gave their time to help compile the section on speciality-specific insights and questions, including (in no particular order):

Dr Vikas Sodiwala
Consultant in Emergency Medicine, United Lincolnshire Hospitals NHS Trust

Dr Lucy Kean
Consultant Obstetrician, Nottingham University Hospitals NHS Trust

Dr Neelima Reddi
Consultant Psychiatrist, Surrey and Borders Partnership NHS Foundation Trust

Dr Muaaze Ahmad
Consultant Musculoskeletal Radiologist, Barts and the London NHS Trust

Dr Helga Becker
Consultant Anaesthetist, Dudley Group of Hospitals NHS Foundation Trust

Mr Hiro Tanaka
Consultant Orthopaedic Surgeon, Royal Gwent Hospital

Dr Deepti Radia
Consultant Haematologist, Guy's and St Thomas' NHS Foundation Trust

Dr Stuart Bloom
Consultant Gastroenterologist, University College London Hospitals NHS Foundation Trust

Thank you to our tireless au pairs, Lisa and Juliane, for going the extra mile (lots of miles!) in childcare, so that we could achieve our goal of completing this book, as well as to the many doctors attending our courses or coaching, for having helped in providing our extensive question lists, as well as some of the example answers used within.

Finally, a big thank you to the editorial team at Oxford University Press for unfaltering support and considerable patience.

Contents

	Introduction	xi
1	The strategic approach to getting the right job	1
2	Job applications	9
3	Pre-interview visit	37
4	Understanding you and your interviewers	53
5	Interview preparation	81
6	The interview	145
7	Interview candidates	169
8	Interview questions	175
9	Political and hot topics in the NHS	189
10	Specialty-specific interviews	197
11	Presentations in interviews	229
12	Psychometric testing in interviews	243
13	New ways of interviewing	251
14	If you do not get the job	259
15	Getting the job—what next?	265
	Index	277

Introduction

To most, gaining a consultant post represents the culmination of many years spent relentlessly developing through study and experience and is therefore perhaps one of the most significant or defining moments in your life. Despite increased mobility between jobs and employers, it remains true that the vast majority of consultants never move, remaining in post for 30+ years. Consequently, it stands to reason that getting the right post is extremely important, and you could say that this is a key purpose of this book.

If you look at an average service, new consultant posts arise rarely and are often hotly contested. The greater the prestige of the service, the higher the likely degree of competition. However, you gain certification at a specific time point and most newly certified doctors want to gain a consultant post as soon as they possibly can. This means that when the 'perfect' job arises, you want to make sure that you stand the best possible chance of gaining an offer because it may be many years before another post in the same service is advertised. We are now getting much closer to the true purpose of this book—your success, in the moment that you most desire it.

The consultant interview represents the gateway to the post you really want. It can feel like success or failure hangs in the balance, dependent upon a 30- to 60-minute snapshot in time during which you are required to demonstrate a lifetime's devotion to medicine. In truth, success is influenced long before you end up in a room full of inquisitive people, and as the book unfolds, you'll learn the strategies, tips and tricks necessary to excel at your consultant interview and gain that specific job that you have worked so hard to get.

Ideally you should be reading these pages some 6–12 months ahead of certification. However, if interviews are looming, the contents become even more vital and so we urge you to read quickly! There's a great deal to do to put you in the right condition to get that post and so let's get stuck into it right now.

Purpose of the interview

So what is the purpose of an interview? Perhaps it would be better to start with what an interview actually is. The generally accepted definition is that an interview:

> is a meeting between a prospective employer and a potential employee for each to ascertain whether or not they are suited to each other based on the attributes of the job, the skills required to conduct it and the attitudes necessary to fit in to that environment.

This is no simple exercise when one considers just how much an employer might want to 'check out' to ensure that someone is suitable for a post and would make a good team member. The greater the sense of positive feeling that an employer has, the greater the likelihood of them offering you the post, and from the candidate's perspective this is probably the key purpose of the interview—to engender the right type and degree of positive feelings so that the employer offers them the job. In truth, however, to leave this until the interview falls far short of the necessary preparation you need to undertake to get to 'yes' on the day.

When an employer seeks to appoint a consultant, they are acutely aware that they are appointing a highly expensive person with whom they will most likely be 'stuck with' if they make a mistake (it remains incredibly rare for healthcare organizations to seek to remove doctors for any reason other than safety or conduct). When one considers that the appointment is at a senior level, that the new appointee will start in post with exactly the same authority as their existing fellow consultants and that they have the ability either to deliver or undermine success for a service and a Trust, it is easy to see just how much importance is placed on the consultant interview on all sides.

This understanding is helpful in defining a strategy to ensure that you get called forward for interview and offered the exact job you want. When you understand the principles and apply the right process, you can bring to bear your energy and drive single-mindedly to the best effect.

The Pareto Principle applied to the consultant interview

Joseph M. Juran, the renowned management thinker (now sadly deceased), is widely accredited with describing the Pareto Principle, based on the findings of the Italian economist Vilfredo Pareto, who in 1906 noted that 80% of the land in Italy appeared to be owned by roughly 20% of the population and then went on to discover that 20% of the pea pods in his garden contained 80% of the peas. The observations are further strengthened by noting that the richest 20% of the world population control just over 80% of the world's income. The Principle has been widely accepted in many observations, including:

- 80% of sales tend to come from around 20% of the customers
- 20% of the bugs in software programmes tend to be responsible for 80% of system crashes
- 80% of healthcare is consumed by 20% of the population

But what does this mean to us? The Pareto Principle is used in business and many other environments to create a directed focus on activities that create the best possible return for the time expended (80% of the result comes from 20% of the things we do). With so much to do and so many things that we could do, it makes sense to devote our time to interview preparation based on the Pareto Principle, as a strategy for ensuring that we deploy ourselves productively and in a timely fashion. The key, of course, is knowing and understanding exactly which 20% of activities fall into the valuable category and which 80% produce comparatively little extra return for effort expended. It's not that you won't engage in them, but it would certainly be better to devote your attention to the 20% first. After all, you just never know when that perfect job will occur, or do you?

Channelling your energy intelligently

So, in the Pareto Principle we find the basis for intelligently channelling our energies into the sort of activity that can transform your journey towards a consultant post. This book is designed to give you that direction in large amounts, focusing your attention on areas of vital importance, including:

- The whole strategy of getting the right job
- The application process and your CV
- The pre-interview visit
- Understanding some basic psychology related to interviews
- How to influence successfully
- Being prepared for the sort of questions you may face
- Approaching presentations and exercises
- Converting the interview into a job offer

Ironically, although we are going to direct you to engage in the 20% or so of activity that can make all the difference between success or failure, we are quite used to the phenomenon that 80% of the applicants for a post will probably only have discovered 20% of those vital activities, giving you a substantial competitive advantage. Makes it sound like valuable reading, doesn't it?

How to use this book to maximum effect

If you have plenty of time and are looking at this at least 6–12 months before your certification, then we advocate starting at the beginning! However, if you are reading this just as you are completing your first application, thinking 'I wonder what I can do to enhance my success', then we stress the importance of starting with Chapter 2 on job applications, then moving on to the pre-interview visit in Chapter 3.

It's possible that you are reading this having already been short-listed, in which case we'd advise starting with Chapter 5 (Interview preparation) and reading swiftly, before moving on to Chapter 9 (Political and hot topics in the NHS) and Chapter 10 (Speciality-specific interviews). These latter chapters are where you will find more detailed information that will help you answer questions effectively at interview, and in a way that gives you the greatest chance of getting the job.

However late you have left it to buy this book, do not start with Chapter 8 (Interview questions). Just practising interview questions without a clear strategy for answering can be highly destructive to your chances of success. It's a bit like commencing surgery without having first studied anatomy. These things tend to have a certain protocol or chronology and the successful candidate fully appreciates this.

Chapter 4 looks at the very important aspect of personalities and psychology within the consultant interview. Many candidates fail at interview because they fail to appreciate how personality influences the choices interviewers make, regardless of the preparation you might have done. Finding the time to work through this chapter will provide immense benefit, not just for your interview but also as a consultant. If you have previously struggled at consultant interview, this chapter is a must and will most likely contain insight into significant contributing factors.

Do you suffer somewhat from nerves? If so, take the time to work through Chapter 6 early. If nerves are not especially a worry to you, still make sure you have read this chapter at least 48 hours before your interview, as part of your overall last-minute optimization process.

Today, some interviewees are asked to do presentations (Chapter 11) or psychometric testing (Chapter 12). If you are to do psychometric testing, you will be informed in advance, as it takes time to analyse the results. The same, however, cannot be said about presentations. We have known candidates turn up for interview not expecting to have to do a presentation, who have then been asked to do one there and then without much preparation. Better to be ready!

Chapter 13 looks at some of the new ways of interviewing and is useful reading for all candidates. Much interview questioning remains traditional and semantic in nature, but there is an increasing trend towards behaviour-based interviewing and this is covered comprehensively in this section.

Finally, we very much hope you get the job. If (when) you are successful, take time to read Chapter 15, so that you start out on your new journey in the best possible manner. It's also possible that you don't get the job first time out. In which case you need to dust yourself off and start again. With this in mind, we've preceded the chapter on success with one on how to deal with an unsuccessful outcome and utilize it to improve your fortunes next time out. You'll find this invaluable information in Chapter 14.

Our book will have been successful if you both enjoy reading it and get the job you really desire. We believe that both are perfectly possible and so, without further ado, we'd like to get started. Enjoy the journey!

Chapter 1
The strategic approach to getting the right job

Introduction

The majority of doctors will remain a consultant in the same post for 25–30 years. Despite this, many juniors wait until 3 months before their Certificate of Completed Training (CCT) date, and then apply for the first few jobs that come along, simply hoping for the best that they will get a job where they will fit in and be happy. In this chapter we consider simple strategies that will help you get the right job for you, rather than just any job.

In an ideal world this preparation should have started 2 years ago. However, if you are just picking this book up for the first time, having already started applying for jobs, even at this stage there is still lots of advice that can reduce the chances of you making a wrong decision that might affect you and your family for many years.

USEFUL TIP: Start preparing for your consultant post at least 2 years in advance.

The last 2 years as a Specialty Registrar (StR)

A consultant job marks the accumulation of many years of hard work. It also defines our life both in and outside work for the next 30 years. Consequently, it is important to get the right one. Preparation for getting this post ideally needs to occur at least 2 years before the first interview by careful review of your CV with the help of your educational supervisor, focusing on clinical and non-clinical experience, audit, research, teaching and training, involvement in leadership and management to ensure that you will have the correct skills and attributes at the right time. Looking at specific or example job descriptions, and particularly the essential and desirable short-listing criteria, by going to the National Health Service (NHS) Jobs website (www.jobs.nhs.uk) (Box 1.1) will provide clearer guidance on what will be needed both within your speciality and within the type of institution you would like to work.

Box 1.1 NHS Jobs website (www.jobs.nhs.uk)

- The majority of NHS consultant posts are advertised on this website
- Gives instant access to
  - Consultant job descriptions
  - Essential and desirable criteria for appointment
- Register with the site as early as possible. This will allow you to look at
  - The consultant posts being advertised in your field
  - Review job descriptions and essential and desirable criteria
  - Plan your pre-consultant training and experiences to maximize your potential to be short-listed in the future

Box 1.2 asks a series of questions which you might want to consider when reviewing your progress towards developing the right experience to get the type of consultant job you would really like. Not all questions will be relevant to everyone. It is very important to recognize that, although courses and training are important, more and more the successful candidate will be the person who is able to show what he/she has done as a result of that training. For example, very soon all trainees will have done a leadership course and this will no longer act as any type of discriminator. The people who will be screened in at short-listing will be those who have used that learning to lead a project or team. Box 1.3 is an example of the essential and desirable criteria for a consultant post.

Box 1.2 Developing the right experience

- Clinical experiences
  - Is there a specific special interest I wish/should develop?
    - Time out of programme
    - Experience abroad
  - Is there specific training I must have attended, e.g. Advanced Life Support Courses?
- Leadership and management
  - Do I need to attend a training course?
  - What have I done as a result of the training?
    - Led a clinical improvement/service redevelopment project
    - Attended directorate meetings
    - Represented my colleagues
- Audit
  - Have I done an audit which follows the audit cycle?
  - Have I lead an audit project?
- Other aspects of clinical governance
  - What exposure have I had to the following?
    - Risk management
    - Patient and public involvement
    - Evidence-based guideline development
    - Bench marking
- Teaching and Training
  - What experience have I had?
  - What feedback have I had?
  - Have I developed any innovative teaching methods?
  - Have I been on a 'train the trainer' course?
- Research
  - Have I done any original research?
  - Could I publish a case review?
  - Could I be the local lead for a multicentre trial?

Box 1.3 Example of essential and desirable criteria Consultant Rheumatologist

Requirements	Essential	Desirable
Qualifications	MB BS (or equivalent) Registered with GMC MRCP or equivalent On GMC Specialist Register for Rheumatology (or within 6 months of CCT date) Broad experience of rheumatological medicine	Distinctions, scholarships, prizes Other degrees, e.g. BSc, MSc, MD, PhD A sub-specialist interest complementary to those of the current consultant staff
Audit	Understand the principles of audit	Evidence of participation in audit projects
Research	Understand the general principles, scientific method and interpretation of literature	Evidence of personal research projects and their presentation Publications in peer-reviewed journals
Motivation	Punctuality, reliability, enthusiasm Initiative Common sense	
Personal skills	Evidence of leadership Organizational ability Able to take responsibility and cope with stressful situations Able to get on with other members of the multidisciplinary team Credibility and integrity A sympathetic approach to patients and relatives Ability to establish good professional relationships with others	Critical and enquiring approach to knowledge acquisition To have undertaken a postgraduate communication skills course An understanding of corporacy in the NHS
Management	Evidence of organizational ability	Attended an NHS Management Course appropriate to consultant duties

Other requirements	Clear, concise and well-presented CV An interest in teaching and education Clearly formulated career goals Physically and mentally fit, with satisfactory occupational health clearance Basic IT skills for the use of email and Microsoft Office	Experience in the training or development of trainees in medicine Outside interests Intermediate or advanced IT skills

If you are very fixed on the areas you would like or are able to work, it is advisable to contact the lead clinician and find out when future posts are likely to become available. Let them know when your CCT date is and that you would really like to come and work with them. This can make all the difference to the timing of any job advert as they are far more likely to advertise a post when they know they will have high-calibre candidates in a position to apply for them.

Whereas you are probably worried about finding a suitable post, i.e. the risk of not having a decent job, potential services are just as worried that when they go to advert they will not have any 'suitable' candidates. It is always worth remembering that you can always move, however disruptive that is, whereas your employer is essentially 'stuck' with whomever they appoint. Consequently, a well-timed job advert, designed to attract someone they already have confidence in, reduces their risk considerably.

Choosing the right job

Besides the type of job that you would like, it is also important to consider the sort of area you want to live in. If you dream of a life of coastal sailing on sunny summer evenings but apply for the first job that comes along, based in a large city in central England, it may mean spending the next 30 years less than happy with your life outside medicine. Alternatively if city life is for you then applying for a rural District General Hospital (DGH) post may not give you the excitement and overall work—life satisfaction or work—life balance that will keep you happy. If you are married, this is something that you cannot decide alone and it needs careful discussion with your partner about what is important for each of you and your family in all areas of your life, e.g. recreation, job, children's education and finance (e.g. ability to do private practice, likelihood of partner finding a suitable job).

Spend time thinking about how you want to spend the next 30 years of your life—both in and out of work. What are your future goals for your life? If you have a partner, discuss this together. Use Box 1.4 and the Wheel of Life (Figure 1.1) to help you. You need to consider what your preferences are both now and going forward for the next 30 years potentially.

Box 1.4 Choosing the right job

- What type of job appeals to you?
  - Academic teaching hospital vs district general hospital
  - Ability to develop a specialism vs being a generalist
  - Ability to develop a thriving private practice
  - Potential to acquire clinical excellence points
  - What type of work environment do I want (dynamic vs steady, for instance)?
  - Am I primarily interested in clinical work or wider health service leadership?
  - Do I want to be in the NHS (the traditional NHS) or a new provider type?
  - Do I prefer a smaller, close-knit team or a much bigger department?
- What type of lifestyle appeals to you?
  - London vs cultural city vs city vs small town vs easy access to countryside
  - What hobbies do I like or wish to develop?
  - What do we like doing as a family?
  - How do I see my life outside work?
  - What type of home do I ideally see myself having?

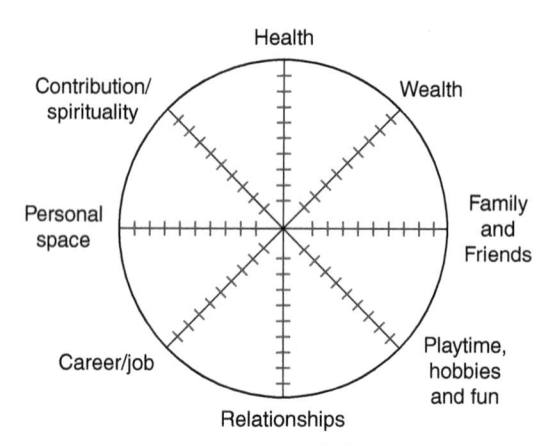

Figure 1.1 Wheel of Life.

How to use the Wheel of Life (Figure 1.1)

The Wheel of Life comes in many variations and has its roots in Buddhist philosophy. It is a well-recognized tool used in life coaching for helping individuals form a game plan for life that is well matched to their life aspirations and areas of key importance. For each area, e.g. health, score yourself out of 10 as to how **satisfied** you are with this area of your life. Please note: you could be 21 stone, spend all day sat on a sofa eating chips and score 10/10 for health if you are fully satisfied. Conversely you could be 8 stone, spend 4 hours a day exercising and still only score 4/10 for health. Only you know how satisfied you are. Put a point on the line where you are. Note 0 is the centre and 10 the outside of the circle. Join the dots together.

How smooth is your wheel? You are very much your vehicle for life. Imagine driving your vehicle with the shape of wheel that you have just drawn. Is your journey going to be smooth or bumpy?

You can use the wheel in several ways:

- To assess where you are now and whether this is what you want
- To start having a meaningful debate with yourself and your partner if applicable about what is important in life going forward, e.g. which areas need enhancement
- When you are looking at a specific job, to assess its likely impact on your wheel and whether this is an improvement or degradation from both the present and your ideal picture
- To periodically reassess your life goals, to ensure that your game plan and career plans remain aligned as your life evolves

Preparing to get the right job even before it is advertised

Most people don't start preparing for an interview until the job has been advertised. This is too late if you really want to have maximum chance of getting just the job you want.

Consider Bob. Bob has a sensible strategy for ending up in the job that he wants and he started his preparation a 'very' long time before the job was advertised:

- He thought very carefully about what his ideal job looked like and what lifestyle he wanted to attain
- He narrowed his selection down to a series of towns and services that fitted the bill—his 'hot list'
- He approached those services proactively
    - He made it clear that this is where he would like to work (employers are always keen to find people who definitely want to work there)
    - He asked them about when jobs might be coming up
    - He learned what they were ideally looking for

- He determined what clinical experiences were most important to them
- He asked about their research interests
- He then developed a plan to ensure he matched up to their wish list, including ensuring he created substantial evidence of achieving in their important areas
- He entered each rotation or job with a clear picture of what he wanted to get out of it, how it matched to his ideal job and set himself clear developmental goals
- He made sure he had ample opportunities to interact with them, e.g. by attending the same meetings, and offering to come and do teaching sessions in areas of interest
- He actively pursued publications in subject areas important to them
- He developed rapport and a productive relationship over time

By the time the job was advertised, he was the natural choice. His CV highlighted all of the important factors pertinent to this specific role. You are up against Bob—be prepared!

Chapter 2
Job applications

Introduction

This chapter deals with the application process. By the end, you should have a thorough understanding of:

- The regulations that apply
- How to apply
- Critical considerations when applying
- How to improve your chances of being short-listed
- Key pitfalls to avoid

All appointments to the role of consultant are governed by specific regulations at both a health service level and an employment law level. All potential employers must adhere to the rules and regulations existing under British law that relate to equality, diversity and discrimination. Additionally, NHS Trusts, Primary Care Trusts (PCTs) and other healthcare bodies employing clinical staff need to adhere to certain regulations that are healthcare specific, e.g. advertising widely and having a Royal College Representative on the interview panel. However, although many still comply with the spirit of the regulations, Foundation Trusts are not required to follow the same rules and this is increasingly apparent as the number of Trusts holding Foundation status increases. Often, their divergence includes dispensing with the Royal College Representative, atypical patterns of advertising and even not specifying a particular CCT. This is a trend that we believe will only increase as Trusts grapple with workforce redesign as a solution to increasing austerity.

As the chapter unfolds, we will endeavour to raise critical considerations that need addressing regardless of whether it is a Foundation or non-Foundation Trust you are applying to. However, regardless of whether a Trust is currently Foundation or non-Foundation, it is likely that all Trusts will become Foundation Trusts over the next few years.

Wherever feasible, we will include specific pointers on how to improve your application's chances of success, i.e. getting you short-listed for the job you really want.

When can you apply?

It is a legal requirement to be on the GMC Specialist Register before taking up a consultant appointment. However, you are eligible to apply for a consultant post when the interview date is within 6 months of the expected date of your CCT (or recognized equivalent if outside the UK).

An Advisory Appointments Committee (AAC) may also short-list a candidate if they think it is likely that he/she will meet the eligibility criteria for admission to the GMC Specialist Register, e.g. if a candidate is applying from outside the UK or is applying for a Certificate of Eligibility for the Specialist Register through the GMC (previously article 14 PMETB).

It is worth considering for a moment what it might feel like if you were one of a group of consultants going to advert for a new consultant colleague and finding either no one or no one of sufficiently high calibre applied. How would you feel? Do not underestimate what this would mean to a group of consultants. Would they behave differently if they knew you would be in a position to apply for their post in 3 months time, had the right experience and special interests and, perhaps more importantly, actively wanted to work there?

There is no doubt the answer would be 'yes'. Consequently, do not be afraid of developing contacts and networks whilst a job is still perhaps simply a future intention for the service involved. If you want to work in a specific area, then proactively approach the Clinical Service Lead a year or so before your CCT to discuss what opportunities might be available and what special interests they might wish to attract. You can then spend your final year actively pursuing the experiences and specialist interests that you now know will:

- Cause that service to wait until you are in a position to apply before advertising the post
- Make it almost impossible not to short-list you and indeed appoint you, assuming you perform well on the day (see later)

Applying for the right job for you

As discussed in Chapter 1, not all jobs are the right job at an individual level. From around 6 months before you are in a position to apply for posts in earnest, it can be extremely useful to regularly review and evaluate job adverts, job descriptions and person specifications. This will help you in two distinct ways:

- By ensuring you have clarity about which types of job will be most suited to you
- In learning how to evaluate jobs effectively by reading beyond the person specification so that you become skilled at picking out the areas of key importance for the prospective employer

As you start to recognize areas of key importance, which will be different from Trust to Trust, consider how you would modify your application form appropriately to truly sell yourself. It is particularly important to do this for the jobs that are most attractive to you. A generic, one size fits all approach to applications is unlikely to stand you out from the crowd.

How are jobs advertised?

With minor exceptions (e.g. a consultant transferring from a university to an NHS post in which the duties are substantially the same), all substantive consultant posts must be advertised. Jobs are usually advertised in one of two places:

- *British Medical Journal* (BMJ) and its website (www.careers.bmj.com/careers)
- NHS Jobs website (www.jobs.nhs.uk)

Some Trusts will also (either additionally or only) advertise jobs on their own website

The secret to successful applications is discovering the job early, therefore allowing you maximum opportunity to get your application right. Because there is no consistency in the way jobs are advertised it is essential to register with both BMJ Careers and NHS Jobs and to set up email notifications of appropriate job adverts. The key to this is setting up suitable criteria and reminders so that you are notified as soon as appropriate posts are advertised. These reminders come as a simple email with a link to the specific post. To access the online BMJ reminders you will need to be a member of the British Medical Association (BMA).

> **USEFUL TIP**: It is worth experimenting well before you can apply for a consultant post to ensure the search criteria you have chosen are locating the jobs that are relevant to you.

Many jobs are advertised earlier and therefore for longer on NHS Jobs. It is vitally important to apply for these jobs as early as possible in case they become oversubscribed, as some of these adverts will carry the option of closing to further applicants before the formal closing date. This is most often seen in adverts for locum consultants.

It is also worth noting that some employers place adverts in the BMJ that are extremely small, sometimes just two to three lines with essentially a web address. This is usually an attempt by the employing organization to save on advertising costs, but means that these adverts can be very easy to miss. Sometimes the strategy is utilized to weed out less-motivated candidates, who may not be prepared to hunt down the full advert online.

Locum job adverts

Locum jobs are often advertised differently from substantive posts. Firstly, there isn't a specific advertising requirement and many are filled without an advert ever appearing. If they are advertised, it tends to be on NHS Jobs and not always in the BMJ. Locum posts are often a route to a substantive post later on and so it is vital that you consider how best to learn about these posts, especially in centres you would be happy to have a substantive post.

Another unique aspect of locum positions is that they often close earlier than their stated deadline. Many will contain the provision for closing early if sufficient applications are received or even simply at the Trust's discretion. Whereas many people wait until close to the deadline when applying for substantive posts it is actually very important to get locum applications in as early as possible. That means being extra vigilant and having your application ready to go as soon as a post appears.

Typical sources of locum posts are:

- NHS Jobs
- Trust's own website

- Word of mouth
- Learned society newsletters

Working less than full time

Although a post may be advertised as whole time, legally it must also be open to part time applicants and to job sharers. However, this is a rather simplistic view and it is worth considering the reality. There is no doubt that some employers and departments are much more open to flexible working than others and some jobs are much more open to part-time working, annualized hours and job-sharing. If you do want to work in these ways, take time to consider the job description and job plan. Could this be easily adaptable to part-time working? What are the main criteria for developing this post? Is it to cover out-of-hours work? If so, could you predominantly do this? Is it to develop a new area of expertise? If yes, how could you persuade the Trust you could do this whilst working in a flexible way?

CVs and application forms

What is the purpose of a CV/application form?

To answer this question fully we need to consider it from both the employer's and the applicant's perspective.

Employer's perspective

From an employer's perspective the purpose is to collect relatively standardized information that allows them to compare candidates with the aim of reducing the potentially larger number of applicants to a manageable, pertinent few, as well as identifying characteristics of individuals that they feel constitute an ideal profile for the job they have in mind.

Applicant's perspective

For you, the applicant, the main purpose of your CV or application form is to get you short-listed. This is often your first opportunity to sell yourself (unless you have been strategically positioning yourself for this post) to your future employer so that they want to look at you further. To do this you need to tailor your application to the specific post by carefully considering the job advert, job description and essential and desirable criteria (see below). The Royal College or Specialty Representative will want reassurance that you have the appropriate training and the shortlisting panel will want to know that not only do you meet the essential and desirable criteria for the post but also that you will deliver for them across all of their expectations for the post. To fully understand what the employer's expectations are for the post, carefully study the job advert and job description, highlighting all of the key areas they describe or in which they discuss what they expect from their preferred candidate.

What happens after you submit your application/CV

Most employers are keen to short-list as quickly as possible following the closing date, to prevent losing the best candidates to another employer. Short-listing is usually done by the interview panel, including the Royal College or Specialty Representative, with each person individually ranking the candidates in order of preference. These rankings are collated by Medical Staffing and the top candidates invited to interview. Where there is only one consultant representing the department at the interview, it is common practice to give the other consultants in the service the opportunity to comment on the CVs. However, ultimately it will be the consultant representing the department that submits a single preference list, in the same way as other members of the panel.

CV strategy

Getting your CV right is an important component in your strategy of getting the perfect job. Consequently, it is important that it has a strategy of its own. Let's start by looking at some of the basic principles:

- The CV must be honest
- People look for gaps, so don't leave any without a sensible explanation
- However objective we are supposed to be, we are influenced by presentation, so make it look good (but not flashy)
- Ensure that any formatting is consistently applied throughout
- Ensure that your CV is logical and easy to follow

Difficult to follow CVs get screened out because when you are short-listing from a hundred applicants, struggling on just one seems awfully hard work.

> **USEFUL TIP**: Ask younger consultant colleagues and friends who are unlikely to be applying for the same post if you can look at their CVs and application forms. This will quickly give you a feel of what looks good (and possibly what doesn't).

In the interview itself it is likely that only the Royal College Representative will refer to your CV as it is their role to ensure you have the right training and experience for the role. If there are any omissions, wrong dates or concerns around you obtaining your CCT, these are likely to be spotted by the Royal College Representative and you can expect some tough questions. If there are specific issues around this, or complicated circumstances that are difficult to understand, then remember to have carefully thought about how you might answer those questions to reduce any further concerns.

> **USEFUL TIP**: Humans naturally tune in or tune out information (known as 'deletion'). If we are looking for a candidate who is going to take on teaching commitments, we are naturally seeking those references throughout the CV, but we may not notice something really interesting that isn't on our horizon. This small piece of behavioural insight is immensely useful. By carefully considering what a Trust or service is looking for, we can cluster that information and put it in a noticeable place.
>
> In our example of a role with a significant teaching commitment, imagine holding two CVs in front of you, one with a distinct section on 'Teaching Experience' and the other with the same degree of teaching experience but listed under each job it pertains to. Which one stands out for the teaching job? The one where it is easy to spot the teaching and the teaching has prominence.

This reinforces the most important aspects of strategy:

- Build/adapt your CV or application for each job, so that you can better present it
- Closely examine and analyse what the most important aspects of the job are, so that you can ensure these have appropriate prominence

After sifting through a hundred CVs and successively getting the list down and down, a CV that has prominent points very relevant to the job, presented in a way that makes them memorable, is more likely to go onto the 'definite' pile. It is worth noting that humans are more likely to remember:

- First items in a list
- Last items in a list
- Outstanding items
- Relevant items not hidden
- Stories

This can help you devise a CV strategy that markedly increases its chances of being noticed, liked and remembered.

Selling yourself

For many doctors the idea of 'selling' themselves or speaking highly of their own achievements is alien. However, even with the group 'doctors' there are huge variations in this and some cultures and personalities naturally emphasize their achievements and others are more reserved about them. When we use the term 'selling' in the context of the consultant application and interview, we really mean being positive about your abilities and achievements and persuading others of the benefit this brings to them. If you are naturally a relatively hesitant person then it is worth considering whether you have brought out or emphasized your best attributes enough.

> **USEFUL TIP**: When we use the term 'selling' in the context of the consultant application and interview we mean being positive about your abilities and achievements and persuading others of the benefit this brings.
>
> **REMEMBER**: Selling is like perfume; a little used wisely is attractive and enhancing. Drown yourself in it and it is a turn off.

It is important to recognize that people don't buy products, they buy benefits. For example, when you buy a new car you look at the benefits that car will bring you and the manner in which it delivers them, e.g. it gets you from A to B . . . fast! We need to look at this in the same way when we are writing our applications to ensure we get short-listed. Some doctors promote themselves by listing only brief facts on their CV, e.g. courses attended or titles of audits done, and hope that the short-listing team will infer the benefits this brings. This is a risky assumption to make, especially if there are a lot of applicants. Equally, a list of simple facts doesn't tell the interview panel much about you or whether you will fit in, just that you have the right experience. With highly structured training there is an increasing danger that candidates start to look very similar to each other because they have been on similar rotations, gained similar experiences and attended similar courses.

> **USEFUL TIP**: Imagine reading through two CVs in application for a job with a significant audit responsibility. CV1 says 'I conducted a substantial audit of neonatal admission temperatures', but CV2 says 'I conducted a substantial audit on neonatal admission temperatures that lead to a reform of the early care policy and a 1.2 degree increase in average admission temperatures'. CV2 would be more likely to get you short-listed because it shows context, purposefulness and application.
>
> At the macro level of special interests, this could mean that if you are a paediatrician with a special interest in respiratory disease and the department wants a colleague with a special interest in child protection and gastroenterology, you would need to draw out your experiences in these latter areas and place those references in places that are easier to pick up on.
>
> **REMEMBER**: We only buy those benefits we want.

So, how do we know which benefits a Trust wants? It is vital that we review all aspects of the documentation available to us to diagnose what seems to be the thrust or theme running through or any specific requirements that have been given prominence. When deciding what are the important aspects to bring out in your application form or CV, take time to consider the wording of:

- The job advert
  - This will often give you a feel of the organization's or service's culture

- You can use this information to highlight personal information that is consistent with this culture*
- The job description
  - What type of person do they want?
  - What are the key skills, qualities and areas of interest emphasized about the post?
  - What are the areas of interest of the department and do they appear to be wanting to augment these or introduce variety?
- The essential and desirable criteria
  - See below

*A word of caution—sometimes a Trust may want to introduce someone who is different to the predominant culture to create balance and new perspectives. This emphasizes the importance of doing your homework thoroughly, and not only from the written information.

Ultimately, a great CV or application is consistent and has a theme running through it that is a good match to the themes in the job description and advert. If the panel 'feels' that this application is close to the 'sort' of person they had in mind, this increases your chance of being short-listed. By being clear about what you bring in terms of benefits, they can see they are short-listing the right type of person who delivers the right sort of benefits. Consequently, when describing the benefits you bring, however uncomfortable it may feel, you need to be explicit, i.e. the benefit must be spelt out so that everyone 'gets it'. Examples of the benefit statement on the end of a factual statement of experience might look like:

> '…which means that I can directly help develop service strategy aligned with the evolving healthcare economy', or
> '…which means that I am equally appreciative of both clinical and business imperatives, ensuring that I work collaboratively and constructively with management'.

Let's look at one more example of taking a common set of factual statements and turning them into benefits. Many people list the courses they have attended to demonstrate that they are committed to developing the right skills. However, rather than just listing them, think about how you have already used the learning from the course and how this employer could benefit. For example:

Core Skills in Patient Experience Excellence, London, June 2010

I learned how patient experience is linked to service finance, allowing me to adapt my handling of patients, to encourage the right behaviours across the team and to increase our chances of receiving full CQUIN (Commissioning Quality and Innovation) reimbursement.

Further examples of how not to and how to sell yourself are shown in Box 2.1.

Box 2.1 Examples of 'how not to' and 'how to' sell yourself

Gaps in training

Poor

I hated the Foundation years so took 2 years out to back pack around the world.

Good

At the end of my Foundation training I took the opportunity to extend my knowledge of both the world and medicine by travelling extensively. I did locum work in A & E in South Africa, New Zealand and Australia. My experiences in South Africa were fundamental in shaping my interest and future training in Trauma and Orthopaedics.

Teaching

Poor

I have taught medical students, junior doctors and nurses.

Good

I have experience of teaching the whole multidisciplinary team including medical students, junior doctors, nursing and ancillary staff. I have attended both Train-the-Trainer and Advance Life Support Generic Instructor courses. As a result of these, I use a wide variety of styles in my teaching, which is frequently rated amongst the highest by the medical students undertaking their emergency medicine attachment.

Audit

Poor

- Audit of compliance with blood transfusion guidelines
- Audit of case notes

Good

I have undertaken a number of audits aimed directly at improving patient care:

- **The use of naloxone in newborn infants**
  This audit was presented at the regional audit meeting and published by x as an example of good audit practice.
- **Management of infants with rhesus haemolytic disease of the newborn**
  I have led a multidisciplinary audit into the management of infants with rhesus disease at risk of exchange transfusion. This audit highlighted areas

for improvement in communication between obstetricians, neonatologists and the blood bank. As a result I:
- Developed and delivered a series of teaching sessions on the management of haemolytic disease of the newborn
- Designed a proforma for improving communication, which has been successfully piloted

I am presently undertaking a re-audit to quantify the actual impact of these interventions.

When facts can read larger than prose

Having made the case not to rely purely on facts to give the right impression, sometimes facts can speak larger than embellishment of the prose. For example, 'I have done over 100 operations for x with a complication rate of <3% (national average 5%)' allows others to draw their own conclusions as to whether you are an expert or not and is more effective than 'I have had extensive experience in operation x', as one person's view of what constitutes 'extensive experience' may not be the same as another's.

When presenting important facts, such as our previous statement 'I have done over 100 operations for x with a complication rate of <3% (national average 5%)', think about how you will ensure it stands out. In any one section of your application, people are more likely to read the beginning rather than the end, so ensure the compelling facts are near the beginning. If the facts are particularly compelling or impressive, you could consider highlighting them still further. In addition to putting the statement up front, consider putting it as a separate line with a bullet point to help it stand out. It may even be helpful to put the statement in bold. However, you do also need to consider who the recipients of your application will be (see Chapter 4), as this works well for some and turns off others. Be careful of not over-using bold as a way of promoting yourself, as it can cause irritation in others or come across as arrogant.

An example of emphasis of key facts could be:

> Surgical Experience
> **I have done over 100 operations for x with a complication rate of <3% (national average 5%)**
> Detail, detail, detail. . . .'

Writing and structuring your CV or application form

A CV or application form is not something you can put together over a few hours, and indeed to be truly successful it may need several weeks of careful preparation. Nowadays many jobs, even at consultant level, only allow for the submission of an online application form, usually via the NHS Jobs website (www.jobs.nhs.uk) or occasionally through the Trust's own website. These forms are not conducive to selling yourself and the NHS Jobs application form in particular has strict word or character restrictions for each section and is almost devoid of formatting.

To overcome these limitations needs practice and careful attention to detail. For instance, use a refinement process to get a short section perfect:

- Write out everything you would ideally want to include, as though it was going into an unrestricted CV
- Put everything into priority order—most important first
- Check your word count
- Systematically work through each statement to 'tighten' the English
- Recheck your word count
- If it still doesn't fit, you might have to take the bottom, least important points out
- Hold these for possible inclusion in an 'Additional Information' section

With this in mind it is important to start completing the static data in the standard consultant NHS Jobs application form at the same time as you start developing your CV (see below for more details). It is a good idea to do this in a Microsoft Word document so that you can cut and paste into the actual application.

> **USEFUL TIP**: Formatting in Word can be lost on pasting into the NHS Jobs application form. You will save yourself a *huge* amount of time if you get used to writing in Word without applying formatting.
>
> **REALLY USEFUL TIP**: Depending on how you have Word 2007 set up, it tends to apply a space after a paragraph, removing the requirement to do a double return. However, when pasting into the application form this spacing is lost, resulting in the paragraphs running together and creating a significantly larger reformatting task. Get used to putting the double return in, even if it looks a bit weird in Word.

Professionally prepared or home grown?

There is no such thing as an ideal CV or application form, only an ideal one for that particular job. Whereas having your CV professionally written can be helpful, often improving the prose value and creating a good focus, there is no substitute for a well-tailored CV written specifically for each job you apply for. Even if your CV is fully prepared already, prior to submitting it you should always double check that:

- You have put the correct name of any hospital you are applying to (it is difficult to sell how much you want to work somewhere when you get their name wrong)
- You have their name convention correct, e.g. including 'Foundation Trust', for instance
- You do not refer to previous applications, e.g. by describing the wrong post or skills needed

- You have definitively and competently demonstrated within your CV that you fit the job description and have all the essential and as many of the desirable criteria as possible
- You have checked each section for spelling and punctuation
- Someone with good English skills has read it through
- You have begun and ended each section with the most important points

Some people will favour a commercial company for CV writing, but remember, they do not know you, will not write in the way you do and therefore will not portray your personality. An alternative to getting a professional to write it is to write the CV yourself and then ask a number of people for comment: a colleague who may recognize other things you should include, someone good at English and punctuation, and finally one or more consultants. Do listen to their advice but ultimately go for what is right for you. It is only you that has to live with the results!

With the increased use of application forms for junior doctor posts we are finding that many prospective consultants will never have written a CV. If submitting a CV is part of the application process, it might be worth asking to see copies of other people's to get a clear idea of how to approach it. Unlike in the commercial world, where a CV is rarely longer than two pages, a consultant CV may be as long as 16–18 pages. Consequently, before starting, decide on a clear structure for your CV (a guide is shown in Box 2.2) and collect together all the information or ideas you have, dropping the information into distinct sections. You also need to decide on a format for your CV (see Box 2.3), including use of formatting, bullets, colours and text size. In 18 pages of text, it is also vital that the short-listing panel can readily find things. This is important on the day too, where they might want to refer to items. If the interview slows down because people are hunting for information, the panel may not ask sufficient questions to get to the bottom of your expertise and could even experience 'frustration'—not something you want to be remembered for. With a clear heading structure, properly applied and inclusion of page numbers you will be able to provide an index or table of contents.

Box 2.2 CV structure

- Title page
- Table of contents
- Personal statement
- Personal details
  - Name
  - Contact details including phone and email
  - Date of birth (DOB) and marital status—not required but if you have nothing to hide and are proud of who you are then why hide it?

- GMC registration
- Medical Defence Organisation details
- Society memberships
- Qualifications
  - Do not list pre-university qualifications
  - Name of degree, date and university
    - If you attained any honours or distinctions, list them
  - Include any postgraduate degrees and examinations
  - If there are several parts to your postgrad exam do not list all parts—only date of final completion
  - Date of CCT
    - If this is in the future, clearly state when you will obtain this
  - Consider placing Advanced Life Support qualifications here, especially if they are an essential criteria for the post you are applying for
- Prizes and scholarships
  - Academic prizes
    - Do not list things you got at school
- Present job
  - Consider including subheadings in this section
- Previous jobs
  - List in reverse order i.e. most recent job first
  - Job title
  - Organization
  - Key consultant colleague
  - Dates (triple check—any discrepancies/gaps will be spotted by the Royal College Representative and you will be questioned on these—it also demonstrates a lack of attention to detail)
  - If you have gaps, explain them honestly
  - Do not describe every individual job in detail—pick the highlights and any special achievements
- General clinical skills, achievements and outcomes, e.g. in paediatrics
- Specialist clinical skills, achievements and outcomes, e.g. in paediatric cardiology
- Leadership and management
  - Training undertaken
  - Experience gained

Have you led a project, did you ever introduce a change within a service, did you represent your junior colleagues, have you attended any directorate or other management meetings, did you ever run the rota, a teaching programme, etc. How did you lead and manage, and what feedback did you get?

- Teaching and training experience
  - Undergraduate
  - Postgraduate
  - Multidisciplinary teaching and training

What have you done and what formats of teaching have you undertaken? Do you have feedback? Do you enjoy it?

- Research (if you have done a specific research project, describe it briefly)
  - Your hypothesis
  - What you did
  - What you found
  - Where have you presented and published data

If you have not done an individual project, have you assisted, have you been part of a multicentre trial, what did you do, what did you learn, how might it be relevant to the job you are applying for, what does it give you?

- Publications and presentations
  - Books
  - Chapters
  - Peer-reviewed articles
  - Non-peer-reviewed articles
  - Presentations

In all of the above it is useful to highlight your name in bold.

- Audit and clinical governance

You may have done a number of audits. Only include those done properly with clear standards which follow the audit cycle. Be absolutely sure you know the outcomes, the actions taken and the results of the audit. Summarize the key findings and outcomes in no more than three lines.

Have you been involved in other aspects of clinical governance, e.g. risk management or patient and public involvement?

- Recent training course (applicable to the job you are applying for, with two sentences summarizing what you have learnt)
- Interests and hobbies
- Referees
  - At least one from your most recent job
  - Include contact details

Make sure you have asked your referees.

> **Box 2.3 Getting the best from Microsoft Word**
>
> Word is very powerful at creating attractive, easy to navigate documents, but to make best use of it you need to plan thoroughly from the outset. Ensure that you have a robust title/heading structure (found in the 'style' drop-down menu):
>
> - Heading 1 (e.g. Arial, 18 point font size, coloured, bold): use for main sections like 'Personal Information' and 'Educational History'
> - Heading 2 (e.g. Arial, 14 point font size, bold): use for sections within the main sections, e.g. under 'Educational History' you might have 'Qualifications', 'Clinical Courses Attended' and 'Management Courses Attended'
> - Body: Arial, 12 point font size
>
> If you have suitably planned and then been disciplined with your use of headings you can now insert a table of contents at the beginning, making navigation very easy for the reader. This instruction can usually be found as follows:
>
> - Insert
> - References
> - Table of Contents
>
> (found under the references tab in Office 2007)
>
> You can format your table of contents so it looks good, is well spaced and matches the rest of your document. Once inserted, you can update it by right clicking on it and updating either just the page numbers (if you haven't altered the heading titles) or the whole table of contents.
>
> **USEFUL TIP**: Alter the table of contents default to your preferred style. This will ensure that when you update the whole table you don't lose your nice formatting.

Does it look good?

Your CV is a sales document and humans are essentially emotionally driven creatures. We might short-list based on a 'feeling' that we can't quite put our finger on. The critical emotion to appeal to is confidence. We say yes, buy things and *short-list* when we have confidence in what we are seeing. The seeing element is also important because 60% of the population process information as pictures out of preference. A good picture to a visual person carries considerable weight but a poor one detracts. This is no different from you visiting a website to buy something. You are more likely to buy when the website is professionally designed than when it looks like a bad amateur has constructed it, again because you have a greater sense of confidence in the company behind the site when the site is a good shop window.

> **USEFUL TIP**: If layout, structure, headings, etc. are beyond your comfort zone or competency in Word, then a good compromise could be to prepare the content as you would like it to run and then ask a graphic designer to do the formatting. There are lots of designers who do ad hoc work, and as far as they are concerned a CV is just a brochure about a person.
>
> If you want to develop a CV that stands out from the crowd, the information in the following section will also help you achieve this without spending hundreds of pounds on a professional CV writer.

Job description, and essential and desirable criteria

(See Box 1.3.)

Your success at application stage will be heavily influenced by how closely you appear to match the job description, as well as the essential and desirable criteria. It is vital that you consider these carefully before committing pen to paper (or fingers to keyboard), as success at short-listing is often a direct result of the quality of your assessment of these factors and your ability to demonstrate a convincing match of your experience to what they are looking for.

The golden rules for increasing your chances of selection, reinforcing what we have built so far, are:

- Personalize each application to the specific attributes of the job you are applying for (don't just cut and paste from previous ones without editing)
- Demonstrate an absolute match to the essential criteria, using examples of actual experience or training where possible to 'prove' it
- Demonstrate a close match to as many desirable criteria as possible, again using examples of experience or training
- Ensure that your application catches the 'essence' of the job description
- Ensure that your application catches the 'essence' of the person specification
- Present it well
- Ensure zero mistakes
- Keep asking yourself 'what's in it for them?', i.e. why should they short-list you?

If a service is looking for skills or experience that they think are essential for someone to be successful in the advertised role, then it tends to be in the essential criteria. However, the desirable criteria are often a wish-list of attributes or skills that collectively the team and wider management would find useful. You can enhance your chances of short-listing by trying to discover which points carry the most weight, so that you can tailor your application accordingly. There is no substitute for good, old-fashioned detective work in this regard, including finding answers to the following:

- What is the service well known for?
- What skills and special interests do the existing consultants have (desirable criteria often represent skills gaps that they want to fill)?

- Does the service have any specific aspirations?
- What skills might be useful for their type of service, e.g. a surgical service in a Foundation Trust that will be introducing Service Line Management (in which case financial management skills might be important)?
- How was the original job advert and the job description worded? Many of the clues as to what they want will be there

The list here is far from exhaustive and it is important to think deeply and widely about why the points are in the desirable criteria—what are they trying to achieve with this person? Although we deal with visits and networking elsewhere, a job that you are really serious about should have detective work that also involves learning first-hand what appears to be important.

When you first write your CV it is likely to be a generic one. However, once applying for a specific job it needs tailoring. That tailoring starts firmly at the beginning. On the front page of your CV, write what job you are applying for—it's a simple thing to do but already it says 'I have tailored this CV for this post—I must be serious about it'. Inside the CV, make sure you do not inadvertently talk about a previous job you applied for (surprisingly common). Go through the essential and desirable criteria line by line and make sure you have completely demonstrated all the competencies required. Once written, revisit your CV and ask the highly pertinent question 'Have I demonstrated competency sufficiently for the committee to have confidence that I meet the criteria?' If you do not immediately think you have justified one of the criteria, e.g. participation in research, then brainstorm what other experience you have that may demonstrate this further. For example, in this case, have you ever been involved in a multicentre trial your department was contributing to? What role did you play? Did you collect data? Were you involved in obtaining informed consent?

What if you don't meet an essential component?

If you don't exactly match the essential criteria, it is easy to think that your application is sunk. However, it is vital to think about whether you have other compensating facets that may be desirable to the service and how you can demonstrate that the missing component is transient and already being dealt with. For example, an application to Paediatrics may require a level of child protection training that you haven't yet attained. You can't say you have it if you don't, but you could say 'I have Level x Child Protection Training scheduled for June 20xx'. In the same way you can apply for a consultant post prior to obtaining your CCT, there is nothing to stop you demonstrating that you are within sight of the remaining essential criteria. The more real the solution, e.g. 'I am booked to attend x', the less of an issue it will be.

Research has shown that you are more likely to get short-listed if you focus on your achievements and outcomes rather than just describing your roles and responsibilities in each post that you have done. It is very easy to forget achievements, think they are not relevant or play them down out of modesty. However, remember that employers are looking for people who will achieve things, and the greatest predictor of that is their level of achievement so far. One way to ensure sufficient focus on achievements is to take time before writing your CV or application form to brainstorm all of your

> **Box 2.4 CV top tips**
>
> - Start now
> - If you have never written one, ask a consultant colleague or two if you can look at theirs
> - Update at least every 3 months
> - Decide on a clear structure
> - Have a personal statement—people want to get an understanding of the real you and what drives you
> - Use Arial 10 or 12 point font for the main body of text
> - Have a footer with page numbers, your name and date
> - Use wide margins of at least 2.5 cm
> - Use 1.5 lines or double spacing in the personal details section
> - Be honest
> - Sell yourself, even if this is alien to you
> - Ask someone who is good at English to proof read it
> - Get a consultant colleague to read it
> - Print it on good quality, brilliant white paper of 90–100 gms density

achievements in each of your different posts and in your life outside work. Remember when considering achievements that you do not need to have done everything personally to have gained valuable experience, e.g. 'I was part of an audit team that improved the quality of care for patients with acute stroke at *St Elsewhere*'.

Box 2.4 gives many more tips for developing your CV.

Personal statements

At an individual level people often have intense opinions on whether personal statements should be included in a CV. Despite this I have never known someone not short-listed as a result of having a personal statement. Personal statements can be very powerful, especially when there are many similar candidates, as this is one of the few opportunities where the person short-listing gets any real feel of your personality, values and drivers.

It is often said that a personal statement should be written in the third person. However, do not be afraid to write it in the first person as this often sounds much more natural and something *you* have written rather than an advertising agency. Think of the personal statement as summing up your career to date, your future ambitions and you as a person. As always, be mindful of the job advertised and of what you perceive the employing Trust would want in terms of added value from a new colleague. However, beware of the following.

Pitfalls of personal statements

Many people write their personal statement entirely on the basis of what they think a Trust wants. However, this is now not a reflection of them so much as a semantic sales statement. That could be picked up on and work against you. If you are passionate about something, include that where it matches, and where it doesn't pick something else to emphasize that is still the real you but better matched to the job.

When writing your statement, keep it short. A personal statement should be no more than eight lines long and ideally take no more than 30 seconds to say.

Personal statement example 1

I am committed to excellence in all that I do, evidenced by obtaining a distinction in the majority of my subjects, as well as leading the rugby team to its best season score. I am a driven, goal-directed individual, which allowed me to train four nights per week during that rugby season, undoubtedly contributing to us lifting the trophy. My naturally supportive approach to team members was heavily reinforced by realizing we would never lift that trophy as a collection of individuals, only if we were a team, and that the team supported the weaker members to become stronger.

Personal statement example 2

I am a tertiary neonatologist with a highly developed special interest in minimally invasive respiratory support and a passion for ensuring that our approach to care is as mindful of the parents as it is of our patients. With considerable experience in involving parents in service reform, I have championed the importance of active, collaborative dialogue with all those affecting or having an influence over a service. My enjoyment of networking has contributed to an appreciation of different people's perspectives, as well as a heightened awareness of my own impact on others. I love people.

NHS Jobs application form

The form itself

Given that so many jobs are applied for through this portal, we'd like to spend a few minutes on some of the technical considerations, starting with how to prepare an application without even having a specific job to apply for.

To set this up you need to register with the NHS Jobs website and then 'pretend' you are going to apply for a consultant post. Once you start writing your application form you can simply save it; just do not submit the form when it is complete. The form is then saved for future reference or adaptation and automatically comes up when you apply for a new job. It is worth noting that if you have not accessed the website for a year your information is deleted. It is always worth saving what you have written/submitted as a Word document.

The main opportunity to write in this form is in the section entitled 'Your present roles and responsibilities', which allows 4000 characters including spaces, i.e. approximately 600 words, for each post you have held. It is really important to draw out in this section all of the qualities and skills that you have developed throughout your training that will be relevant to the consultant post for which you are applying. However, in reality, some jobs give you tremendous relevant experience and others don't, meaning that the section sizes might not do the former justice. Obviously learning to succinctly describe your qualities, skills and experiences is beneficial.

Again we advocate when completing large sections to do these in Word, where you can carefully spell check everything you have written and easily count the number of characters you have used, including spaces, or words, depending on the section structure. These parameters are absolutely fixed within the application form, preventing you from putting too much text in and then cutting it down. It is much quicker to work on it in Word, edit it, cut and paste, etc. until you are happy and then copy it across to the form. When cutting and pasting, ensure that the application form has accepted everything you have written. If your answer was indeed longer than permitted the end will be truncated.

When you come to complete the form for a specific position, we would strongly recommend you print out what you have written and check it carefully to ensure the form demonstrates you have fully met the job description and have all of the essential and as many as possible of the desirable criteria. This also facilitates asking a colleague or someone good at English and grammar and one or more consultants to review it. In truth, it is very difficult to get a good feel for the flow of your application form when it is broken into bits in the form. You will discover much from reviewing it on good old-fashioned paper.

Overcoming the presentation challenge

The areas covered by the form are shown in Box 2.5. However, as can be seen, the application form is not always conducive to promoting yourself as effectively as many of us would like and it does not allow for formatting (not even italics). Unlike in applications for junior doctor posts, all people short-listing see the whole document except your personal details and therefore it is important to consider some useful form structuring tips that present your information in the best possible light.

Box 2.5 Information requested in the NHS Jobs application form

Note: Trusts can vary this form slightly, for example, asking you to describe each job, but this is the standard format used for the majority of consultant jobs.

Personal details

- Name
- Address
- Are you a United Kingdom (UK), European Community (EC) or European Economic Area (EEA) national?
- If you are not, from the above areas do you have tier 2 certificate of sponsorship?
- Disabilities

This information is kept by human resources (HR) and is not forwarded to the short-listing panel, i.e. the panel should not know your name.

Monitoring

- DOB
- Sex
- Ethnic origin
- Sexual orientation
- Religion
- Criminal convictions—unspent
- Criminal convictions—spent
- Relationships with anyone within the organization you are applying to

Again this information is for monitoring only and is not shared with the short-listing committee.

Qualifications

- Essential qualifications (up to five, with most recent first)
- Desirable qualifications (up to six, with most recent first)
- Training courses attended (up to seven)—make sure these relate to the post you are applying for)
- GMC registration, Specialist Register and CCT date if in future
- Any fitness to practise proceedings or current investigation in the UK or other countries. (Are you currently the subject of a fitness to practise investigation or proceedings by a licensing or regulatory body in the UK or in any other country?)
- Any history of being struck off in the UK or other countries. (Have you been removed from the register or have conditions been made on your registration by a fitness to practise committee or the licensing or regulatory body in the UK or in any other country?)

Employment history

- Job title, institution, address and dates of your present job
- Reason why you are leaving (150 characters including spaces, i.e. approx. 24 words)
- Your present roles and responsibilities (4000 characters including spaces, i.e. approx. 600 words)
- Your ten previous jobs (job title, institution, address, dates)
- Information on gaps in employment (no restriction on length)

Additional information

- Describe your experience of clinical audit (max. 150 words)
- Describe your relevant teaching experience (max. 150 words)
- Details of your most relevant research work and publications in peer-reviewed journals (max. 500 words)
- Give examples of your approach to working in a team (max. 150 words)

- Explain your areas of clinical skill and competence relevant to this post (max. 150 words)
- Any other supporting information that you think may be helpful, or that is requested in the Person Specification. You must ensure that this does not contain any duplicate information already provided elsewhere in the application form or any personal details (max. 500 words)
- Type of job you would prefer, e.g. part time, full time, job share
- If applicable to the post, do you hold a certificate to support your responsibilities under IR(ME)R (the Ionizing Radiation (Medical Exposure) Regulations) 2000?
- Evidence of relevant training and experience is required for those justifying or undertaking X-rays, interventional radiology, computerizeded tomography (CT) scans, etc. Please place this evidence within your supporting statement

References

- Must cover at least 3 years of employment and include your last two employers
- Must give name, address, email, telephone and fax

Declaration

You need to tick that:

'The information in this section is true and complete. I agree that any deliberate omission, falsification or misrepresentation in the application form will be grounds for rejecting this application or subsequent dismissal if employed by the organization. Where applicable, I consent that the organization can seek clarification regarding professional registration details.'

Formatting the NHS application form

In substantial sections, or where distinct sets of key points are being made, consider using headings by putting the heading phrase in uppercase to make it stand out.

Bullet points are not available. However, you can overcome this by using [space][-][space]. This effectively creates a bulleted list, but you do need to be mindful of bullet point length, because if it is too long it will line break and look messy.

You can also create faint lines to emphasize separation. These are best created by simply running a line of full-stops one or two lines below the section you have just finished. We find it useful to then copy the first line in which you do this and paste it in when it is needed next. However, remember each of these full-stops will count as a character.

Finally, let us remind you that if composing your sections in Word, do a double return between paragraphs if you want a space between each paragraph in your application form.

Demonstrating competencies within your CV or application form

Team skills

The area of the application form that causes consultant applicants the most anxiety is the section on team working. The section is short and therefore it is quite difficult to say something meaningful. The actual question asked is:

Give examples of your approach to working in a team (max 150 words)

> **Example**
>
> I and my fellow Registrars championed a team communications effectiveness audit and I then facilitated a feedback and improvement forum as a platform to allow us to continually improve. This has resulted in a significant drop in the need for incident reports, whilst also reducing conflict between the surgeons and theatre staff. At school, I was commended for my natural trait of spontaneously helping others after I had finished my own work. I have now worked on five successful, collaborative, multidisciplinary, system-wide audits with people from many departments, each with very different needs. These have led to substantial improvement and, besides stimulating pride around being a team member, they were also a wonderful opportunity to gain insight into the different working practices between different types of professionals and how best to adapt my style to ensure good working relationships that are productive.
>
> Use examples from work that show you get on with others. Use examples where as a team you have achieved together.

Communication skills

There are a number of ways in which to approach this, although it is notoriously difficult to provide proof that you have excellent communication skills. However, one fast way to *undermine* people's confidence in your communication skills is to submit a CV with errors in it. There is a subconscious alarm bell that rings, saying 'If he puts as little attention into this CV at a critically important time, then what else might be overlooked?'

> **USEFUL TIP**: Remember that it can often be difficult to reduce the size of a short list to a manageable number. Communication skills are often cited as essential criteria and if your application has spelling and grammatical errors then you will reduce your chances of making the short list.

The sorts of examples people use to emphasize their communication ability include:

- Communications courses they have been on
- Presentation and teaching courses
- Any distinct projects involving communication skills
- Examples of where effective communications were essential
- Examples from emergency or intensive care environments or rotations (where communication is vital)
- Through 360-degree feedback

Leadership skills

Again, courses are a mainstay of illustrating leadership development, but with most candidates having attended leadership courses nowadays, it has ceased to be a competitive advantage. It is important to work out what else you could cite that 'proves' leadership ability. Again, examples might include:

- Distinct leadership roles you have held
- Lessons learned and practice that has changed as a result
- 360-degree assessment
- Projects that you have led, e.g. audit
- Change that you have led
- Examples of how you have used some of the skills developed on a course

This section emphasizes that leadership development is so much more than a course. Approaching applications, you should be looking for distinct opportunities to take on responsibility and demonstrate that you can successfully lead things.

Referees

As part of the application process you will be asked to name referees. One must be from your present employer. Many Trusts are now asking for a reference from each of your employments over the previous 3 years and the NHS application form enables you to specify that your referees are not to be contacted until after the interview. However, in reality the expectation is that you will say 'yes' to referees being contacted pre-interview. It is courteous to ask your referees before including them on your CV/application form. It is also useful to send them a copy of your CV or application form in case they are approached. This reduces the chances of them undoing your hard work!

> **USEFUL TIP**: When asking referees if they are happy to be named, ask for permission for all of your applications, so that they can sit in the system, e.g. 'Would you mind if I included you as a referee for my consultant jobs applications?' This saves re-asking, which can cause delays, and you simply need to inform the referees that you have applied for another job.

Covering letter

If you are posting your application or CV, always send a short covering letter. These are not always passed on to the short-listing panel so make sure that everything you want the panel to know is included in your CV or application form. However, sometimes they are passed on and it is therefore vital to treat this as simply another strategic part of your application which also has the risk to undermine it if you get it wrong! If you can't write neatly, type it.

> **USEFUL TIP**: A useful strategy for the covering letter is to use it to emphasize why you want this particular job, with an emotionally focused approach rather than fact-based. You can also use it to highlight something that needs extra prominence. It could simply list the key career highlights that lead you to believe you'd be excellent in the role.

Short-listing

Short-listing is done by the members of the interview panel (see Chapter 6). Each applicant is scored against the essential and desirable criteria by each panel member and then ranked in order. The consultant representing your specific speciality may decide to involve his or her consultant colleagues in the short-listing, but ultimately only has 'one voice' when submitting his or her rankings. The Medical Staffing Officer will then amalgamate all the rankings and the top candidates will be invited to interview. It would be rare to ask more than six candidates to interview for a single post. Therefore, meeting all of the essential criteria is not sufficient to guarantee an interview, especially for popular jobs.

What to do when several jobs are being advertised but not the one you really want

Unfortunately there is no easy answer to this question. However, be aware that it is not generally seen as acceptable to turn up for interview and then turn down the post or to turn up for interview and then ask to take a few days (or weeks) in deciding whether the post is acceptable.

More and more consultants no longer see their first job as a job for life and consultants do move, although you may not want to express that idea to the interview committee!

When considering what to do, ask yourself:

- What is the future job market likely to be like?
- How well do I fit the profile of the proposed job that I really want (i.e. objectively assess your chances)?

You may want to use the Wheel of Life in Chapter 1 to analyse how satisfied you would be in each area of your life if you accepted a specific job. This will help you make objective decisions about whether to continue with your application or wait for a better matched job.

Chapter 3
Pre-interview visit

Introduction

The pre-interview visit is one of the most important parts of your interview preparation. Done properly you will:

- Learn of all the issues and concerns of your future colleagues and Trust
- Have a high chance of predicting the types of questions likely to be asked at interview
- Recognise what is important to key individuals on your interview panel, allowing you to phrase your answers appropriately in the interview itself
- Discover the behaviour and psychology of panel members, allowing you to build strong rapport and better tailor the language of your interview answers
- Form a clear idea of whether the job you have applied for, the hospital, the people and the area are right for you so that you can make an informed decision before proceeding to interview

Although this is your opportunity to ask questions and discover more about the department, its members and the Trust, you must remember that the people you will meet will also want to ask questions about you. You need to be prepared for this and carefully consider how you wish to position yourself for the interview. As individuals, we form impressions of other people very quickly and although the interview process is meant to be completely detached from the pre-interview visits, the impression you make will carry through into the interview itself.

Why are pre-interview visits important?

At a very simple level, if you do not go and visit a job before the interview itself, it is highly unlikely you will get the job. A consultant job is still very much seen as a job for life and the panel will want to appoint someone who is genuinely interested in their post and their Trust, evidenced by taking the trouble to visit and have a thorough look around.

> **USEFUL TIP:** If you do not undertake a pre-interview visit it is very unlikely you will get a permanent consultant post.

The two key reasons for doing a pre-interview visit, besides deciding on whether this is the right job, location and Trust for you, are to position yourself as the candidate of choice and to learn as much as possible to help you be successful in the interview.

Position yourself as the candidate of choice

Although the interview should be an independent process, most interviewers go into the interview with a short list of preferred candidates, derived partly from the CVs and predominantly from the rapport they developed with you at the pre-interview visit.

> **USEFUL TIP:** We make impressions of other people within about 30 seconds of meeting them. We then look for the evidence to reinforce our impressions, i.e. validate them.

The pre-interview visit is your opportunity to develop rapport in more relaxed circumstances than the interview, to structure the panel's expectations and to create a will to appoint you that will assist you in the interview itself.

To learn

Pre-interview visits are a fantastic opportunity to learn what you really need to know to succeed at interview because everybody is predisposed to be open and communicative. The sorts of things you should try to learn are:

- What the service is looking for in the new consultant
- Where the service is going, i.e. what its strategy is and where it sees itself a few years from now (its vision)
- Any particular political issues on their minds (both local and national)
- Any specific sensitivities or key requirements
- Other issues, concerns or items of particular interest presently to
  - your potential future Trust
  - your potential future colleagues
- The motivational and behavioural drivers of the interviewers (see Chapter 4)

If you listen well and ask a few key questions, you will be able to both predict and develop appropriate answering strategies for the key questions you are asked at interview. Listen to where they place emphasis, demonstrate more passionate feelings or specifically highlight something as important.

> **USEFUL TIP:** Listen carefully at the pre-interview visit and you will be able to both predict the questions you will be asked at consultant interview (including the political ones) and know how to answer them!

Most interviewers ask questions on subjects that are close to their heart or are a specific issue to them at the present time. If a specific political agenda is keeping them 'awake at night' this is the most likely topic that they will discuss at the pre-interview visit and ask you about in the interview itself.

In the interview itself, you will need to 'sell' yourself to the interview panel. When people buy things, it is rarely just the product they are purchasing. Predominantly people buy the benefits the product gives them, i.e. the outcome they are hoping to achieve. However, people only buy these benefits if they are benefits that they specifically or particularly want. When you are listening (intensely) at the pre-interview visits, ask yourself what benefits are they wanting from the new consultant? What is it that they are hoping the new consultant will be or do? Afterwards, as you prepare for the interview you can think about how you can demonstrate that you bring these benefits, more so than other candidates.

To decide

The pre-interview visit also gives you an opportunity to decide whether this job is the right job for you and whether indeed you should proceed to interview. Remember, it is definitely okay to withdraw from a job before the interview day. It is not seen as acceptable to withdraw from a job having been offered the post at interview, and indeed there is still a heavy expectation that if you are offered the job you should accept it there and then.

As substantive posts become more and more rare, it is likely the candidates will feel less and less inclined to hold off from proceeding to interview out of fear that it may be a while before another job comes along. However, we would like to re-emphasize that you could end up stuck in a job that you are not happy with and this could result in significant personal distress and future life/marriage strains. Equally, we would also remind you that if jobs don't come up so often in your specialty, it is increasingly acceptable to take a job for a few years and then move on to something you see as more permanent. We also believe that there will be a significant increase in fixed-term contracts, as Trusts become less sure about the future and consequently less inclined to make substantive appointments. As this becomes the norm, it will help reduce some candidates' feelings of guilt associated with taking a job that they do not see as their job for life.

When should you go/make contact?

There are a number of times when it would be appropriate to make contact or visit a department, and not all of these are immediately prior to interview. Typical times include:

- Pre-advert
- On advert
- After short-listing

Increasingly, busy staff are reluctant to receive visits following advert but prior to short-listing. Obviously, they need to remain accessible by phone to answer any enquiries or queries about the post. This trend is set to increase as fewer jobs attract ever-more candidates. Consequently, unless you specifically want to restrict your visiting to after short-listing, it can be a good idea to make a pre-advert visit, ideally before even they know they are going to be advertising the job.

Pre-advert

If you know that you would like to work in a specific location, then it is a good idea to proactively approach the lead clinician at least a year before your CCT and then keep periodically in touch. Remember, the purpose of pre-interview visiting is about positioning yourself as the ideal candidate. It is also about forward planning. There are a number of things to establish during this visit. Are there any jobs on the horizon? When will they be advertised? What special interests will the post have as requirements?

For many departments, there is nothing scarier than going to consultant advert and not knowing if there are going to be any good applicants for your post. If a department knows you are out there, that you are a good candidate and that you are keen to apply for their post but cannot apply for two more months in view of your CCT date, then they will most likely wait for you. After all, they have probably had to wait quite some time to gain approval for the post and so a few more months for the right candidate would seem like a small price to pay.

On advert

If the job has been advertised, *always* phone the person whose name is specified on the advert to discuss the job further. This shows that you are genuinely interested and enthusiastic about their job. Ask them if you can visit now or should you wait until after short-listing. Remember that some departments, in order to keep their workload down, will not see people until after short-listing.

If you are able to visit before short-listing, keep things relatively informal and only see a few key people in the department itself at this stage. An example might be the lead clinician, the consultant whose post this was if it is a retirement post and/or a consultant with the same interest as you. At this stage, bothering senior people like the medical director is likely to prove counter-productive.

After short-listing

However busy your present job is, you *must* visit the department after short-listing. If you do not visit and do not take time to see the key people then it is very unlikely that you will get the post. It is easy to put these visits off and to find excuses why you are too busy to go or how you cannot let your present colleagues and employer down. However, this is one of those times in your life when it is vitally important to put yourself first and make this a priority! You will not get a second chance.

Even if you met some people before short-listing took place, you will still need to go back and meet the other people on your interview panel. It may also be appropriate, depending on how informal your first visit was, to re-see the lead clinician. In any event, this is the opportunity to add in senior, prominent people, who may well be part of the interview panel and who certainly will have much information to share about the Trust and its challenges.

There is no doubt that every department is different and it is not always easy to know whether you are being over- or under-keen in their eyes. Talking to one of the senior secretaries or the last consultant in through the door can be very helpful in giving you a feel as to what is the appropriate behaviour in that department, when it comes to visits. To a degree, the expectation on potential candidates to engage in pre-interview visits is partly driven by the psychology of the existing team. There are definitely consultants who would see the pre-interview visit as a necessary evil rather than an opportunity to gain early and first-hand experience of potential candidates. The majority of people however feel that the practice of pre-interview visiting remains essential and a clear demonstration of someone's commitment to joining that particular service.

If you are an internal candidate it is still expected that you will sit down with all the key players. Remember, you have a lot to gain from these meetings in terms of interview strategy. Do not think they all know you and therefore you do not need to see them. We have seen many an internal candidate fail to get appointed because they fell into the trap of believing the job was already theirs. Arguably, you need to work even harder to demonstrate that you are not taking the job for granted and that you are especially keen to have it.

In the past, trainees had specific time to undertake pre-interview visits for consultant jobs written into their contracts. This is no longer the case, but most departments remain supportive of this activity, given that your fellow consultant colleagues have all done the same thing.

Who should you see?

- Immediate clinical colleagues
  - Depending on the size of the department you are about to join, it may be appropriate to meet all your future colleagues. Remember that getting your consultant job is a bit like getting married. You could be stuck with these people for 30 years. At a very minimum, try to meet the service lead and the two colleagues you will work with predominantly
  - Sometimes there are clinical colleagues who may not be on the panel, but if you do not see them it may have consequences if they choose to canvas hard against your appointment. The Clinical Service Lead is a good source for asking which clinicians you must see and whether there is anything you should know before you do
- Peripheral but important clinical colleagues
  - Consider whether there are other key clinicians, within a different service area, who you ought to meet because of close working relationships, e.g. a neurologist and neurosurgeon, cardiac anaesthetist and cardiac surgeon, neonatologist and obstetrician
- Senior Nurse/Senior PAM (Profession Allied to Medicine), e.g. radiographer
- Clinical Director
- Directorate Business Manager
  - This is becoming particularly important with the increasing likelihood of specific service developments in your speciality or role, as well as the possibility that your speciality could be delivered in new ways as part of the ongoing changes to our healthcare delivery. It may also be appropriate to consider meeting the Director of Finance in these circumstances, especially if the Trust has been in a turnaround situation
- Chief Executive Officer (CEO)
- Medical Director

- University Representative on your interview panel (if relevant to the post applied for)
- Chairperson of the Trust, if on your interview committee
- Panel chairperson
  - Note some interview panels will not allow you to meet the Chair of the panel
- Any other individual on your interview committee
  - Often the Chief Executive will be represented by a different director on the interview panel, e.g. the Director of Nursing or Director of Finance. All directors can ask tough questions, so if any of them are on the panel, meet with them in advance to get a better lie of the land. If you are lucky, they may deliver you some gems of knowledge you would never have previously known about. Without doubt, you will be better prepared for the questions they will ask

> **USEFUL TIPS:** Arrange to see the Medical Director and the Chief Executive at the *end* of your pre-interview visits. You will be more informed and will be able to ask more pertinent questions.
>
> Make sure you informally talk to the trainees. They will very quickly give you the low-down on whether this is a good place to work, as well as any tensions at a consultant level.

As well as formally meeting the people outlined already, always informally chat to the secretaries and the junior doctors. Junior doctors will very quickly give you a feel of whether this is a good department to work in and secretaries have more influence than you think over their consultant colleagues.

Additional important pre-interview considerations

- Don't try to just guess who to see
  - Ask the person whose name was on the original job advert
  - Sometimes there are people who may not be on the panel, but if you do not see them it may have consequences
- All hospital management structures are different and so it is okay to ask about the management structure and who you should see
  - The HR department should be able to send you a management structure or organogram (which it is a good idea to get anyway)
  - Ask the consultant whose name was on the original job description who you should see and whether there is anything you should know
- Do not just see people who are on your interview panel
  - Think about who you would or could see to ensure that you had the best understanding of this post. Who would help you learn what you need to know to succeed at this interview? For example, if this is a new post with a remit to develop a new service, meeting with the business manger would be essential. If this was a post leading a multidisciplinary team, e.g. psychiatry, meeting wider members of the multidisciplinary team would be very powerful and helpful

- Ask yourself what would I want to get out of seeing each person? Why would I be seeing them? If you can see a good reason then add them to your list

It is very important, if at all possible, to meet the Medical Director and Chief Executive. In most smaller hospitals this is both possible and expected. In larger hospitals, the Chief Executive and Medical Director may not agree to meet you. Remember, if they say 'no' to you they are also saying 'no' to all the other short-listed individuals. Don't take it personally.

We would strongly advise leaving your appointments with the Medical Director and Chief Executive until the end of your pre-interview visits

- This enables you to have a much more constructive dialogue, as you will be clearer about the specific issues facing both the department and the organization
- You will feel much more informed by then and will be able to ask the most constructive but also the most effective questions in terms of building your understanding of the Trust and the issues they face

Some Chief Executives are now using short (10-minute) telephone interviews to chat with short-listed candidates. If this is the case, you have to be hyper organized with a clear set of questions to ask, ordered from the most important down to the least important in case the time runs out.

How should you organize your pre-interview visits?

There are a great many potential people to see, so try to organize your pre-interview visits as soon as you are short-listed. In an ideal world set aside 2 days to do this, but, depending on your existing commitments, you may have to try to get to see everyone in a single day.

The following is important when organizing pre-interview visits:

- Discuss who you should see with the person whose name was on the original advert or job description as the point of contact
- Contact Medical Staffing and ask who will be on your interview committee (they are usually quite happy to provide this information)
- Contact the secretary of the person whose name was on the original job advert and see if she/he can help you or at the very least provide you with the contact details of everyone you need to see. Most secretaries will be kind enough to do this for you
- Do not try to cram in too many appointments too close together
- You will need at least 30 minutes to see most people
- Give yourself time to walk from one appointment to the next (it doesn't create a great first impression if you turn up looking like a sweaty wreck because you have run from one end of the hospital to the other)
- Try to see the Clinical Service Lead first
- Try to see the Medical Director and the Chief Executive last

> **USEFUL TIP:** If a secretary has been particularly helpful in organizing all of your pre-interview appointments with staff, consider stopping by with a small box of chocolates to thank her (or him). It is important to have the secretaries on your side and not against you. Chocolate, where there is a valid reason to give it, seems to work wonders!

Preparing for the pre-interview visit

Firmly remembering that this is a marketing exercise as well as an information gathering one, it is very important to consider in advance what you want to take away from the pre-interview visits, along with what impressions you would like to leave. In particular, what key issues do you want to explore and what do you want their views on?

Advance preparation

Review the Trust's Annual Plan, Quality Accounts, Vision and Strategy, etc.

These documents may well have been made available to you when the job was first advertised online. However, there is always additional useful information to be had by searching the Trust's internet site, especially the section 'About our Board'. If you are struggling to find the information that you really need, contact the HR department or the Trust's public relations office and ask them to send you the information.

> **USEFUL TIP:** When you apply for a consultant post, make sure you download and save all the documents that were attached to the original electronic advert, e.g. the Trust's Annual Plan, so that you can easily access them for your pre-interview and interview preparation.

Consider the following:

- What type of organization are they (e.g. Foundation Trust, social enterprise) and what does this mean?
- Do they wish to become a different type of organization and what does this mean?
- Have they made a previous failed application to become a different type of organization and, if so, why did it fail?
- Are they likely to merge with another Trust?
- Do they have distinct links with another Trust and, if so, what are that Trust's plans?
- What is their 5- to 10-year strategy?

- Does their medium- to long-term strategy appear to adequately address the competitive marketplace?
- Where does your service appear to feature in their 5-year strategy?
- What is the strategy for related services that may have a knock-on effect on your own service? For example,
  - The impact of developing feto-maternal medicine on neonatal services
  - Developing a speciality that relies heavily on radiology support
- What key government initiatives or other national issues may have an influence on your future service or this Trust and which you may wish to explore with them?

Review the job description and job plan

- Do I really know what I will be asked to do?
- Is there an opportunity to develop the areas I wish?
- Is there already someone with a special interest in my area of expertise?
- Does the workload fit the job description?
- If I want to work part-time how might I make it work?
- Are there things in the job plan that are unclear?
- Will there be an early review of the job plan?

Read your CV/job application

Make sure you thoroughly know what is written on your CV. At the interview itself, all candidates will be asked the same questions. The pre-interview visit is an opportunity for all those with a stake in the decision, therefore, to ask you questions they cannot ask everyone else, e.g. about mutual colleagues you have worked for or written papers with, your extra-curricular activities, a project you have done which they would be interested in doing themselves and more.

It is always useful to print off some spare copies of your CV and take them with you. Not everyone will have had the opportunity to read your CV or indeed seen a copy. However, we would strongly advise you not to thrust them upon people as this could be seen as canvassing. However, if someone asks you whether you have a copy, then that is a different matter.

Talk to your present consultant

- What are the issues facing your speciality at the moment (always better to go in appearing knowledgeable about and sensitive to critical issues)?
- What political 'hot potatoes' relevant to your speciality do you need to be aware of?
- Does your present consultant know anything pertinent about the department or the people you have applied to?

Preparation on the day

Remember that you are trying to set a good impression *as a consultant*. Consequently, it is important to consider the following:

- Dress smartly
- Be punctual

- Be prepared to share information about yourself and your family
- Carry some spare copies of your CV with you

What else should I do at the pre-interview visit?

One of the key purposes of the pre-interview visit is for you to learn as much as possible, to help you in the interview itself. You will do this predominantly by actively listening but also by having a few key questions to ask as back-up. Remember, this should not be an interview of you, although do expect people to ask general questions about you, as well as asking for your opinions on various matters, as they try to build rapport. Do not see these questions as trying to catch you out. However, do remember that many people are very wary of appointing colleagues they do not feel that they know anything about. At the end of the day, the most important thing in a colleague is someone you can get on with. Box 3.1 highlights some key do's and don't's of the pre-interview visit.

Box 3.1 Some do's and don't's of the pre-interview visit

- Do have a few key questions—see examples
- Do not go armed with a whole list of questions that you subsequently work through. You will not necessarily learn and may infuriate the individual you are seeing who had specific things they wanted to tell you
- Do not get stressed or emotional (refer to Chapter 6 for advice on reducing this)
- Do not make adverse comments about other people even if the people you are visiting do
- Do take a note book
- After each visit write down:
  - A few key points you have learnt
  - What was important to the person you have just met
  - Any specific sensitivities
  - What was important to the person in terms of their personality (Chapter 4), e.g. were they challenging and action orientated, friendly and reliable team players, or quiet and structured, working to a clear set of guidelines and evidence base?
- After each visit ask yourself:
  - Will I enjoy working with this group?
  - Are any tensions acceptable to me?
  - Will I have the opportunity to develop a clear presence and role for myself?

Questions to ask and discussions to have at the pre-interview visit

Clinical Service Lead for the department

- Ask the Clinical Service Lead to show you round—many questions and discussions will form as you do this
- Detailed discussion regarding what the job actually entails
- What does the job really mean in reality?
- How does the department work and from where is it controlled?
- Were they looking for a specific special interest or just generally trying to extend their skill mix?
- What opportunities are there to develop special interests and/or take on specific roles, e.g. teaching/research?
- What are the research interests of the department?
- Where does he/she see the future direction of the department?
- What are the issues facing the department at the present time?
- What would they like to see from a new consultant colleague?
- What are the relationships like within the department—both Dr/Dr and with other professionals—is it a cohesive group?
- How is clinical governance run within the department? Are there any specific clinical governance issues?
- Is there anything else I should know that I have not asked about?

Clinical colleagues

It is useful to ask similar questions to all your potential clinical colleagues. You will begin to learn about them as individuals. You may begin to undercover tensions within the department, if they exist, and this will help confirm whether or not you are making the correct decision to proceed to interview. Questions to ask include:

- How do you see this post working (and fitting in)?
- Is there a special interest that needs filling within the department?
- What issues are facing the department at the present and in the near future? What do you think that will mean for services on the ground?
- What are your special interests?
- What are your research interests?
- What do you hope to get from a new consultant colleague?
- What are relationships like between management and the department? (if you have time). What gives rise to this?
- What is it like working in this hospital?
- What is the area like to live in?
- What recreational opportunities are there?
- What are the schools like? (Where do existing consultants send their children to school?)

Remember this should be seen as a job for life and people expect you to want to know about more than just the hospital.

Nursing/PAM lead

- What do the department staff hope to gain from this appointment?
- What are the issues for nursing/PAM?
- What does patient feedback show about the department?
- Are there any specific initiatives under way to measure or improve patient experience?

Clinical Director/Associate Medical Director/Divisional Director

You need to see the clinician who has direct managerial control for the department. These people can have a variety of titles, but it is usually one of the above. If you are unclear who to speak to, ask either Medical Staffing (who should have a managerial plan) or the Clinical Service Lead.

- What does the Trust hope to achieve by establishing this post (this may be less relevant if it is a replacement post)?
- What are the critical issues for the directorate?
- What is the ethos of the hospital, e.g. cutting-edge teaching hospital vs friendly good quality care?
- Where does he/she see your speciality in 5 years' time in this hospital?
- What are the key issues facing the hospital at the present time?
- What are likely to be the dominant future key issues?
- What is the Trust doing in relation to present political issues, to ensure that it survives and thrives?

Directorate Business Manager

Depending on the job you are applying for, meeting the Directorate Business Manager may or may not be appropriate. However, if you are applying to a role or specialism which involves a significant service development component, it is essential to spend time with the Business Manager exploring the issues in developing this area of service. You may wish to discuss key stakeholders, effects of political agenda, etc. The Business Manager will also have a good insight into the political and government issues affecting your service and the Trust.

University Representative

- What is the university's relationship with the hospital?
- Where does the university see the future of your service?
- Is there specific university research in your area (consider both local and multi-centre research)?
- What are the University Representative's research interests?
- How is research likely to develop in your area in the Trust?

- Will there be an opportunity for you to do research if you would like to?
- Are there specific issues for research within your area/the Trust at this present time, both internal and external?

Medical Director

The Medical Director will usually want to talk to you about clinical governance and revalidation within the Trust but may also talk about strategic direction. He/she will usually do most of the talking, but it is useful to have a few key questions which should have been informed by your early discussions as outlined above.

- What are the key risks for the Trust?
- How is clinical governance organized within the Trust? Are there any pan-directorate, or pan-primary/secondary and tertiary care initiatives?
- What is the strategic direction of the Trust?
- How is the Trust dealing with the key political agendas?
- How does the Trust work with its key stake holders, e.g. Commissioners and General Practitioners?

Chief Executive (CEO) (+/− Chairperson of the Trust)

In some large Trusts, the Chief Executive no longer meets consultant candidates. However, hopefully in most hospitals this will continue. You need to recognize that the Chief Executive's time is precious and that you need to be organized. He/she may only have 10 minutes set aside for your meeting. If as advised you have left this meeting towards the end of your visit or visits you should have a key list of questions you want to hear the Chief Executive's views on. Make sure as you talk to him/her that you are able to show that you are a well-informed individual. Do not just ask what the strategic plan is but concentrate on an aspect relevant to you and get a greater understanding. If your service is not within the strategic plan, ask if the hospital has specific plans for the development of your area.

Canvassing the interview committee

The word 'canvassing' is defined as soliciting votes. In the modern world, canvassing the interview committee is deemed unacceptable. This does not mean that it does not happen and there is no doubt that conversations occur at meetings between consultants about their excellent and less-from-excellent registrars who are potential consultant candidates.

However, the old way of getting your consultant to pick up the phone and recommend you to Bob once the job has been advertised has essentially gone. So has the use of references to significantly determine who will get the job. In most consultant interviews, as in interviews for roles outside medicine, references are only reviewed after the successful candidate has been decided upon. In these cases, the reference is used to confirm that there is no significant reason why you should not be employed, e.g. you have been referred to the General Medical Council (GMC).

It is important to state in your application if you have a relationship with anyone in the Trust or on the interview panel who may be seen to influence the panel in any way. This does not mean this person cannot interview you or that you will be looked on in a different light, but you put yourself at risk if the relationship is not declared.

Do not confuse canvassing and pre-interview visits. Finding out as much as possible about the job in advance is vitally important. This is a particularly important message to doctors who have trained predominantly overseas and do not perhaps fully understand the UK system. These doctors often think it would be deemed wrong to meet the people interviewing them in advance of the consultant interview, yet if they do not do this they are very unlikely to get the job.

Chapter 4
Understanding you and your interviewers

Introduction

This chapter seeks to demystify the complex area of human behaviour and motivation in a manner that makes it not only accessible but also useful to someone facing an interview situation. Far from being filled with complex, interrelated behavioural constructs, we have simplified a genuinely complex area sufficiently to allow practical application in the form of conscious competence.

A thorough understanding of what makes people tick is a significant competitive advantage in an interview. This section is in sufficient depth to give you the edge, but if you would like to understand more about behaviour, difference and influencing, then we'd strongly recommend attending a good course on the subject. It will benefit your interview and indeed the rest of your working life.

Can and should we consider 'classifying' individuals?

Some might consider that delving into human psychology in interviews represents a risky departure from the factual and predictable into a less 'tangible' field. We see it differently. An otherwise good candidate who ignores interpersonal difference at interview runs the risk of being inadvertently declined, not because he/she is not worthy of appointment but because he/she is simply a poor behavioural match to the decision makers.

It is vital that we appreciate the decision to appoint is as much an emotional one as a logical one, however much we would like to kid ourselves otherwise. Interviewers hold a mandate to assess candidates for 'fit' to the department they will join. After all, you may well work with your new colleagues for many years and those years could seem long for everyone if the fit is not good. Fit is very much an emotional judgement, rather than an objectively detached one. Whereas many inputs will form the ultimate decision to appoint or not, likely fit with fellow department members will be an important consideration, with roots firmly in 'gut feeling' rather than rational assessment.

What is important is that you adopt a simple and easily manageable framework for behaviour that allows you to adequately and smoothly adapt your approach with confidence. In this chapter, we will share with you just such a framework, as well as highlighting both the advantages to be realized and the pitfalls to be avoided.

Understanding difference and its relevance to interviews

Imagine an interview panel where the whole panel was comprised of doctors from the department you wished to join. You wouldn't be unreasonable in assuming that the majority of them were just like you, thought like you, would answer questions like you and would even choose the same language as you. If you'd done your homework thoroughly, you'd have even confirmed this through the pre-interview visit. You could rest assured that your own default style of communication and choice of answers would most likely be on track.

However, the likelihood of that reality is slim. Interview panels are made up of diverse individuals, with different psychologies and a wide variety of contexts. This difference ensures that candidates have to not only formulate a sensible answer from a clinical or service perspective but also tailor both their answer choice and communication style to the individual asking, whilst never forgetting the other individuals on the panel. That requires an understanding of the individuals, an ability to spot or find out how they are wired and knowledge of how best to adapt your natural style to deliver the right impact.

Life through the lens of others

To help illustrate difference between individuals and demonstrate how it influences the interview situation, we are going to introduce three members of the interview panel for a post in paediatrics and examine their different reactions to certain circumstances and answers. Bob, the candidate in question, does not have a significant understanding of behaviour and he tends to approach situations on the basis of what feels right to him, with a healthy degree of caution towards others and a desire not to be overfamiliar or pushy without getting to know someone first. He finds interviews a nerve-wracking experience and often finds himself worrying that he might not perform well. This job is in a location that he knows his family would be happy in and the heightened level of importance he places on being successful is playing havoc with his calmness.

Brenda is a Consultant Paediatrician of 10 years' service. She is hoping to appoint a colleague who will fit in well and be a friendly and supportive team member. In particular, she is keen to find someone who would be sympathetic to their desire to move out from under the seemingly autocratic control of the divisional lead and help them develop a truly patient—parent-centred service.

Rupert is Clinical Director for Women's & Children's Health and a Consultant Gynaecologist with a significant private practice. He is secretly hoping for someone who can take a more proactive leadership role in paediatrics, which he currently feels he spends too much time on because of the 'nice but ineffectual' manner in which they go about running their service.

Gerald is Medical Director and a Consultant Haematologist by background. He applied for the post of Medical Director whilst serving as Clinical Governance Lead because he felt that he could do a better quality of job than the previous incumbent and to ensure that important safety matters with solid audit data behind them received the appropriate attention they deserved from senior management.

Brenda welcomed Bob with a warm smile and a friendly, gentle handshake, much like his own. He started to relax. She led him through to the interview room and introduced him to Rupert and Gerald. Rupert stood up and enthusiastically shook hands with a fairly vice-like grip. Gerald, on the other hand, said a pleasant hello but continued to remain seated. They all sat down to begin. Already, Bob was feeling most drawn to Brenda, who seemed lovely, and a bit unsure of Gerald, who seemed a little detached. He hadn't 'worked out' Rupert yet, although he felt a bit overpowering.

After some fairly benign questions around the contents of Bob's CV, the panel started in earnest to ask their set of interview questions. Rupert had the first question, which was a succinct 'The Trust has aggressive cost-improvement targets and you need to drop pay costs by 15%. What would you do?' After carefully thinking about this, Bob answered 'I think it's really important to consider the terrible impact this has on the people involved. I think I would try to find a way of sharing the difficulty out fairly across the department's staff to avoid significant distress on a few'. He noted that Brenda seemed to be nodding and he went on to expand, largely to her how he might do this.

Brenda then asked whether he had been in conflict with a direct colleague before and, if so, how had he handled it. Bob flinched, remembering an argument that had gotten out of hand with a fellow middle-grade. It had ended with some very hard discussions with a consultant in which he was told that he should have dealt with it earlier and more forcefully. Bob opted to utilize this advice and explained the importance of not letting conflict take hold.

Gerald asked the final question, which pertinently was on clinical safety. 'You're on service and the nursing staff call you to say that the ST2 has administered a wrong dosage of a drug, the same problem that occurred with the same ST2 last week. What would you do?' Bob quickly answers that he'd immediately go and inform and reassure the parents and assess the patient for any ill effects. He goes on to explain that he'd then sit down with the ST2 because they must be feeling awful, perhaps making them a cup of tea and asking them to take a break. Obviously an incident form would be necessary too.

The panel thank Bob for coming and say that they will be deliberating immediately and should be able to inform him of the outcome within the hour if he wished to remain around. The deliberations were not straight forward.

Brenda said that she thought Bob was lovely and would certainly fit in. She said she particularly liked his empathy for staff and patients and he seemed very caring. Rupert rolled his eyes and said that he thought he was a weak candidate because 'he needed to take hard staffing decisions but hadn't, wasn't very resilient about disagreements and even his handshake was wishy-washy'. Gerald said that he had concerns over Bob's attitude to safety. Whereas he agreed that assessing the patient was an early priority, he expressed that 'he seemed more interested in protecting the ST2, who clearly had issues, than following a rigorous process. There was no mention of how he would address the performance issue, inform the right people or conduct a formal assessment of how it had happened'. On the basis of a 2 to 1 vote against, Bob was not appointed.

This is not atypical and unfortunately Bob has resonated with someone just like him but failed to address the needs of two people who are very different. In this example, Rupert would have responded better to strong, forceful, practical answers that proactively dealt with the hard issues, without being influenced too much by individual sensibilities. This would likely have felt uncomfortable to Bob, who clearly has a high degree of concern for individuals. Gerald would also have found this high people-focus disquieting. He would have been more reassured by a cold, dispassionate, analytical approach to the objective facts of the different situations, recognizing the breadth of problems and working logically and sequentially through the issues to conclusion. The greatest challenge here is that each panel member listens to all answers but their judgement of the answers is heavily influenced by their separate psychologies. To get this right, Bob needs to construct his answers to deal firstly with the needs of the question originator and subsequently with other panel members. A mastery of this will set Bob well apart from the masses at interview and serve him well throughout life.

Simplified classification framework

There are many questionnaires, systems and descriptions of behaviour, each with their own merits and disadvantages. More familiar ones include Myers Briggs Type Indicator®, Strength Deployment Inventory® and Insights Discovery®. You don't need a degree in psychology to understand this area, but you do need to develop sufficient mastery so that you can use the understanding practically in the interview situation, preferably on the hoof. Consequently, we are going to describe a simplified framework that is easy to grasp and practical to use. We make no apology for that simplification and are confident that the framework is sufficient to improve interview success without over-engineering a solution.

All that said, human behaviour is obviously much more complex and we want to make the point that people do not fall into nice neat boxes (or islands, in our case). We recognize and understand this fully, but the simplification here is robust enough to get the job of improving interview technique right without overwhelming you with complex behavioural and psychological academia.

Three key classifications

Our simplified approach or model is based around three islands and the cultures and behaviour of the people who live on them. Rupert, Brenda and Gerald were each typical islanders but from different islands. So let's understand our islands and their inhabitants more.

We'd like you to imagine a cluster of three different islands, each with a fairly homogenous community of inhabitants, different from the other two neighbouring islands. Life has evolved on each island in relative isolation and they now have very different cultures, embedded behaviours and values. Each community is driven by a distinct set of principles and although they will engage in the behaviours common on other islands, they have certain ways, rules and facets of behaviour that to them represent the 'right' way of proceeding through life. This 'hard wiring' drives their decisions, opinions, preferences, likes, dislikes *and* their interview behaviour or choices.

Island of Opportunity

Rupert was from the Island of Opportunity. The inhabitants of our Island of Opportunity are best described as driven individuals with a strong desire to achieve and succeed. They feel good about themselves when they are moving forward, getting things done, winning things and acquiring evidence to the effect that they must be successful, such as a car to be proud of, a position of authority and responsibility or a nicer house in a better area. If you happened to be on the island early in the morning, you'd find that the inhabitants are up and ready for what the day has to throw at them, driving themselves hard and being energized by the challenge. They don't shirk away from dealing with difficult problems and tend to face them head on, practically and pragmatically. As you wander around this island, you notice that they prefer to get stuck in to practical things rather than spending time discussing matters, and when they are forced to contemplate something you notice a growing unease that they aren't 'doing' something. Overall, they are task-focused, achievement-orientated, outgoing individuals who don't suffer fools gladly and have a high respect for people who deliver on their goals.

Island of Team Spirit

Brenda was from the Island of Team Spirit. The inhabitants of this island are very different. As you arrive on this island you notice how warm and friendly they are. They seem genuinely pleased that you've come to visit them and they make you feel welcome by tending to your wellbeing—a drink is offered early and nothing seems too much trouble. As someone offers to show you around, you get a strong sense that these islanders really enjoy helping people and notice that they tend to place others' needs and wishes before their own, gaining satisfaction from having done the right thing or having been of service to others. There's a selflessness about these islanders. As you wander around, you see evidence of a well-developed community spirit, with social events and team sports. It seems important to these islanders to get on well together and you rightly surmise that their evidence of success is not in the cars they drive or the positions they hold so much as the quality of relationships they develop, their empathy and sensitivity towards each other and the gratitude or value placed in their service unto others.

Island of Intellect

Gerald was from the Island of Intellect. This is again a very different environment from the other two islands. The first thing you notice is a strong sense of order. Public transport runs on time, there are well-developed systems and processes and everything seems to have its place and purpose. It's not an ostentatious place and you'd best describe people's lot as 'appropriate to their needs'. As you enter the island you experience the formal immigration procedure, professionally and courteously delivered but without too much concern for individual sensibilities. You surmise that there isn't much room for departure from the protocol. At the end of the day you notice that the inhabitants tend to withdraw to their own spaces, preferring to re-charge their batteries away from others rather than with. They're not unfriendly, but you do notice a 'professional distance' and it's clear they find overfamiliarity uncomfortable, being very happy in their own company. Consequently, as you wander round, you see that running seems to be a common free-time activity and you notice the island has more than its fair share of bookshops.

As you have probably gathered, life from one island to the next is significantly different. The islanders from one island have a very different outlook on life from the others. They are driven by different values, make different choices, notice different things, notice things differently and have different interests. Consequently, in interview situations, they pick up on different aspects of answers and would 'rate' answers differently from each other. Even their choice of language is different and this too can have a bearing on how an answer is judged. They interact with each other differently too. In our earlier example, you may have noticed that Rupert shook hands vigorously and Gerald abstained altogether. These differences are simply cultural characteristics of the people from different islands.

What's important to each?

Next, we'll examine what's most important, noticed or prominent in the minds and lives of different islanders. By understanding this, it gives you considerable insight into what they might be looking for in your answers and, indeed, what turns them off.

We'll examine this from two standpoints:

- What's important to them in life
- What's important to them in interviews

What's important to them in life?

Island of Opportunity (Rupert)	Island of Team Spirit (Brenda)	Island of Intellect (Gerald)
• Achievements	• Relationships	• Principles
• What I get done	• How I get it done	• Whether I get it right
• Leading	• Following a trusted leader	• Autonomy
• Competence	• Support	• Self-reliance
• Winning	• Participating	• Time out
• Being promoted	• Being liked	• Being respected
• Status	• Acceptance at face value	• Independence
• Challenge	• Social interaction	• Space

Rupert doesn't suffer fools gladly. He's direct, to the point and likes to take charge. He drives himself and those around him hard and expects people to go the extra mile, just like he does. He plays competitive sport and would always prefer to have a match rather than a friendly. Having challenges in life stimulates him and when he overcomes them he expects the recognition for his achievements. He has worked hard to build his private practice and is naturally entrepreneurial. He respects those who are confident, not afraid to stand up for what they believe and proactive.

Brenda has a high degree of concern for people. She likes to help where help is needed and considers herself both a team player and highly loyal to her patients, colleagues and service. When she gets to know someone she is open and warm. She likes working amongst people and shies away from isolation, in which she feels lonely. She likes to see the right thing done and shuns selfishness or self-interest. She will lead but it's not her favourite position in life and she much prefers to be of service to a strong leader who she trusts and has confidence in. She likes to be recognized for her efforts, but a simple 'thank you' is all it takes to deliver that recognition. She doesn't like the limelight and prefers a few quiet words of gratitude rather than an award. She forms deep friendships and puts in the effort to make them work.

Gerald is an independent character, very happy in his own company. He likes life best when it has a rhythm or routine to it, rather than rapid or consistent change. He's cautious by nature and portrays a certain 'professional distance' with colleagues. His own space is important to him and constant interaction leaves him craving the peace and quiet of his office with the door closed. Gerald likes notice to do things and an intelligently thought-through plan. If he had a mantra it would be 'seek first to understand' and he likes to have the rationale for decisions, so that he can be confident they are right. Despite his liking of his own company, he is a strong, confident character who won't be pushed around. In fact, the harder he is pushed, the more resolute and steadfast he becomes. He prefers to be self-reliant, rather than dependent on others, resulting in him being a low delegator who prefers to tackle work on his own, methodically and with considerable attention to detail. He is risk averse and prefers to get things right first time through careful planning and preparation.

What's important to them in interviews?

When considering what's important to Rupert, Brenda and Gerald in the interview situation, we need to consider three different areas:

- The introduction and building rapport
- The answers that we give to questions
- The manner in which we answer questions

We will cover the introduction and building rapport in a later section, as well as going into how to adapt questions to be more suited to a particular island inhabitant. At this stage we'd simply like you to understand how one's island culture influences what's important to you in an interview situation.

Rupert is looking for strong confident answers that are brief and to the point. He respects decisiveness and so if you're going to present two different possible courses of action it is important to clearly articulate which one you would decide upon. He will place more weight on what you did than what you thought and so it is equally important to identify the steps that you went through. Rupert will be particularly interested in your leadership ability. His own leadership style is likely to be more autocratic than transformational and so to earn the most Brownie points you may wish to emphasize examples where you clearly took charge. The manner in which you answer questions will be a significant influence on Rupert's decision. He is looking for somebody who stands proud and makes good eye contact. In Rupert's eyes, submissiveness is not a mark of respect to his senior position so much as a sign of weakness. Where he offers an opinion he is happy to be challenged as long as you are prepared to defend your position. A well-articulated argument confidently presented is the mark of someone in charge of his or her life and not a life in charge of him/her.

By contrast, Brenda is looking for a little more humility in the answers. Too much confidence could come across as arrogance to Brenda, something that might give her cause to think that you could be difficult to work with. Answers need to be delivered in a much more gentle style with less energy and preferably a soft smile. When probing leadership, Brenda will be looking for evidence that you have an inclusive or transformational style and achieve things with people or through people, not in spite of people.

If you have an example of something that you achieved in difficult circumstances by taking people with you, this would increase Brenda's belief that you are a team player. Brenda would warm to human-interest stories and so it is a good idea to have a bank of examples around work that you have done with others, as either a member of the team or the leader of the team. In Brenda's eyes, having worries, fears and other emotions is perfectly human and not a sign of weakness. In fact, cold hard clinical answers could lead her to believe that you do not have sufficient empathy and might not be good company as a colleague. Across the interview it will be important to show the real you, including the values that you have and how you like to interact with other people.

Gerald's focus in the interview will be far more formal and concerned with the detail, accuracy of the background and signs of technical weakness. He is far less concerned with your interpersonal interactions and far more concerned about identifying areas where your knowledge and skills may not be up to scratch. He will respect answers that you have carefully thought through and constructed in a logical order. Opinions tend to turn him off, unless they can be backed up with evidence that suggests or proves that the opinion is correct. It is particularly important not to express an answer that you do not wish to be quizzed about in-depth. Gerald is most likely to spot gaps and anomalies in answers, which to him would seem imprecise and consequently worth exploring. This high propensity to spot problems will also lead him to spot anomalies in your CV. If there are gaps in your CV then it is important to have logical explanations for them and be ready for probing. In contrast to Brenda, Gerald prefers answers delivered factually and unemotionally. As far as he's concerned, if an answer is correct then individual sensibilities need to be ignored. Gerald does not like risk and so it is best to either de-emphasize episodes of risk or demonstrate that you recognized the risk and took appropriate action to mitigate its chances of occurring.

Your interpersonal impact on different interview panel members

Your own cultural characteristics could have adverse impacts on the rapport you build with different panel members and how they feel about your style, approach and life in general. It's important to consider which island you feel most akin to and how that might be perceived by others. What you need to decide is whether their tinted viewpoint would stand in the way of you being appointed. If you feel that there is a chance that you may not be appointed on the basis of someone's impression of you, then you must resolve to adapt your answers to better match up to the key players on the interview panel.

Decide which island is most like you and then see how you might be perceived by the other two islands and how you can modify or adapt your approach to have more beneficial and less adverse impacts.

From the Island of Team Spirit's perspective

Rupert, from the Island of Opportunity, can come across as rude, bullying and without regard for people's feelings to Brenda. It is his direct style and task focus that give rise to this, not helped by his apparent self-focus, evidenced by his acquisition of shallow status symbols. She does recognize that he gets things done, but she can have a tendency to feel that this is at the expense of people. Rupert would reduce these feelings by emphasizing his loyalty to the team, his desire to help and by adopting a little more humility with a little less confidence. A warm friendly communication style would go a long way to building rapport with Brenda. Rupert has a tendency to get straight down to business. The lack of small talk or preamble can suggest to Brenda that Rupert is self-focused.

Gerald, from the Island of Intellect, can be very measured and controlled with his answers. Whereas this is admirable in ensuring that answers are well thought out and properly articulated, the delivery devoid of emotion can come across to Brenda as slightly cold and unfriendly. Whereas Gerald would see objective professional detachment as a strength, Brenda might see it simply as a lack of empathy. Gerald's tendency to withhold personal information about himself and instead stick to the facts makes it quite difficult for Brenda to discover the real him. Consequently, Gerald can be seen as having ulterior motives or hidden agenda or things to hide, which can result in Brenda not developing a sense of trust, which for her would be very important. To counteract this, Gerald would be well advised to develop a series of small stories or examples that demonstrate the real him and in particular how he would be a good team player.

From the Island of Opportunity's perspective

Brenda, from the Island of Team Spirit, can come across as weak, a pushover and unfocused to Rupert. Her more personable communication style and her tendency to include preamble can result in Rupert thinking that she has a lack of application to the task at hand and that she is easily distracted. Brenda can come across as subservient to people in authority. Whereas there is nothing fundamentally wrong with this, it does add to Rupert's perception that Brenda is weak. Brenda could improve her perception in Rupert's eyes by making strong eye contact, speaking with authority and demonstrating confidence in her answers. If Rupert offers a different suggestion or an alternative viewpoint then Brenda would do well to stand her ground firmly but politely. Rupert could have concerns that Brenda's deep appreciation of people could lead to her avoiding taking difficult decisions where it involves letting somebody down. Again Brenda can improve her perception in Rupert's eyes by having a range of examples where she did indeed take difficult decisions that were necessary but not always pleasant.

Gerald, from the Island of Intellect, can come across as slow, rigid in his approach and obstructive. This arises out of Rupert's desire to move on and Gerald's desire to be cautious, methodical and sure of himself before committing to action. Gerald could improve this view by cutting back on some of the detailed explanation that he has a tendency to include in answers, instead focusing on the action or outcome of his thought process, rather than the reasoning. Rupert is much more interested in what he's going to do than why he decided to do it. Gerald could further improve his perception in Rupert's eyes by having a range of examples or instances when he had to adapt what he was doing to fit with the needs of others or because of an alteration in plan. This would help demonstrate his flexibility. Rupert responds well to a degree of passion which he is unlikely to get from Gerald. If Gerald is aware that he can come across as dispassionate, then he can look for opportunities to demonstrate how he showed tenacity in something that he cared deeply about. Because Gerald can be highly principled he needs to be on guard against coming across as too black and white. In Rupert's eyes there is always more than one way and Gerald would do well not to demonstrate a fixed point of view, despite his tendency to believe that there is a right way of doing most things and pointing this out.

From the Island of Intellect's perspective

Gerald can see Rupert, from the Island of Opportunity, as reckless and pushy. Gerald tends to view Rupert's high propensity to early action as meaning that Rupert doesn't think things through particularly carefully before he starts doing. This, to Gerald, would increase the likelihood of mistakes being made or the danger of running up a blind alley that he would have avoided with a more careful thought process. Rupert has a tendency to simply give the endpoint, conclusion or action from his thought process, without going into the rationale in more detail. He would reassure Gerald more if he shared a little more of the thought process behind his conclusions. Gerald can see Rupert as a risk taker and given that Gerald is risk averse, this adds to the perception of recklessness. Rupert can reduce these feelings by demonstrating that he appreciated the risk, carefully considered it and took action appropriately, perhaps having a backup plan if the risk had been realized.

Rupert can rub Gerald up the wrong way by pushing him too hard to make a decision when Gerald is not ready. In the interview situation, Rupert needs to be on guard against airing his frustration at people he sees as slow, perhaps instead recognizing the value in carefully considering the course of action before leaping into it.

Brenda, from the Island of Team Spirit, can seem too emotional or familiar to Gerald and overinfluenced by sentiment. Her warm and friendly style, coupled to a high degree of attention to ensuring that somebody is okay, can come across as smothering to Gerald, who prefers a detached professional exchange. Gerald can have concerns that Brenda's objectivity is clouded by her feelings for the individuals involved in any particular scenario. As far as Gerald is concerned, what is right must prevail over what is preferable. Brenda needs to demonstrate that she has carefully considered the facts of the situation and the intended outcome and made an unemotional, objective decision which she is prepared to carry through. Brenda would be well advised to have a range of examples of scenarios where she had to take tough decisions that weren't always in the best interests of everybody but were demonstrably the right course of action.

When meeting Gerald for the first time, Brenda needs to be aware that her desire to form warm relationships can cause Gerald to withdraw defensively. She is best served by a simple handshake delivered in a formal, detached manner.

Differing communication styles

Given that we have comparatively little opportunity to learn about interview panel members in advance of the interview itself, differing communication styles is one of our more useful ways of recognizing them.

Island of Opportunity (Rupert)	Island of Team Spirit (Brenda)	Island of Intellect (Gerald)
• Direct	• Warm	• Detached
• Bulleted or brief	• Cautious or shy	• Methodical
• Action orientated	• Softer	• Carefully thought through
• Task focused	• People focused	• Measured
• High energy	• Bubbly	• Guarded
• Passionate	• Hesitant	• Comprehensive
• Intense	• Friendly	• Monotone
• Powerful	• Personal	• Precise
• Confident	• Use of preamble	• Dispassionate
• Self-promoting	• Use of the word 'sorry'	• Detailed
• Use of the word 'I'	• Use of the word 'we'	• Use of the word 'it'

The safest approach in an interview situation is to match the style of communication to the person you are addressing.

You could address individuals in turn and adjust your style 'on the hoof' for each. Make eye contact with whoever you are addressing and match your style to them and then change it when you move to the next person. If that sounds risky, then simply address answers to and match the style of the person asking.

Distinct islands have distinct word preferences too. The following words would be typical of our different islanders:

Island of Opportunity (Rupert)	Island of Team Spirit (Brenda)	Island of Intellect (Gerald)
• Task	• Like	• Accurate
• Action	• Feel	• Precise
• Goal	• Support	• Appropriate
• Achieve	• Help	• Evidence or proof
• Results	• Worry	• Facts
• Opportunity	• Thank you	• Information or data
• Best	• Do you mind?	• Method
• Winning	• Care	• Risk
• First	• Kind	• Problem
• Progress	• Tea? Coffee?	• Logical
• Targets	• Appreciate	• Correct

If you imagine listening to somebody using a high density of words from one of the above columns, you probably get a distinct picture of what that person is like. Get used to listening for 'overuse' of these words. We'll deal later with how to use these words to improve the resonance of your own answers.

Self-awareness—understanding your own wiring

Understanding yourself and your own behaviour is critical to gaining an ability to be flexible and adaptable when it serves you best. If you consider how Bob approached his interview in our previous sections, you will now realize that he was simply going with what his subconscious told him was right. Had the whole interview panel been wired just like Bob this would have been the perfect approach. In our example, Bob was wired quite like Brenda, from the Island of Team Spirit, and you will notice that it was Brenda who found Bob most acceptable. Although Bob's answers would have been reasonably competent, it was what he chose to emphasize and how he delivered it that gave rise to Rupert's and Gerald's opinions of him.

Developing self-awareness

There are a number of very practical things you can do to both develop self-awareness and learn how to adapt your style (see Box 4.1).

How you answer interview questions will be heavily influenced by your underlying wiring. If you think back to the question Bob was asked concerning cost-saving measures involving dropping pay by 15%, his gut instinct was to immediately think about the impact on the individuals concerned. There is nothing fundamentally wrong with this answer. Indeed, Brenda thought that it demonstrated Bob's empathy with the situation and the people. However, Rupert and Gerald had very different reactions. Rupert, who would have been conscious that if the Trust was in trouble then the longer savings remain outstanding the more unstable the Trust may be, could see Bob's answer as avoiding the critical issue that savings must be made in favour of protecting the people, which may not be appropriate in this case. Gerald would have been concerned that Bob's answer was unduly influenced by his emotions and his desire not to upset people and consequently was not objective. Self-awareness and insight would have allowed Bob to address the concerns of Rupert and Gerald too.

Recognizing an individual's pattern

Being better able to recognize which island an individual is from significantly enhances your ability to consider your style, impact and answers. The pre-interview visit is extremely helpful, as your more casual interaction will allow you to learn much about individuals. Always try to look for as many 'signs' as possible and avoid putting too much reliance on any single observation.

Box 4.1 Developing self-awareness

Your golden rules

Write down on a piece of paper all of the golden rules that you live by in life. When you feel that you have a comprehensive list of these rules, ask yourself the question 'Why are these rules important to me and which island does this suggest I come from?' More importantly, ask yourself 'If I stated these rules to somebody from one of the other islands, how would they react to them or what would they think about them?'

Practising with a friend

Find a small group of friends or colleagues who you can identify as being distinctly from one island or another. Get them to ask you a series of interview questions, to which you will respond with very natural answers. Then ask them what they liked and disliked about the answers and how the answers made them feel about you as a potential employee or candidate. Once you have learned how your natural style comes across to them, ask them how you could have altered your answer to have greater resonance, or to generate greater confidence that you would be a good candidate.

Understanding rapport

List out on a piece of paper all of your current colleagues who you feel you have a very natural rapport with. Then list out all of your current colleagues where communication or interaction feels slightly unnatural. Over the coming days or weeks observe these two groups and notice what words each group uses, what body language or mannerisms they employ and why it is that you feel either comfortable or uncomfortable with them. When you examine your collected observations, you will most likely notice that the people you are most comfortable with are probably from the same island as you. Equally those who you are less comfortable with are more likely to be from other islands. You will notice distinct traits or behaviours in the uncomfortable group. You need to ask yourself if these traits or behaviours would feel comfortable or uncomfortable when you place yourself on another island. This exercise will help you develop considerable self-awareness of your immediate impact on others and how to adapt it to build rapport more successfully.

Recognizing Opportunity Islanders

Typical signs or behaviours of Opportunity Islanders include:

Factor	Behaviour
Home	Large house in a good area, latest gadgets
Car	Sports or status car, maybe rare
Hobbies, Sports and Interests	Competitive sports, extreme, status, team captain
Family	Purposeful visits, protective relationships
Friends	Lots of acquaintances, practical relationships, peers
Preferred Jobs	Practical, risky, visible, status, leading
Work Patterns	Hyperbusy, long hours, get stuck in, punctuality
Office	Organized, certificates and pictures, big desk and chair
Manner	Direct, down to business, energetic, forceful

Recognizing Team Spirit Islanders

Typical signs or behaviours of Team Spirit Islanders include:

Factor	Behaviour
Home	Warm and inviting, lived in, very personal
Car	Often utilitarian, e.g. People carrier, or with identity
Hobbies, Sports and Interests	Team sports, social activities, dinner parties, charity
Family	Regular contact by visit and phone, close relationships
Friends	Numerous friends with lots of activity
Preferred Jobs	Team environment, caring professions, people serving
Work Patterns	Erratic, easily distracted, breaks with others, compliant
Office	Personal—photos, plants, cards, chair for guests
Manner	Warm, cautious until they know you, considerate

Recognizing Intellect Islanders

Typical signs or behaviours of Intellect Islanders include:

Factor	Behaviour
Home	Carefully chosen, efficient, sensible
Car	Safe, reliable, good economy, low depreciation
Hobbies, Sports and Interests	Gym, running, chess, collecting, time to oneself
Family	Set times, distinct pattern, when you 'should' be there
Friends	Comparatively few, intellectually similar, loyal
Preferred Jobs	Research, isolation, systematic, intellectual stimulation
Work Patterns	Distinct routines, guidelines, early, sense of order
Office	Impersonal, orderly (caution), isolated, functional
Manner	Professional, detached, cautious

Considering your interview panel

The challenge that we face with identifying the underlying wiring of our interview panel is that we don't spend much time with them before the interview itself. That means that we must use every available opportunity at our disposal to pick up those signs. Opportunities include:

- Utilizing information that we are already aware of, e.g. their specialty or job
- Information that we can uncover through research, e.g. specialist interests
- Talking to them directly in the pre-interview visit
- Immediate signs gained from first impressions

Existing information

What someone does as a job can be heavily influenced by their underlying wiring. It's important to consider the 'nature' of the job, for instance does/is it predominantly:

- Practical? (Opportunity)
- Involve an element of risk? (Opportunity)
- Involve lots of direct patient interaction? (Team Spirit)
- Involve working in isolation? (Intellect)
- Require a detailed, methodical approach? (Intellect)
- Quite technical? (Intellect)

- Involve quite strong or proactive leadership? (Opportunity)
- Very team orientated? (Team Spirit)

Because the nature of the job tends to influence whether we would apply for it, certain specialties and jobs have a much higher proportion of some islanders than others. The following may be useful in gaining clues as to which island someone may be from. Again, as with any single reference, we need to act with caution.

Specialty/Job	Typical Islands
Surgical specialties	Opportunity
Paediatrics	Team Spirit
Psychiatry	Intellect—Team Spirit mixture
Laboratory specialties, e.g. Pathology	Intellect
Emergency Medicine	Opportunity
Radiology	Intellect
Medical specialties	Team Spirit or Intellect or a mixture of the two
Obstetrics & Gynaecology	Opportunity
Neonatal medicine	Intellect (but watch for Opportunity too)
Anaesthetics	Intellect
Medical Director	Opportunity or Intellect or a mixture
Senior Academics	Opportunity—Intellect mixture
Managers and Senior Managers	Opportunity
HR	Intellect or occasionally Team Spirit

If you take the trouble to make a basic assumption prior to interview, then aim to validate it when you are introduced.

Research

For key players on the interview panel, it is worth digging through Google and Medline to see what you can uncover about them. For instance, a string of references on Medline for a non-academic appointment suggests that the development of understanding (Island of Intellect) is important to that individual. Opportunity Islanders often engage in competitive sport and you will often find references to them as team captains, etc. Consider individuals' roles on committees. What is the committee for? Committees of movers and shakers often attract Opportunity Islanders, whereas safety, planning, drugs and therapeutics committees tend to attract more Intellect Islanders. Engagement in education, for instance as educational supervisors, suggests a possible Team Spirit Islander.

> **USEFUL TIP**: Research done on the interview panel or key players also demonstrates that you have done your homework—an admirable trait in a future colleague!

Pre-interview visit

This is an important opportunity to gain some real, first-hand insight into potential panel members. It is important that you maximize the opportunity to learn about the department/Trust and the individuals. Even if you don't get the chance to meet up with all of your potential future colleagues, remember to ask about them, for instance any special interests they have.

> **USEFUL TIP**: Every time you learn something, write it down in a notebook with a page devoted to each individual and then review what the overall picture looks like—what is it telling you?

It is useful to have a whole series of questions that you can ask almost everybody, each of which could give you some island clues (as well as provide information of value anyway, of course). We propose the following:

- Why did you apply here? (What were their reasons?)
- What do you like best about this Trust? (e.g. its strong academic reputation—Intellect or Opportunity)
- When you first considered a new colleague, what type of person were you ideally looking for? (We tend to choose islanders similar to ourselves out of choice)
- What do you do in your spare time? (On the pretence of discovering free-time opportunities)
- What are your ambitions for the department? (Opportunity Islanders often have big plans, whereas Intellect Islanders often have very detailed plans involving resolving weaknesses or problems. Team Spirit ambitions tend to be modest and geared towards improving patient care and support)
- Where do you believe the department needs strengthening? (e.g. leadership—Opportunity Islander response)

It is important to listen beyond the factual nature of the answer itself to the motivation or reason that seems to be running behind it. If appropriate, ask 'why' as it will often give you better information than 'what'. Remember:

- What car?—BMW (could be Opportunity or Intellect)
- Why a BMW?—safety, fuel economy and resale value (almost certainly Intellect)

First impressions

Hopefully, with the preceding guidance you are not walking in to the interview cold. However, if you are, you can still gain a great deal of insight from the initial impressions. We give a lot away in our mannerisms and how we relate to others, often without even realizing it. The following may be helpful signs:

Island	Typical signs
Opportunity	• Firm handshake • Strong eye contact • To the point, little small talk • Power dressing • Seated in the dominant position • Time conscious
Team Spirit	• Soft handshake • Warm greeting • Enquires after your welfare • Offers you a drink, makes you comfortable • May engage in small talk • May seem nervous themselves
Intellect	• Reluctant handshake or no handshake • Comparatively little eye contact • Might seem aloof or otherwise preoccupied • Quite formal • May deal with the 'rules of engagement' • Measured behaviour, i.e. self-control

It is best to have a picture already built up and to be utilizing this opportunity to see if your original thoughts were correct. However, it is also worth remembering that an individual can be a mixture of Islands and this would be reflected in a mixed pattern of behaviours. Equally, there are no absolutes because we are all so individual. The above pattern is simply 'indicative' that a person may be from a particular island.

Applying the principles in an interview situation

Hopefully you now have enough of an understanding that you can recognize a particular islander and have a perspective on their world, including what's important to them. We now need to focus on how to use this information to your best advantage in the interview situation. To do this, we need to understand a little more about how wiring influences behaviour.

From stimulus to behaviour

When we meet people, talk to them, answer a question, provide a CV or even do something, we are providing a *stimulus* that evokes a behavioural response. If that behavioural response is a positive one, we are more likely to get appointed, and if it is a negative one, despite highly competent answers, then we are less likely to get appointed. You could be forgiven for thinking that this isn't objective or fair and that recruitment should be based on an objective assessment of someone's capability. This is true but ignores the basic facts that we are mostly slave to our subconscious and have very little time to assess a future colleague. Consequently, gut feeling will play just as much a part as objective assessment. Some would even say that the CV is the objective assessment and the interview is therefore more about fit, etc. Either way, you want to ensure that you provide the right stimulus *and* the right answer to maximize your chances of being appointed.

The precursor to most behaviour, including the decision to appoint, is an emotion or collection of emotions. The sequence of activity goes as follows:

$$\text{Stimulus} \rightarrow \text{Meaning} \rightarrow \text{Emotion} \rightarrow \text{Behaviour}$$

Consequently, your goal in the interview is to evoke the right emotion or collection of emotions in each individual on the panel so that they automatically arrive at a decision to appoint you. That means considering the meaning they'd need to get from your answers and applying the right stimulus or words to evoke all of this. If all that sounds complex, then the following framework will make it much easier.

Simple framework

We utilize a process known as THINK, FEEL, DO, although it runs in reverse order, commencing with asking exactly what it is that we want someone to do. We then ask ourselves what must that person think and feel in order for that outcome, decision or behaviour to be the natural extension of those thoughts and feelings. Both the thoughts and feelings and the 'do' should be influenced by our understanding of an individual's underlying wiring. Let's look at a simple example.

Imagine those old-fashioned days when you had to specify either a smoking or non-smoking room when you booked a hotel. Let's say you specified a non-smoking room, but when you turn up at the reception desk they informed you that all the no-smoking rooms have been taken. You suspect that there are non-smoking rooms if the receptionist simply rearranges the bookings.

What would the receptionist need to *think* and *feel* in order that rearranging the bookings (*do*) would be her natural behaviour?

We need to consider that receptionists work in a customer-facing role in the hospitality industry. In the absence of any signs that might suggest otherwise, we could reasonably assume that the receptionist was from the Island of Team Spirit. Consequently, we now need to ask ourselves what would a Team Spirit Islander need to think and feel in order to rearrange the bookings?

- That you were disappointed but in no way angry with the receptionist
- That rearranging the bookings would be a kind and appropriate thing to do
- That you would be genuinely grateful for the help
- That she would be doing the right thing for the hotel

In this case, those thoughts and feelings would be delivered more through the manner in which you handled this than what you actually said. This would come most naturally to Brenda and least naturally to the other two. It is easy to surmise that Rupert might try to use authority and argument as his strategy to get the room. Gerald would be more inclined to rely on the principle that as he had booked a non-smoking room he should be entitled to the no-smoking room. Neither approach is likely to positively resonate with the Team Spirit receptionist.

Let's examine how we might apply this to answering questions, especially how we might adapt them to better match the underlying wiring of panel members.

Adapting question responses

Let's consider how we might bring Brenda to a natural decision to appoint Bob. We must first clarify *exactly* what we want her to do:

Do:
  be certain that Bob is the right person for the job and therefore appoint him.
  Now we need to consider what Brenda must think and feel in order for that to be automatic:

Think and feel:
  that Bob is a kind and caring individual
  that Bob would be supportive as a team member
  that Bob would not upset existing staff
  that Bob places the needs of the patient before his own
  that Bob would be loyal to the Department

We can now test this out by asking ourselves whether Brenda, who we have identified as Island of Team Spirit, would feel a natural inclination to have confidence in Bob as the preferred candidate, sufficient to appoint, if she thought and felt the above. Once we are happy that we have the right set of thoughts and feelings to create, we can start to consider how to tailor the answers to our questions and our overall approach to generate those thoughts and feelings. This will be achieved by firstly building rapport with Brenda, so as to put her in the right frame of mind, and then emphasizing past experiences that demonstrate the above. For instance, when Rupert asked about job cuts, recognizing the impact on the individuals and taking measures to protect their welfare would have resonated positively with Brenda. However, it didn't resonate positively with Rupert because he would need a different set of thoughts and feelings to feel certain that Bob was right for the job.

This dilemma between positively resonating with Brenda but not negatively resonating with Rupert is relatively simply resolved by phrasing the answer to account for both sets of needs. This might sound something like the following:

> 'If the Trust is in severe financial deficit then it is vital that action is taken swiftly, or it places even more jobs at risk. However, if job cuts are arbitrarily decided without sufficient consideration of the impact on individuals or groups, then it can inadvertently sacrifice the future for the present by reducing morale and leaving the Trust short of individuals who may be vital for future performance. Step one would be to rapidly analyse who is essential to the future success of the department. Step two would be to work out a strategy that makes maximum use of natural staff turnover to move to the new staffing structure. I would ensure that all staff fully understood the rationale for the changes, linked firmly to their future job security, and were actively involved in helping create and implement the new strategy. It is possible that this will not create the magnitude of change necessary to drop pay costs by 15%. In which case, we might have to consider additional measures, always with three key principles in mind:
> - Change needs to happen swiftly to induce stability and sustainability
> - Always minimizing the impact on individuals
> - Never at the expense of quality and safety'

In this example, as we have three different islanders, the answer has been tailored to ensure that each of them has their primary needs addressed. Rupert should come away feeling that Bob would take decisive action to address the issue in a timely manner. Brenda should come away feeling that Bob has taken difficult decisions firmly with staff in mind, trying to avoid specific job losses where possible. Gerald would be reassured that Bob's approach to workforce redesign would have future performance as an underpinning driver, along with a high concern for quality and safety. This answer should be a win all-round and demonstrates that Bob has a depth of thought process beyond his own immediate experience.

Island thoughts and feelings in the interview situation

The following is a good generic guide to what different islanders need to think and feel in order to have confidence in and certainty to appoint a particular candidate. In each case, we need to consider that candidates are up against each other and therefore these thoughts and feelings need to be stronger for you than the others.

Island	Typical thoughts and feelings
Opportunity	• Strong leader • Decisive • Practical • Goal-focused or task-orientated • A peer, rather than a junior • Self-assured or confident • Competent
Team Spirit	• Warm and friendly • Considers people • Places patients first • Demonstrates empathy • Supportive and loyal • Likeable • Open and honest (integrity)
Intellect	• Quality and safety focused • Risk averse • Cautious (doesn't leap to action) • Considers things carefully • Doesn't take snap decisions • High attention to detail • Cause and effect thought process

You will notice from the above list that Rupert has a natural tendency to look forward towards things that he wants, whereas Gerald also considers things that he wants to avoid. Rupert is primarily concerned with what you can do, Brenda with who you are and Gerald with how well you do what you do.

Delivering the answers

When a specific individual asks you a question, it is important to address that person first but without ever forgetting that there are other panel members who will be listening. The skilful adapter would frame the answer so as to deliver the interviewer's element of the answer first whilst making eye contact directly with him/her, before addressing other panel members with their own specific bits, again making eye contact as he/she does so.

In our job-cutting example it was Rupert who asked the question and, consequently, you would need to emphasize the importance of swift, decisive action as the first point, whilst making eye contact confidently with him. Given the people element to this question, it would then be prudent to deal with sensitivity whilst making eye contact with Brenda and then move on to the importance of considering quality and safety, as well as having a robust solution, whilst making eye contact with Gerald.

Further example

Have a go at creating an appropriate answer to Gerald's question below, accounting for all three islands.

The question is as follows:

> 'You're on service and the nursing staff call you to say that the ST2 has administered the wrong dosage of a drug, the same problem that occurred with the same ST2 last week. What would you do?'

You will find an example answer in Box 4.2.

We strongly advocate practising this process again and again. Within this book you will find a wide variety of interview questions, many with example generic answers. Try adapting these answers (or coming up with your own answers) to account for different islands.

> **USEFUL TIP**: Ask friends and colleagues from different islands to rate how positive they find your answer, including what they both like and dislike about it.

Box 4.2 Possible answer to the practice interview question

You're on service and the nursing staff call you to say that the ST2 has administered a wrong dosage of a drug, the same problem that occurred with the same ST2 last week. What would you do?

When constructing an answer to this question, it is important to establish what each person is looking for. Gerald will be most concerned with how you deal with the immediate safety concerns, as well as your root cause analysis and solution to preventing it happening again. Brenda will be most concerned with how you deal with the people involved, both the patient and the ST2 and possibly the nursing staff. Rupert will be primarily concerned with whether you are decisive and how you might deal with any reputational issues that could affect the department's status.

The answer probably looks something like this:

'Firstly, I would immediately assess the potential for harm arising out of an incorrect dosage and then immediately inform the patient, offering an apology and reassuring them that there are unlikely to be any ill effects. I would make it clear who to contact if they were at all worried. Secondly, I would rapidly assess whether the circumstances of last week's incorrect dosage was similar to this week's. Armed with this initial assessment, I would reassure the ST2 that no harm had been done but that we did need to deal with the problem of incorrect dosing. I would have this conversation away from other staff and reassure the doctor that there are unlikely to be any further repercussions unless the patient makes a complaint or we can't rectify the cause of repeated mis-dosing, which is obviously an important safety issue. I would explain clearly how we will examine the dosing issue, emphasizing that the goal is to ensure that the doctor has confidence in administering drugs directly. Finally, I would talk to the nursing staff and reassure them that the doctor concerned and myself have a distinct plan to avoid this happening again. Obviously, we would need to complete an incident form, as well as notify appropriate senior personnel in the Trust.'

Developing rapport

Building rapport is very much about first impressions. Rapport is a very individual sense and it is just as important not to inadvertently break it as it is to try hard to build it. There are two general strategies for ensuring you stand the maximum chance of developing good rapport with each panel member.

Matching our first impressions guide

Earlier, we provided an island-by-island guide on how to recognize individuals based on first impressions. Ironically, at a subconscious level, each islander would be developing a first impression of you based on a very similar set of factors. The safest approach is to match as closely as possible the first impressions you see in each panel member. This is likely to be the behaviour they are most comfortable with and will most likely lead to the strongest rapport.

Matching body language (mirroring)

Rapport can be formed at a physiological level. As you progress through the interview, notice how each person sits, what they do with their arms, how they hold themselves, their head position and any other distinctive aspects of body language. When you are addressing them, as naturally as possible, try to match their specific body language. When two people have rapport, you will find that this matching process takes place automatically. However, we can induce it by subtly adopting similar body language to that which they are displaying. It is obviously important to ensure that you don't do this in an obvious manner, or you run the risk of them feeling copied and wondering why (unless they have read this book!).

Tailoring presentations

It is common in the modern consultant interview to have to make a short presentation. We tend to view this as simply a different form of answering questions. However, the principles that we use in answering questions are equally applicable to presentations. It is quite useful to consider who may have set the presentation and therefore what they were trying to evaluate. Regardless of this, the closer a presentation matches the underlying wiring of the interview panel, the more impact it is likely to have.

Most of us construct presentations in a form that would work for us. This, of course, is perfect for people just like us. However, given our emphasis of the difference in people, you can probably see why this might not be appropriate for all panel members.

The basic strategy is to tailor the presentation first and foremost to the key players on the interview panel. You need to decide which panel members carry the most weight in the decision to appoint. This will obviously be heavily influenced by the make-up of the panel and therefore it is important to establish this ahead of attending the interview. Given that all panel members have some impact on the decision to appoint, it is important to ensure that the presentation emphasizes information or aspects of the subject matter that relate to all three islands.

The following guide will help you formulate a presentation that resonates with each island:

Island	Presentation
Opportunity	• Brief • To the point • Conclusion first, then underpinned by evidence • Emphasizes practical value • Delivered with conviction and confidence • Thought-provoking • Light on evidence, heavy on use
Team Spirit	• Personable style (chatty discussion) • Includes feelings about things • Emphasizes benefits to people • Relaxed presentation • Recognizes others' contribution
Intellect	• Structured and orderly • If it's mentioned in the agenda, cover it! • Clear cause and effect logic • Sound rationale • Identifies weaknesses and constraints • Delivered professionally, even dispassionately • Identifies alternative conclusions, if appropriate

Brenda is more concerned with how it is delivered than what it says, as long as the contents don't negatively resonate with her values around people, help and support. Rupert is most concerned with what he can do with information, how it improves his ability to achieve or how it simplifies what he needs to do. He does not need all of the rationale and workings. In fact, if this is included you run the risk of him switching off, hence the importance of commencing with the conclusion and then underpinning it with the evidence. This ensures that Rupert gets the practical value of what you are presenting while still delivering the evidence that is so important to Gerald. Gerald wants to see that you have clearly thought things through and he will be looking for holes in your argument. He is the most likely to ask detailed questions afterwards and you will earn extra Brownie points by having a couple of additional slides that address the most likely ones. It is equally appropriate to consider producing a professional-looking handout that expands on the information. This says to Gerald that you have carefully considered the subject matter and gone into sufficient detail, whilst demonstrating to Brenda that you must really want to come and work with them because of the effort you have gone to. Rupert would be impressed by the document (predominantly the cover) even though he is unlikely to read it.

Chapter 5
Interview preparation

Introduction

This chapter focuses on the preparation you will need to go through to be successful at the consultant interview. Many candidates wrongly think that the key to interview success is to know about everything political that has ever happened to the NHS or their speciality. Unfortunately this belief sets them up to be unsuccessful. The key is to take time to learn as much about yourself as possible so that you can use every interview question as an opportunity to promote why you should be given the job.

In this chapter we explore:

- An appropriate preparation plan
- Key sales techniques
- Key rules for answering questions effectively
- Key tips for answering specific types of question, e.g. the negative question or the opinion question

The preparation needed for answering political questions is addressed in Chapter 9. Guidance on how to approach answering questions within the interview itself is addressed in Chapter 6, e.g. not understanding the question asked.

The purpose of interviews

It goes without saying that the purpose of the interview is for the interview committee to appoint the right person for the job. In general this will be the person who they feel:

- Will most fit with the ethos of the team, service and Trust
- Is a safe doctor
- Will be both a leader and a team player
- Will proactively develop the service
- Will work collaboratively with Trust management

However, not all interview committees want all of the above in all cases. For instance, although many Trusts are currently looking for proactive, business-focused goal achievers (because there is a shortage!), some may simply want a quiet, methodical clinical professional. At the pre-interview visit it is vitally important to get a sense of what the key players really do want so that at interview you can effectively promote the benefits you will bring to the post in that regard.

It is equally true that not all panel members are the same. Many panels are made up of people with divergent requirements. Again, at the pre-interview visit it is essential to differentiate who wants what and then make sure you address those needs or desires appropriately, focusing more heavily on the key players, as they carry more weight in the decision. We will explain how to achieve this successfully later in the chapter—see 'Meeting the needs of more than one interviewer'.

> **USEFUL TIP**: At the pre-interview visit, you must get a sense of who the key players are, how much weight they carry and what they personally want.

What the employer really wants to know is:

- Can you do the job?
- Will you do the job?
- Will you fit in?

Unfortunately, they will not make it easy by simply asking you those questions directly, so you will have to demonstrate these things for them through three elements of your interview strategy:

- Developing rapport to build feelings that you fit in
- Providing evidence to prove you can do the job (evidence is a loose term here as it is mostly examples of things done or previous behaviour that leads to this sense of 'proven')
- Selling the qualities and skills you have which are important for this specific post. Again you will deliver this best by demonstrating your previous experience and behaviour in specific situations, e.g. leading a project, but also through careful wording, real moves and emphasizing specific aspects of your capability or experience

Preparation plan

It is true to say that both over- and under-preparation can result in failure at interview. Whereas under-preparation will likely result in you being unsuccessful, over-preparation has certain risks attached to it that can be mitigated if you are aware of them.

Under-preparation can result in:

- Disorganized answers
- An inability to answer a question, i.e. you don't know
- Rambling, often a function of the first two
- Failure to get the real you across (or even recognize what needs to be got across)
- Failure to shine, against a more shiny 'pack' of candidates

Over-preparation can lead to:

- Rigidity of answers, i.e. they are over-rehearsed and inflexible
- Failure to answer the actual question asked
- Seen as 'failing to listen' because you give information that you know but which doesn't contribute to the answer quality
- Impression of a dry, impersonal, dispassionate character, almost robotic

Clearly the goal is to engage in a sensible and appropriate level of preparation and that requires an effective preparation plan.

Appropriate preparation

For many people, interview practice starts with practising a whole pile of questions. This should come later in your preparation, not early. Ideally, plan to cover the following over a number of days:

- Understanding the real you—self-awareness and self-knowledge
  - Review your CV and experience—know this inside out
  - Work through the 'getting to know the real you' exercise
    - Even if you have done this previously for a different job application you will need to re-do the exercise and consider how the examples you have used benefit the organization and service you are now applying to
- Review key topics, one theme per day
- Practise specific key interview questions

As you go through your preparation, it is important to constantly consider the following in your thoughts and reflections:

- What does this specific interview panel want in a consultant colleague?
- What were the key issues raised in my pre-interview visit?

What does this interview panel want in a consultant colleague?

In general, panels are looking for the following attributes in a consultant colleague:

- Safe
- Team player
- Leader
- Proactive—will make a difference
- Fits with ethos of hospital and service
- Business-focused, as well as clinical

We do need to appreciate that we can't apply a global principle here as different individuals have different things on their wish-list, e.g. the Chief Executive may want a consultant to come in and shake up the service by providing strong leadership and direction, whilst the Consultant Representative may want someone who is a good team player, works quietly and will not rock the boat. You will have an understanding of all of this from the pre-interview visit. You need to get a sense of what the key players want and ensure you cover all bases in the interview.

> **USEFUL TIP**: Build yourself a grid or table of the key players so that you can fill in the blanks of who they are, the weight they carry, what they want, how they are wired, etc. If there are outstanding boxes in important areas, commit to filling them through research.

It is important also to recognize that panels usually want very different qualities and attributes from a locum consultant colleague compared to a permanent consultant colleague. Often the key qualities for a locum are someone who can hit the floor running and just get on with the job with little support. Needing someone who is going to lead significant service development is unlikely to be a specific requirement in these instances but the ability to deliver education successfully may climb the list in terms of importance (locums are often utilized to take on educational commitments to allow substantive consultants to focus on other things—it is important to find this out—ask!).

The interview as a sales pitch

Unfortunately (or fortunately), it is not politically correct to ask many of the questions that interview committees would really like to ask and so they tend to ask you benign questions, such as what the audit cycle is, what key performance indicators (KPIs) should we have in your speciality or how would you manage a drunken colleague, all in the hope that they will be able to reach a sensible conclusion.

Many interviewees naively believe the purpose of these questions is to answer them factually and correctly—often failing badly at an interview for the job of their dreams. The key to getting the job is not answering but responding to the questions as if each one was as an opportunity to sell or promote yourself. We will come back to 'responding' in more detail later in the chapter.

> **USEUL TIP**: The key to getting the job is not answering but responding to the question asked. You need to see every single question as an opportunity to sell or promote yourself, or to deliver a 'tick' against a vital criterion for appointment.

Sales techniques

We know that most doctors didn't go in to medicine to become sales people and therefore the principles and techniques are somewhat alien. We hope that the following guidance will demystify the topic sufficiently for you to develop a fairly competent ability to present yourself in the right light.

All good sales people know that when it comes to selling or promoting something, you really need to:

- Understand your product (which in this case is you)
- Understand the needs of the person investing in the product (the interview committee)
- Understand what benefits they hope to get from this investment

If they are to sell or promote effectively, sales men and women recognize that people do not buy products, e.g. a vacuum cleaner; rather they buy the benefits that vacuum cleaner brings, e.g. the ability to remove dog hairs. Already you can see that the benefit is not a generic one but specific to the individual, i.e. someone with a moulting dog wants dog hairs removed and therefore is 'in the market' for a vacuum cleaner that does just that. If you don't know that your vacuum cleaner does that and don't recognize that this person wants that, then you might not sell many vacuum cleaners! The same principles apply when going for a consultant interview—it is more important to understand what they want than to simply tell them what you are good at.

Once a good sales person is clear about the needs and challenges of the 'client', he/she then utilizes two techniques:

- Stress the benefits and qualities of the product most relevant to those needs and challenges
- Give examples that demonstrate the strengths of the product in that regard

For example, a BMW may be fast, look good and have status, but if the person buying is wanting space, safety and a good resale value then it is these that need emphasizing. The BMW would be an excellent choice but it isn't going to be bought by *this specific client* unless these attributes are clearly identified and backed up with something of substance.

Sales people also know that they are most likely to get a sale if you, the client, decide and act there and then. This is difficult in an interview as the committee retires to consider all of the candidates. Consequently, with a detached decision-making process, a good sales person would recognize that it is important for the panel to remember the person and his/her answers. This is best achieved through stories and examples rather than semantic answers. For example, asked about the qualities of a good clinical leader, it would be perfectly acceptable to provide a list of the most important ones. However, this is likely to be similar to other candidates and afterwards results in candidates all 'merging' into one. Better would be to answer something like 'When I was undertaking my fellowship in Australia, I discovered that . . .'. The panel is far more likely to remember your fellowship in Australia and, assuming the answer you gave was sensible, chalk that up as a plus point in the discussions afterwards.

Examples that demonstrate your strengths

- Remember past performance or behaviour is the best predictor of future performance or behaviour. If you spontaneously led a clinical service improvement in the past you are much more likely to do it again in the future. If you have dealt with a specific type of ethical problem, you can talk about the specific example or case you had
- You are remembered for your stories and examples. These are what make you stand out from the other interviewees. The more you talk about what you have actually done the more you stand out from the other candidates and the more your answers will be remembered

Imagine your interviewer having a series of coat hangers on which to hang information about you, which in turn will help you stand out from the crowd. Stories and examples are the garments that you need to hang on these hangers in the interviewer's mind. The more vivid the garments, the higher the likelihood that panel members will notice them and remember them. It is these particular garments that help you to stand out from the crowd and ensure you are remembered when the panel is making its decisions. This concept, known as authentic recall, will substantially enhance your ability to get appointed by making you stand out to a panel that is looking for an 'outstanding' candidate.

> **USEFUL TIP**: Remember, people buy benefits and solutions, not products, so always sell your attributes that most closely match the panel's wish list.

Stress the benefits of your skills and qualities

- Remember, these are only a true benefit if they benefit the employer, i.e. they are what he/she wants or needs
- When you talk about a course, emphasize what it has helped you do or be good at—spell it out and don't assume that they will just 'get it'

There is a huge difference between 'I have been on a leadership course' and 'The leadership course taught me how to set direction effectively, which I then utilized to run my next audit project. I noticed that this improved compliance with the audit and reduced confusion around what we needed to do'.

Techniques to help you sell/promote yourself on the day

Many people, but by no means all, feel uncomfortable talking about themselves and particularly their positive achievements. For some this feels inappropriately egotistica, almost unethical or embarrassing. However, if you do not do this nobody else is going to do it for you on the day of the interview and your chances of getting the post will be markedly reduced. If you are going to do this successfully on the day of your interview and it is not your comfort zone then you need to train your brain accordingly and this takes practice.

The 'getting to know yourself' exercise (see below) is designed to get you thinking about all your achievements and examples that could be used to promote you. It also gets you to think about your character traits. Once you have completed this exercise you need to start learning to talk out loud about these things, which can feel uncomfortable when you start to do it with other people. A good idea is to start with a partner, close friend or someone who is also preparing for interviews but not for the same job. Always warn people what you are trying to do, especially if they are close to you, or they might think you have turned into an overconfident alien when they married you for your humility! If this feels uncomfortable, an alternative is to answer out loud in front of a mirror. You need to practise this until it becomes comfortable, or you risk struggling in the interview itself.

As you do this training, do not underplay your achievements. Indeed, quite the opposite, you must learn to actively boast about them but in a calm, confident way. For each skill or quality that you have recognized from the 'getting to know yourself' exercise try talking about it for 30 seconds in a positive and persuasive manner.

Particularly concentrate on the benefits this quality or skill will bring the particular organization whose job you have applied for.

> **USEFUL TIP**: Imagine that the interviews have produced neck-and-neck candidates and it all hinges on this answer—you have to *persuade* them that this will make all the difference to them in the future. How would you frame this benefit?

Getting to know yourself

To be able to sell or promote yourself you really have to get to know yourself. Unfortunately, this is the area candidates often spend the least time on as they assume they know themselves well. However, there is a big difference between having a memory of what you have done or where you have been and being prepared to answer questions confidently and like a good sales person.

Time spent here is what makes the difference between those who succeed at interview and those who fail—remember the Pareto effect (see Introduction). The panel want to know about the real you, not the textbook you. You need to spend time being comfortable in selling yourself and being able to convince others that you bring added value.

In order to get to know yourself you need to:

- Understand your skills, qualities and attributes
- Develop examples of the benefits of these from your past experience
- Understand what the employer wants and how your specific skills, qualities and experience benefit him, i.e. know which aspects of you are most important for this interview
- If you have already written it, know your CV/application form inside out

The 'getting to know the real you' exercise (see Box 5.1) is fundamental to your interview preparation and must not be missed. To do this properly requires several days of brainstorming so that you:

- Become clear about the qualities and skills you possess
- Develop a series of examples and evidence from your past which demonstrate these
- Are clear how these qualities and skills will benefit the organization

If that sounds like we are repeating ourselves, it is, because this really is one of the most important differentiators between good candidates and ones who get appointed. Appointment is often because of how the candidate performed 'on the day' and it is this sharing of knowledge about yourself that holds much of the key to that.

At this stage it can be useful to carry around a notebook with you so that each time you remember an example or achievement you can jot it down. You'll find that at the start this doesn't come easily. You'll ask yourself a question like 'What examples do I have about being a leader?' Your first attempts at answering this will probably not

Box 5.1 Exercise—getting to know the real you

For each question, in addition to thinking about your qualities or skills:

- Give an example or evidence that demonstrates or reinforces your answer
- Think about how theses qualities or skills would directly benefit the employer
- Is this a benefit they want? If not it is not a benefit!

Questions

- What are my strengths?
- What are my unique skills, both clinical and non-clinical?
- What added value do I bring?
- Why will I fit into this department?
- Why will I fit into this Trust?
- What sort of colleague am I?
- What makes me a good doctor?
- How do I know I am a competent doctor?
- How would others know I am a good doctor?
- What sort of team player am I?
- How do I lead?
- What makes me a good leader?
- How do I teach?
- How do I know I am a good/excellent teacher?
- How do I demonstrate to people that they can trust me?
- How do I deal with stress?
- How do I relax?
- What are my weaknesses (do not overplay these)?
- What have I learned from the courses I have attended?
- Consider your personal experience in:
  - Leadership
  - Team building
  - Service/clinical development
  - Education and teaching
  - Clinical governance
    - Risk management
    - Audit
    - Critical incident reporting
    - Patient and public involvement
    - Root cause analysis
  - Dealing with difficult patients
  - Dealing with difficult colleagues
  - Ethical issues

> For all of the above areas of personal experience ensure you have examples that demonstrate your competency but also reflect on what you have learned from these experiences and what you would do differently in the future.
> - **Convince yourself that you are the right person for the job**

impress even you, but as time unfolds instances will spring to mind and it is important to capture them when they do or risk losing them. Brains don't like to repeat themselves, but equally they have a tendency to avoid giving you the best answers when you demand them, preferring to chuck them out at inconvenient moments like Sunday dinner with the family. Chances are, if you don't write it down, it will disappear and may not come back again.

As you collect your examples remember to:

- Be honest; however, this does not mean down-playing yourself
- Use *your* answers not someone else's

Think beyond the questions asked in the exercise to the essential and desirable criteria for the job and what you have heard at the pre-interview visit. This will provide you with further ideas of what you need to demonstrate to the interview committee to show them that you are the best person for the job. At the very least, ensure you have a really good example or evidence for every aspect of the essential and desirable job requirements, as well as anything specifically raised as an interest by panel members.

Remember, you may be able to use a single example to demonstrate a number of different skills or attributes. On the day of the interview, however, you need to have a series of examples at hand depending on what questions are asked. Therefore, at this stage, try to avoid using the same examples for lots of different questions. The more examples the better. You do not necessarily have to use them all!

You will need to redo the final part of the 'getting to know you' exercise for each individual job you are applying for or if you are not successful at your first interview. It is essential that the benefits you bring are tailored to the specific job and organization, something which you are unlikely to demonstrate if you just have a picture of the 'generic' you.

> **USEFUL TIP**: You are remembered for your stories and judged by your past, so ensure that both are vivid and supporting of your 'case' to be appointed.

Do not forget the final part of the exercise: 'Convince yourself that you are the best person for the job'. If you cannot convince yourself, you are unlikely to be able to convince others. Whilst you are not sure you are the best person for the job, you will probably not get the job, although the person you think is going to get it probably won't either.

Matching your experiences to their requirements

We have emphasized just how important it is to match your examples and stories to the specific requirements of your interview panel. There are a number of ways to develop a clear picture of what the employer wants and it is important to use all of them. They include:

- The job advert and job description
  - What types of descriptors, e.g. 'dynamic', did they use?
- Essential and desirable criteria
- Review of the hospital's strategic direction
- Listening carefully at the pre-interview visit and asking a few strategic questions (see Chapter 3)

Questions to ask yourself

- Where do they see this hospital or service going and what do you have to offer them in this regard?
- Where do they want to develop expertise or new skills and how does your expertise fit with this?
- What additional non-clinical skills do you have that they appear to need, e.g. audit or clinical governance?
- What type of personality would serve them best and who are they most likely to develop rapport with (see Chapter 4)?

If you have not yet had to complete your CV or application form, think about how you can utilize the information you have obtained from this exercise to ensure you are short-listed. Equally, it is important to remember that just because you put some of this information in your CV/application it *does not* mean you cannot talk about it on the day. You will be surprised how few interviewers can remember what you wrote in your CV, especially when they have gone through 150 to get to this point.

Box 5.2 gives practical help and ideas of how to work through the 'getting to know yourself' exercise.

> **USEFUL TIP**: Everything in your CV can be and should be used to sell yourself at the interview. If it doesn't add, then it distracts.

Know your CV

If you have already written your CV and are reading this section for the first time, then a key part of getting to know yourself is to ensure that you know your CV/application form inside out (see Box 5.3).

Box 5.2 Getting to know yourself

Example 1

Understanding your skills

Let's take teaching as an example of a skill. Don't just think 'I have good teaching skills'. Ask yourself what is it you do in teaching that is specifically good, e.g. perhaps you take time to understand your medical student's needs or you always ask for and reflect on feedback.

Building examples/evidence

When did you last teach the students (highlights this is a normal activity)? How did you teach them? What subjects do you teach them? What do you want to impart from your teaching? What did your students do as a result of your teaching? What feedback did you get from the last group of students? What did you do as a result? How did your feedback compare to their other teachers?

Understanding what the employer wants

For example, at the pre-interview visit you learn that the number of medical students is increasing in the department and you become aware that the department needs to start demonstrating to the Deanery that its teaching in your discipline is effective.

Example 2

Understanding your qualities and attributes

Let's take 'proactivity' as a quality. What do you mean by this?

Building examples/evidence

Many people state proactivity as a strength because they believe this is what the interview committee want to hear. Indeed, this is frequently the case. However, without any evidence to back it up you are unlikely to be believed—this could just be a word you learned on an interview course!

What evidence do you have that you are proactive? Have you noticed any deficiencies in care and proactively led a clinical improvement project to resolve this? As a result of your concerns, have you ever developed an audit project? Have you sorted out additional advanced training because you recognized it would be useful?

Understanding what the employer wants

At the pre-interview visit, the Chief Executive stressed a number of times how he needed a consultant who would proactively move services forward given their new Foundation Trust status and the hotting up of the competitive market.

Box 5.3 Know your CV/application form inside out

- Be able to confidently explain all gaps (in a positive way)
- CCT date (are you confident you will get it when you say you will?)
- Are there any deficiencies in your training (how will you change this into a positive)?
- Audit projects/research (only include completed audits and research)
- Prizes/Distinctions and honours
- Additional qualifications

If there are any gaps or weaknesses on your CV, make sure you have developed strong answers and explanations for these areas; for example:

- If you did research for 2 years 3 years ago and you still have not submitted your MD, why not?
- If you lack experience in teaching or a specific clinical skill, how will you develop it as a consultant? What have you already organized to increase your experience? (It is quite common not to match the person specification precisely. Successful candidates already have a plan in place to fill the gaps, so that it is just seen as work in progress)
- If you have no published articles/research papers and are applying for a teaching hospital post, then why should you be appointed? (Think of other compelling reasons beyond just the production of papers)

Update yourself on the messages behind the headlines in the CV; for example:

- What did you actually do to win that prize?
- What were the criteria and standards for that audit project you did 4 years ago? What were the key findings? What actions were put in place and what did the re-audit show?
- What were the key findings in the five research papers you contributed to?
- What did you do when you taught the nursing staff regularly and how did they respond to that?
- If there is anything unusual (and positive) in your CV it is more likely to be noticed and discussed. Can you confidently talk about it and sell it as a benefit to the Trust?
- Are your hobbies something you do regularly? If you've put down reading, who is your favourite author and what are you reading at the moment? If you put netball, have you played it in the last 5 years and to what standard? (Could this be an example of either teamwork or leadership if you were captain?)
- What have you learned from the training courses you have listed and how have you put this learning into practice?

If you have not submitted your CV yet and cannot answer some of the above questions, then consider leaving the information out. For example, you are better listing one good quality audit than five audits of which only one is a good one. Don't list anything that you don't have to where the subject matter has skeletons you don't want out of the closet, e.g. a failed audit project, unless the learning experience was particularly powerful. We are not suggesting you hide something specific, just avoid highlighting what doesn't serve you well.

By the time you have completed the exercise on 'getting to know yourself' and fully reviewed your CV you should have a significant 'tool kit' filled with a range of evidence that you can use to support each of the responses you give at a consultant interview.

Key topic areas to explore

Having taken the time to thoroughly get to know yourself, the next area of preparation is to consider key question topic areas. As you do this, again think beyond what you need to know generally and be specific about what evidence you have to demonstrate competence and expertise in these areas and how it will benefit the service and the organization.

Split your research and assessment of self into distinct topics to avoid the risk of overfocus on one area and underfocus on another. Only sign yourself up as ready when you are confident that you have a significant armamentarium for each area, matched to what you have discovered about the Trust specifically. For instance, rather than just thinking about the changing NHS structure, go deeper and discover how this might be affecting this particular Trust and what strengths you bring in that regard. Table 5.1 covers key topic areas and who is most likely to ask you questions in them.

Table 5.1 Key topic areas

Topic	Interviewer
CV/CCT and training	Royal College Representative
Service development	Chief Executive
Teaching	University Representative
Research	University Representative
Clinical governance	Medical Director
Political issues	Medical Director/Chief Executive
Leadership and management	Any
Team player	Any
Specialist interest	Any
Communication	Any
Ethical dilemmas	Any
Professional dilemmas	Any
Hobbies/dealing with stress/personal	Chair

To help guide your research and thinking at this stage have a brief look at the interview questions in Chapter 8 but do not start trying to answer them yet. Chapter 9 discusses a strategy for directing your reading around the NHS and political topics. Remember to review the notes you wrote following each of your pre-interview meetings, as this will help you to focus on areas for further exploration.

Question practice

Only start practising questions when you have completed the other areas of preparation. The goal of preparation is to ensure that you have the ability to answer questions both competently and with you and the job in mind. That gives you the mental flexibility to adjust your answers according to who is asking the question and how the question is asked. It is important to consider that if you concentrate only on practising questions there is a possibility that you will learn answers off by heart and therefore come over as rigid and boring in the interview, or even that you haven't truly answered the question asked. Practising questions is important though and when you do practise, consider all of the following:

- Practise out loud—we often waffle to ourselves when we speak in our head, or fail to notice what we have actually said
- Practise in front of a mirror—very useful for noticing your body language, e.g. are you smiling? Do you look passionate?
- Use a Dictaphone, so that you can listen to yourself objectively afterwards
- Write down key words as a 'revision aid'
- Consider using video—then you can concentrate on the questions and not looking at yourself (until afterwards)!

Use of video

Many people have access to devices that can capture video. A good idea is to set yourself up a little 'interview suite' at home, with a mock panel (secretly, the best way to do this is to 'borrow' the children's soft toys and assign each of them a role, e.g. Medical Director). Set up your video camera to have a slightly off-centre view of your upper body. You can purchase a mini-tripod for a few pounds and this makes set-up much easier. Then practise questions, captured on video, as though asked by specific and likely members of the panel. This will give you the opportunity to gain some great insight into how you adapt answers for individuals, as well as how well you maintain eye contact with different panel members.

> **USEFUL TIP**: Create yourself a mini-assessment guide and rate yourself out of 10 on how well you did at maintaining eye contact, appearing confident, tailoring answers to individuals, etc.

As you practise questions, always remind yourself about the purpose of the interview:

- To develop rapport—the panel will need to collectively 'warm' to you
  - What did you learn about the personalities of the key players at your pre-interview visit and how does this influence your approach?
- To sell and promote you—the panel need to be shown that you are the best person for the job
  - What is important to this panel?
  - Consider:
    - Job description
    - Job advert
    - Person specification
    - Pre-interview visit findings

As you practise your answers consider how you might change your approach depending on who asked you the question. This will be discussed in greater detail later and in other chapters.

When practising questions it is worth considering where panels get their questions from as it will help you focus your efforts.

Where do interviewers get their questions from?

- The issues that are close to them, e.g. staffing issues, junior doctor training, clinical governance, strengthened appraisals, hospital-acquired infection initiatives
- Their experience
- The internet
- Recent ethical challenges
- The media and recent journal reading

Before attending interview, it is vital that you review what is pertinent today and especially what is pertinent to this Trust. Have they been in the news recently?

Overview to answering questions

Bring the interview to the panel

It is very important in the interview to use every single question as an opportunity for the panel to learn more about you, presented in such a manner so as to ensure that it is you they want. Remember, you are in control of your responses and you need to use each question to demonstrate you are the best person for the job. If you literally answer the questions you are asked the panel may learn little about you, and your answers may simply just put you in the pack with the rest. Therefore, rather than simply answering the questions, you need to learn to *respond* to each question.

Example 1: Responding not answering
Should all doctors do research?

Answer	Response
I think it is important that all doctors do a period of research. It helps them to learn how to properly critique research publications, how to obtain valid consent and how to use statistics appropriately, and gives greater understanding of some of the difficulties associated with doing original research	I think it is important that all doctors do research. When I did my MD on the effects of apnoea and bradycardia on cerebral blood flow, I learned many skills which I believe will be important for me in my consultant role. My projects involved leading a team of three research nurses and as a result I had to learn skills in setting clear direction for the team and motivating staff when things did not always go as planned. I also learned how to critique original research, which will be of immense value in this post. It will be important that our new respiratory strategies and guidelines are based on the best evidence available which will only come from appropriate review of the literature. Also, my research taught me valuable skills in applying for and obtaining an MRC (Medical Research Council) research grant, obtaining ethical committee approval and writing up papers for publication in prestigious journals such as the *Lancet*. These are all skills that I would like to exploit if I were to be successful at this interview. In summary, I think all doctors should do research. It has given me extremely valuable skills which will be of immense benefit as a consultant with a special interest in respiratory neonatology.

Example 2: Responding not answering

What makes a good team player?

Answer	Response
A good team player is someone who takes their fair share of the load, contributes to both the unpleasant tasks and the preferred ones, is supportive of their team mates and avoids causing divisions within the group.	In my experience of working in a number of very different teams, I have seen examples of both good and bad team players. Whilst doing my research, I worked with someone who didn't take fair share of the workload and he was never available for the tasks nobody wanted to do. I noticed how much bad feeling this created and since then I have always strived to balance my favourite activities with those that simply need to be done. Last year, I worked with somebody who appeared to disagree with everything the others said. Whereas his different viewpoint was valuable, it became very obvious that to disagree with everything had detrimental effects on the team. I learned that a good team player chooses when to disagree because it is important versus when to keep quiet and let others take the lead.

It is important to recognize in both the examples above that the question was still answered, but in the 'response' each answer was used as a springboard to sell specific skills, insight or learning that the interviewee had.

To help you see how this works, spend some time listening to the *Today* programme on Radio 4. When politicians are being interviewed you will notice that whatever question they are asked not only do they answer the question (assuming they do actually choose to answer the question asked), but also they ensure they use each of their responses to get certain messages across. Their motivation may be a little off but their process is a good example of adapting responses to deliver key messages.

For some people, answering questions in this way will seem very uncomfortable to begin with. It is important to recognize, however, that if *you* do not promote yourself, no one else will! If you are humble and down-play or do not describe your achievements you will most likely not get the job. Equally, it is important to remember that just because you wrote it in your CV, it doesn't mean everyone will know or appreciate its contents. The CV is no substitute for truly selling yourself face-to-face and, consequently, it is extremely important that if you are wired naturally to be humble that you spend time now practising talking about yourself out loud to other people with a view to arriving at a place where extolling your own virtues is straightforward and natural.

Part of this approach to 'response' as opposed to 'answer' is about maintaining control and ensuring that you create the conditions to shine. This should not be a point of luck, i.e. hoping they will ask the questions that you know how to answer best. Leading the responses to places of confidence allows you to exemplify strengths whilst avoiding weaker areas. Let's examine a simple example. Imagine being asked about your knowledge of clinical governance. Thanks to your earlier research you know that your true strength is in audit, where you have a number of good examples of excellent work, and your weaker area is in incidents and root-cause analysis, which you have just not had exposure to. Consequently, your answer may look something like this: 'I have a strong belief in the importance of clinical governance in running an effective clinical service and this has ensured that I have developed both my knowledge and skills in this area. For instance, recognizing that clinical governance encompasses clinical improvement just as much as it does mitigation of risk, I have undertaken two significant clinical audit projects, one on ABC and another on XYZ, both specifically designed to support an improvement process in an important aspect of care. Right now, I am strengthening my skills in root-cause analysis to enhance my ability to lead clinical improvement in situations involving adverse events or incidents'. You can see that this answer leads the listener into your area of strength and allows you to deliver some significant proof, as well as emphasizing improvement in your weaker area, without ever stating that this area is weak.

> **USEFUL TIP**: It is up to you what you say or don't say, but it is preparation and practice that delivers the ability to exercise this level of control.

What you can see is that you have a far greater control over the impression the interview panel develops than you probably imagined. Successful candidates seize control of this process and ensure that the interview panel develops an impression that is consistent with them being appointed. The danger of simply delivering factual information, without adaptation, is that the impression left may be one that is either negative or with doubt remaining. It is vital that you do not leave this to chance if you are to maximize your chances of being appointed.

> **USEFUL TIP**: The best way to never leave the interview panel with a negative message, impression or doubt about you at the end of any answer is to take charge of the impression left.

This process is most regularly forgotten by internal candidates, where it is very easy to assume that everyone already knows what you can do, meaning that you do not need to promote yourself by responding to each question, instead simply relying on factual answers. Ironically, it is even more important for internal candidates to promote themselves so that they avoid the accusation that they simply assumed they would be appointed and didn't try. As an internal candidate, the safest mindset to adopt is that you are already one pace behind the external candidates and therefore must try harder to leap ahead. This discipline forces you to put the effort into preparation and adapt question responses accordingly.

> **USEFUL TIP**: Do not assume that the panel has read or can remember everything on your CV. You must create the opportunity to bring out the salient points.

Consider 'think, feel, do'

It is useful to have a framework or set of principles that help you adapt your answers appropriately. We advocate a simple technique called *think, feel, do*. It works as follows.

When asked a question, pause and ask yourself what does this individual and this panel need to *think* and *feel* in order to promote me to this post. *Think, feel, do* highlights the concept that all of us are influenced by first thinking and feeling something, which then leads to us doing something. Whereas each of us has a different balance for thinking versus feeling, this does illustrate the importance of emotional drivers in decisions, rather than just rational ones. Once you are clear of the '*do*', then to get the right outcome you need to develop the right thoughts and feelings in the people who you want to take action. In the context of your consultant interview the '*do*' is you want the interview panel to appoint you. What will they need to think and feel from your answer to their question for appointment to be the natural extension of those thoughts and feelings? Your goal is to create the right feelings or emotions to generate the right behaviour, e.g. show an Island of Opportunity person (Chapter 4) that you are confident and can take charge in stressful situations or show an Island of Intellect interviewer that your answers are well ordered, structured and consider all the issues.

> **USEFUL TIP**: Always ask yourself 'What would this person or panel need to think and feel in order to be confident in appointing me to this job?'

It's a conversation not a test

It is important that you see the interview as a conversation rather than an examination or test. This will help you to relax but also ensures that the panel get to know something about you as a person instead of simply evaluating what you know. If they are unable to learn anything about the underlying you, your chances of getting the job are slim. To help in this, it is best to use the sort of language that you would hear in normal conversation and avoid using too much jargon, technical terms or formal definitions.

Key rules to answering questions

The following represents a sensible set of rules to adopt when answering questions:

- Actively listen to the question entirely before starting to formulate a response
- Always pause before answering to consider how you will structure your response

- Respond not answer—promoting you as the candidate of choice
- Tell the panel the key message up front, in case key players have a short attention span
- Always back up your answer with your evidence/examples
- Conclude with and emphasize why this is a benefit to the Trust or department
- Do not talk for more than 2 minutes on each response
- Do not assume they have read your CV—everything pertinent on your CV should be talked about and emphasized
- People tend to remember things when they hear them more than once or where the salient point is isolated from the background information
- Give no more than three key messages in any one response, always leading with the most important first if at all possible

Active listening

It is common for interviewees not to listen properly to the question being asked. This can occur for a number of reasons but the commonest are worrying whether you will be able to answer the question or leaping too early to formulate an answer before hearing out the remainder of the question. When this happens, the response tends to be waffled and often dries up towards the end. Despite the fact that you are going to respond rather than answer the question and have a series of examples to illustrate your response, your response does have to fit with what was actually asked. To improve self-awareness, understand that the candidates most likely not to listen sufficiently are the action-orientated, goal-directed individuals who are wired to talk rather than listen.

If you are one of these individuals, it is especially essential that you train yourself to listen more effectively as part of your interview preparation. A simple way to do this is when seeing patients, avoid asking a whole series of questions and instead ask your patients to tell you their history. Try listening without interrupting (you will be pleased to know most patients can succinctly describe their problems when not interrupted). When your patients finish their history, repeat back to them the salient things they have said. Did you get it right? If you naturally struggle with active listening you will probably want to interrupt patients or will be thinking about what you are going to ask them next even as they tell you the history. It is important to control both of these tendencies in order to improve your active listening skills.

When practising interview questions, ask a colleague to interview you and assess your apparent ability to listen actively and respond accordingly. They can score you out of 10 on how well you appeared to listen, the degree of understanding of the question you appeared to develop and how well your response dealt with the specific question asked. The self-awareness developed in this area contributes to an increased level of self-control, which in turn helps both your responsiveness and your adaptability.

Pausing

When you have been asked a question it is a good idea to pause for about 10 seconds before responding. Many people are worried about leaving a gap between question and response, thinking that this may come across as you not knowing the answer. This is rarely the case and the pause will enable you to do a number of things:

- Ensure you are clear what is being asked—if you are not, then ask them to clarify the question (see below for the correct technique to do this)
- Consider what the purpose of the question actually is; e.g. if someone is being challenging or aggressive towards you, the purpose is more likely to see how you respond under those conditions and not the content of the answer itself. It is important that you respond to the purpose by demonstrating a calm and considered approach even when pushed
- Consider who the interviewer is and what their purpose is at interview, e.g. the Royal College Representative is there to ensure you have the right training but will also need to develop confidence in you as an individual, which will relate heavily to his or her psychology. You must *plan* to deliver what they *need* to be confident in saying 'yes' to your appointment
- Utilizing the concept of '*think, feel, do*', consider how you can best use this process to demonstrate you are the right person for the job
- Decide what three items you are going to choose from 'your tool kit' of skills, qualities, behaviours and examples to promote during this answer
- Choose a structure for your answer, generally involving placing the key point at the front

Again, it is the goal-directed, action-orientated individual who is least likely to pause sufficiently, although this can also happen to warm and friendly people-orientated individuals who find silence a little awkward. However, failing to pause can be catastrophic downstream, sometimes causing a cascade of unwanted events:

- You do not answer the question well
- You answer but do not respond
- You do not promote yourself
- You ramble because you have no structure
- You fail to shine because key points are not matched to individuals or question purpose

If, when you start practising your questions, you notice that you do not tend to pause, it is essential that you practise until this is natural. It will seem very uncomfortable at first, but you will significantly enhance your response by doing this. You can also take some comfort from the fact that the interview panel are more likely to be impressed by you considering your response than having the, most likely wrong, immediate response at your fingertips.

Clarification

If you do not understand the question that has been asked then it is important to clarify the question before answering. Remember that some interviewers are not very clear in the way they ask questions. It may not only be you who does not understand, it may also be other members of the interview panel. However, you should not feel obliged to answer until you have clarified what has actually been asked. The manner in which you ask for clarification will likely decide ultimately the degree of clarificat' that you get. If you just ask the interviewer to repeat the question they may take you at your word and you may still be none the wiser about what is expected of you. A better strategy, therefore, is to use one of the following approaches:

'If I understand you correctly, you are asking me. . . .'
'If I heard you correctly, what you would like me to do is. . . .'

If you felt that the question had been asked sensibly but you simply failed to catch all of the question, it is completely appropriate to ask something like 'Could you just repeat the question please to ensure that I definitely heard it correctly?' The danger of not gaining this clarification or repetition is that you answer what you think you heard, which can sometimes be significantly different from what was actually asked.

Overall structure

Having a structure for your answers helps you to keep on track and reduces the likelihood of meandering in your answer (see Box 5.4). Different questions lend themselves to different approaches, but in general remember the adage:

- Tell them what you are going to tell them, then
- Actually tell them, then
- Summarize what you have just told them but in a different way

Box 5.4 Structuring your answers—all in 2 minutes!

Pause and think (10 seconds)

- What is the question about?
- Think, feel, do
- Decide on three examples, skills or topics to sell yourself, e.g. teaching, leadership and IT skills
- Structure

Opening (10 seconds)

- The answer
- Structure to question

Body (90 seconds)

- Topic 1—example and benefit
- Topic 2—example and benefit
- Topic 3—example and benefit

End (10 seconds)

- Summarize in one sentence
- How will the post, department or Trust benefit from these skills and qualities?

Word order is important in ensuring that all panel members get the benefit of your key points. Consequently, it is really important that you get your main key point across confidently and up front. This is because a significant number of panel members will be from our Island of Opportunity, i.e. of the action-orientated, goal-directed personality (Chapter 4). These individuals have a short attention span and will make decisions rapidly about your answers. If you do not put the key point at the very front, you risk them switching off before you have made it. Do not underestimate how fast that switch-off can be.

The middle section of your answer is where you provide the evidence and examples that make the panel want to appoint you. The more this flows as a story the greater the chances of it being recalled when the panel sits to determine who should be appointed.

In your final sentence you need to summarize what you have just said but in different words, whilst also stating the benefit to the service or organization. It is very important that you end your answer positively, ideally concluding with a specific benefit that matches your experience with their requirements.

> **USEFUL TIP**: The more you repeat your key messages, the more likely they are to be remembered. The more you repeat your key messages, the more likely they are to be remembered. The more you repeat your key messages, the more likely they are to be remembered. Got it? The more you repeat your key messages the more likely they are to be remembered.

Timings

It is essential that your responses are clear. A good strategy is to keep your answers relatively short, recognizing that the longer you talk, the more likely you are to inadvertently hide the key messages that you were planning to deliver in the jumble of additional information you have thrown in.

Despite the enormous responsibility and impact of appointing a new consultant, your interviewers have a relatively short attention span for listening to your answers. It is therefore important that your answer takes no more than 2 minutes. If you do not currently believe the 2-minute rule, attend an interview course and time how quickly you switch off when listening to other people's answers, especially where they are semantic or generic in nature.

> **USEFUL TIP**: Ensure all your answers are less than 2 minutes in length, delivered confidently and with conviction, emphasizing the benefits that you bring.

Starting and ending on a high

Have you ever delivered an answer to a complex question, where you knew that the middle portion was just about right and yet you were conscious that you didn't start

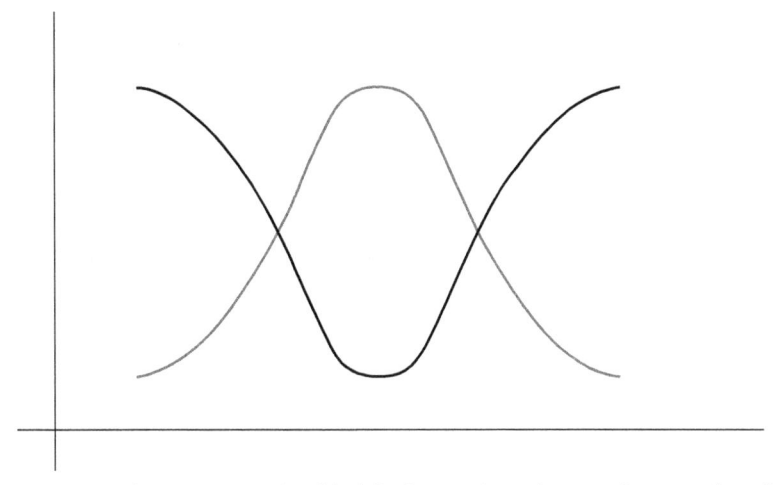

Figure 5.1 Interviewer concentration (black line) versus interviewee performance (grey line).

well and lost it a little towards the end? This is a common finding, related to the mismatching of interviewee performance in answering questions and the interviewer's propensity to concentrate.

As Figure 5.1 shows, the vast majority of interviewees start relatively weakly when answering a question, peak in the middle and tail off towards the end, having run out of things to say. Unfortunately, the interviewers do exactly the opposite, instead listening intently at the beginning, wandering off in the middle and jolting awake at the end, i.e. they are most likely to be analyzing your performance at the very moment, unless you practise well, when your performance is likely to be at its lowest point. Knowing this allows you to practise and to adjust your word order to better suit concentration levels. This is why it is so important to get your answer in at the beginning of your response and to summarize it again at the end of your response.

It is also important to start your answer with something positive. Despite your present reality, it is important that the Chief Executive feels you are a can-do, positive person who will not spend all their time moaning about their lot.

Another common failing is that the answer tails off at the end or appears to dry up. It needs a confident conclusion that emphasizes pertinent benefits or a close using words likely to be heard by the majority of your interview committee. Without tailing off, it is also important to let the pitch of your voice drop slightly at the end of your answer. This signals to your audience that you have finished what you wish to say. If you do the opposite, i.e. finish with an increase in pitch, the panel my be left wandering whether you still have more to say. Clearly, building rapport is an important part of interview strategy and that starts with making it as easy as possible for panel members to conduct the interview smoothly.

Deliver a strong conclusion

Remembering that we tend to recall things at the beginning and end of sequences, it is vital to ensure that we get the conclusion right, as well as the start. As with the beginning of your response, it is important that you conclude with something positive. Practise trying to use your conclusion to link your answer with the specific requirements of the job or the organization, i.e. the benefits they are hoping to gain from your appointment. This is a powerful position to leave people in. For example:

> 'So, as you can see, I have extensive experience in teaching, with excellent feedback. However, my experience in developing neurology e-learning, which has received exceptional feedback from medical students specifically, should prove immensely valuable as the number of medical students doubles next year here at St Elsewhere's.'

> 'In conclusion, I believe that the extensive training and experience I have gained in laparoscopic lower GI tract surgery in my post-CCT fellowship will be an asset to the department as it strives to develop new, innovative, efficient, cost effective ways of delivering GI surgery ahead of the competition.'

Stop when you have stopped

A common mistake made by a significant number of candidates is to start talking again once they have completed their answer. Silence is not a sign that you haven't said enough. It is more likely that the panel is just not fluent at moving from one question to the next or that the individuals on the panel are digesting what they have heard. The practice of talking again once you've completed your answer, arising out of poor discipline or embarrassment at silence, is a recipe for disaster and usually has the effect of hiding any key messages that were in the original answer. Re-starting is most likely to occur if there is a significant silence following your response. Please do not read anything into silence and it is especially important not to read into it 'I must have given a poor answer and therefore I must say more to rescue it'. Again, if this is an issue that you recognize in yourself, then it is something you can practise with a colleague or partner.

> **USEFUL TIP**: Do not be afraid of silence. In no circumstance start re-talking, however long you have to wait!

Three key points per question

In general, people will remember no more than three key points from each response you give. Although it is tempting to put more points into an answer to help demonstrate your worth, you do put yourself at risk. By loading more points in, the panel actually may not remember your three most important points at all or these may become watered down. By only putting across three distinct key points, each different from each other, your answer is much more likely to be remembered and the key points seen to be prominent.

For example, if you are asked a question about audit, a three-point answer may look something like this:

- You recognized and acted upon a problem in service delivery which you thought could be improved and enhanced (proactive)
- You led a small team to deliver both the audit and subsequently the action plan (leadership skills)
- The audit was presented by you at the annual Trust audit competition where you won a prize for audit that contributes to an improvement in care (winner)

USEFUL TIP: Each response should contain no more than 3 key points or it risks losing impact and the key points won't be remembered.

Specific structures

Within the context of the overall principles described above, there are a number of ways in which you might want to subsequently structure your answers, as illustrated by Table 5.2.

Table 5.2 Answer structures for different types of interview question

Structure	Uses
Patients, staff, service, Trust	NHS changes, e.g. revalidation
Different groups of staff	Teaching, clinical governance
Advantages and disadvantages	Opinion questions
Positives and negatives	Opinion questions
Academic and non-academic posts	Research
Time scales, e.g. short term and long term; immediate and later; before, during and after an event	Service development, ethical dilemmas, description of specific events, e.g. breaking bad news
Patients, colleagues, organization	Professional dilemmas
Situation, task, action and results	Behavioural and competency-based questions

Having a structure or focus for your answers helps you steer the key points and examples and assists you in controlling the messages the panel receives. If you share the structure with the panel as part of your response opening, it will help reinforce, especially to Island of Intellect inhabitants, that you are organized and structured in your thought processes. Let's look at how that might sound:

> **Example 1**
>
> **Tell me about your experience in clinical governance.**
> 'The three areas of clinical governance I have most experience in are audit, risk management and the development of evidence-based guidelines. . . .' (principle of three)

> **Example 2**
>
> **What do you think will be the effects of developing networks in speciality x?**
> 'In my experience of working in a relatively new network, the formation of networks has implications for patients, staff and outcomes. . . .' (principle of three and people-focus)

> **Example 3**
>
> **How would you deal with a drunken colleague?**
> 'There are three key issues that spring to mind, two immediate and one subsequent. The two key things I would need to consider immediately in this situation are patient safety and the immediate support of my drunken colleague to return home. Thirdly, when he is sober, I would need to sit down with my colleague and explore in more detail the specific event and the underlying factors that led to it. . . .' (principle of three, safety, people, permanent resolution, prioritization)

Use of language

The correct and intelligent use of language can have a massive impact on your likelihood of getting the job. Subtle changes to word order, use of certain words and phrases and matching of language style to the recipient can all contribute to greater impact and resonance. Let's start with an example to demonstrate this further. The University Representative asks two candidates about teaching medical students.

What should we teach the medical students in gastroenterology and how should we teach it?

(Please ignore the different lengths of the answers and concentrate on the phraseology, structure and key points made.)

Candidate 1	Candidate 2
The teaching would need to follow the syllabus that the Deanery will have set out. I know in this department the teaching is based on 8-week attachments to the ward. During the attachment the consultants will teach medical students on both the ward round and in a weekly tutorial. . . .	I have been fortunate enough to be teaching medical students in gastroenterology and general medicine throughout my registrar training. From the feedback I have received, I have found medical students learn best when you use a variety of different training media. I like to do a mixture of bedside teaching and case-based teaching within the classroom setting. I have developed a number of interactive cases which include blood results, X-rays and histology slides and I am presently developing these into an e-learning package. Medical students come on short attachments to gastroenterology and so I want to pass on my passion for gastroenterology as a career option. Of course most of them will not end up in gastroenterology and so I also think it is important that the students understand common diseases which they may meet in a number of different medical careers, for instance inflammatory bowel disease, bowel cancer and alcohol liver disease.

Review the two answers and ask yourself which candidate do you think will most likely get the job? What language did they use that will help them achieve this? What key principles are they applying? What important personal attributes are they demonstrating? Without even considering the psychology of the interviewer, if you were drawing up a list of advantages for each candidate, what would you list for each of them?

Use of the word 'I'

It is important to appreciate that you are being appointed as a colleague or peer, not a junior. Consequently, it is important to see yourself as an equal with the other people around the interview table. Besides demonstrating confidence and the courage of your convictions, use of the word 'I' is a powerful way of doing this. It also implies confidence and the ability to lead. For example:

- 'The way I approach this type of problem. . . .'
- 'When I am teaching. . . .'
- 'Personally I do. . . .'

Wherever possible, try to turn each response round to the first person and avoid any natural tendencies to use the term 'we' except when answering questions about matters such as teamwork, where it would be more appropriate to demonstrate that you are one of the group rather than an individual.

Use of the present tense

Building on from the use of the word 'I', try to use the present tense as much as possible. For example, 'When breaking bad news to a patient I do . . . '. Compare this to 'When breaking bad news you should . . . ' and consider its impact if every other candidate answered the question in the same semantic manner. As an interviewer I would be wondering whether this candidate has ever broken bad news. Have they just read a textbook on how to do it but never applied it?

Practise trying to turn questions around so that you answer them in both the first person and the present tense. This emphasizes the value of video or dictaphone feedback because it is not always easy to notice or remember what you said, even though you will be confident about the general substance of your answer. Let's look at some examples.

Example 1

How would you deal with conflict between you and a patient's relative?
'When I think there might be a difference of opinion between a relative and myself I immediately. . . .'

Example 2

What makes a good team player?
'When I was working at St Elsewhere's, I was a member of two clinical improvement teams, both with very different styles of working. In both cases we delivered our intended improvements and so I concluded that a good team player needs to be flexible in how he or she works, and since then I have always asked myself the question "Am I imposing my style on others?"'

(In this example, faced with the teamwork question, you can see how the candidate has successfully blended use of the word 'I' to demonstrate confidence and self-assuredness with 'we' to emphasize being a team member and acknowledging that it was the team that achieved the results.)

Example 3

What are the issues facing cardiac networks?
'From my experience in both a large regional unit and a DGH over the last 12 months, I think there are three key issues affecting networks today....'

(The answer is a confident one, but you are probably realizing that the manner of its delivery can make all the difference between arrogance and a simple reflection of appropriate past experience.)

Use of language that implies you have a breadth or depth of knowledge

There is a big difference between letting somebody know that you have done something and emphasizing that this is regular and normal. Using the right adverb is a very powerful way of doing this and highlights the importance of not shortcutting the communication process in the interests of brevity. Again, let us use an example to demonstrate this.

A future consultant colleague asks you about supporting trainees

Candidate 1	Candidate 2
I meet with trainees in rheumatology at St Elsewhere's to ensure they feel supported	I *regularly* organize meetings with the trainees in rheumatology at St Elsewhere's to ensure they feel *fully* supported ...

Candidate 1 almost makes it sound like it is a chore, whereas Candidate 2 suggests that this is embedded behaviour that he/she is deeply committed to as the right thing to do. The only difference between the two answers is the appropriate use of some powerful adverbs. Consider using the following adverbs:

- Typically
- Regularly
- Generally
- Essentially
- Quickly
- Frequently
- Mostly
- Safely
- Very
- Finally
- Firstly
- Secondly

Use numbers where possible

You have probably heard the phrase 'a picture tells a thousand words' and so we would like to introduce an equally valid phrase of 'the numbers tell their own story'. For example, 'I have done over 100 caesarean sections without complication' is more powerful than 'I have done lots of safe caesarean sections' or 'I have extensive experience of doing caesarean sections'. No one can argue with the number of procedures you have done, but they may argue or disagree with your definition of 'a lot' or 'extensive experience' or more importantly draw their own conclusions, which might not be the right ones.

Use your examples

When people talk about real examples they tend to be much more fluent and conversational. This is yet another reason why getting to know yourself and developing your tool box of examples is so fundamental for success at the consultant interview. Use of examples is critically important, but if they also flow naturally they sound much more confident and less rehearsed.

This emphasizes the difference between building an armamentarium of examples that you can draw on to illustrate points versus having a series of rehearsed answers involving examples.

Use active verbs

Wherever possible, try to use active verbs rather than passive verbs. With active verbs, the subject of the sentence (which should be you) does the action. With passive verbs the subject of the sentence has the action done to them. By using the former you convey the message that you have high-level skills, are doing this thing regularly and you proactively engage in action. Let's look at some examples of this.

> ### Example 1
> **Active verb**
> 'At St Elsewhere's I organize the monthly audit meeting.'
>
> **Passive verb**
> 'The monthly audit meeting at St Elsewhere's is organized by me.'
>
> ### Example 2
> **Active verb**
> 'I immediately discussed the situation with the patient's relatives.'
>
> **Passive verb**
> 'The situation was discussed with the patient's relatives immediately.'

Again, it is important to understand your own natural tendencies and to retrain these to utilize the right phraseology.

Use adjectives that are important to the panel

This represents another form of matching you to the specific requirements of panel members. In essence, if the panel wants someone who will fit in and be a team player, you need to ask yourself 'What adjectives can I use within my various answers to illustrate that I am this type of person?' If they want someone who is going to develop or shake up a service, what adjectives will suggest you have this ability? If they want someone who quietly gets on and achieves, what words can you use to convey this aspect of your character?

We have expanded on this in the section on answering questions about your strengths.

Speed and pitch of speech

In general, when answering interview questions you want to speak slightly slower than you would do in normal conversation, unless you have a naturally slow speed of speech. To be clear, we are not suggesting that you draw out your answers or speak sufficiently slowly that the panel members think you are treating them as stupid. However, it is important to appreciate that for most people the natural tendency is to speak slightly too fast for others to grasp unfamiliar topics. Most of our answers will be unique to us and we therefore need to ensure that we give the panel members the best possible chance of hearing and understanding what we have to say. If you have a specific point you want to emphasize, slowing down more at this point will provide this. However, it is also important to ensure that slowness does not mean boring and you will need to modify the tone of your voice to generate enthusiasm and passion at appropriate times.

Enthusiasm

One of the common reasons candidates are unsuccessful at interview is that they appear unenthusiastic. This is particularly noticeable to those interviewers who are from the Island of Opportunity, where passion and enthusiasm are inherent in their natural speech patterns, and is most likely to occur in candidates who swim between the Islands of Team Spirit and the Island of Intellect. It is therefore very important that you are able to speak enthusiastically and passionately when answering at least some of the questions you are asked and an absolute imperative when asked the question. 'If offered this job will you accept it?' This question in particular requires an enthusiastic answer delivered with passion and absolute conviction, with an immediate, strong, clear 'YES!'

So, how can you appear enthusiastic if it is not your natural style? As always it comes down to practice. Think about something that you are naturally passionate about. Talk about this out loud whilst observing yourself in the mirror or videoing yourself. Watch or review your facial features—see how much you smile (smiling naturally conveys enthusiasm). What else did you do?

- What happened to your breathing?
- Did you use your hands in an animated way?

- What happened to your voice?
- Did it speed up a little or seem naturally to go higher?

When you are clear what you do when you speak naturally about something you are enthusiastic about, try talking about your training or audit experience whilst utilizing all the physiological behaviours you have observed. Like all things, you won't get it right first time, you may even feel pretty stupid initially, but with perseverance you will gain control of this important component of behaviour.

Habits and tics

When practising interview questions, try to become aware of any habits, mannerisms and verbal tics that you might have, or be developing. For instance, starting your answer with 'That is an excellent question' or 'That is an interesting question' might be okay occasionally once in an interview, but when all of your answers start in that way it is very frustrating and likely to lose you marks.

Another common verbal tic is repeated 'erms' through each answer. Often individuals are unaware they do this. It can therefore be incredibly useful to either tape yourself using a Dictaphone or ask a trusted friend to practise a few questions with you to see if you have any such habits. For many people this is a natural pause mechanism and can be overcome by developing confidence in your answers and mental flexibility about how to use them.

Not all habits and tics are verbal. Our facial expressions or behaviours may give us away when we are unsure about a question asked or are being more creative than we ought to be with our response. Common behaviours are a dry cough, twiddling hair, ear, necklace, etc, closing your eyes and pulling a face. Again, the most useful way to find out if this is an issue for you is either to observe yourself in front of a mirror when answering questions or ask a partner or trusted friend to watch you. Do not worry if you cannot resolve a habit or tic completely. However, being aware of it will help you to control it or control for it, e.g. not wearing a necklace at your interview, making sure you have got a glass of water or ensuring good eye contact to reduce eye closure. We do not recommend shaving your hair off!

Smiling

It is really important that you remember to smile when practising your interview questions. You are going to definitely need to do this on the day. Smiling makes you both look and feel more relaxed and as a result your answers will be much more conversational. It makes you appear naturally confident, as well as resulting in the interviewer thinking you are interested in the subject you are talking about. Practise smiling at the beginning of your answer, try to remember to do it part way through and definitely smile as you conclude your answer. The more natural this is, the higher the impact. To be clear, we are not advocating a Cheshire cat, forced grin!

Types of question

Questions on your clinical training and experience

The Royal College Representative is going to ask you questions about your experience and training. Their role is to ensure that you are qualified for the job advertised and that you have had the appropriate training. If you have your CCT at the point of interview, this has already been established. If you do not have your CCT, you will be asked about how confident you are that you will get it when you say you will. It can be useful to have thought about evidence or points to 'prove' that your conclusions are not misguided, especially where CCT is contingent on additional exams. We have expanded on this in a subsequent section.

It is very unusual but not unheard of to be asked as a candidate to tell an interviewer about your CV. If you are asked this question, remember that this does not give you free rein to talk for hours—you still only have your 2 minutes to get your key messages across. Therefore, practise summarizing your training as succinctly as possible. Do not describe every job you have ever done; rather, summarize the experience you have received, especially in your later years and that is pertinent to this post. For example:

Example 1

'I have spent 4 years training in endocrinology in two major teaching hospitals. I have developed special interests in maternal endocrine disease, especially diabetes and thyroid disease, and spent 6 months working with the feto-maternal medicine team at University Hospital. This unit has developed specialist services for both these areas and attracts women with complex health issues. I am passionate about clinical governance and audit. My most recent audit on the management of women and their babies with hyperthyroidism resulted in a significant change to practice that subsequently delivered a significant reduction in hospital-bed days.'

Example 2

'Before specializing in paediatric A&E, I spent 5 years training in general paediatrics. I have spent the last 2 years specializing in paediatric A&E, at St Elsewhere's, a very busy teaching hospital with 20,000 paediatric A&E attendances annually to a mixed paediatric and adult A&E department. I have a special interest in teaching. I am an APLS trainer and have recently been appointed as course director. I have co-developed a teaching programme in paediatrics for my A&E colleagues and teach GP trainees as part of their training scheme.'

Example 3

'I have been fortunate enough to gain excellent training in anaesthetics, resulting in the award of my CCT last month. I have developed a special interest in neuro-anaesthesia and undertook a 6-month period of training at the National Neurology Hospital last year. I have now anaesthetized over 400 complex neurosurgical patients and have specialist skills in. . . .'

It is important to give key specific facts rather than go into too much minutiae or detail. Try asking yourself what would this particular employer want to know about my clinical experience and how does it relate to the job I am applying for? The key is to highlight those aspects of training and experience that are important to this specific role. For example, if the employer wants an anaesthetist with a special interest in XYZ you need to highlight both your anaesthetic experience and your experience specifically in XYZ. Regardless of how much experience you have in ABC, there is no point highlighting, or allowing it to take valuable interview time, if it is not what the employer wants.

For each of the specific skills that you have highlighted in your CV, try to develop short statements (two to three sentences maximum) which describe not only the skill but also the benefits that the skill brings, e.g. 'I have spent the last 3 months acting up for an absent colleague, which means that I am more likely to hit the ground running and be useful earlier'.

Questions on your CCT

If you do not have your CCT, you will be asked a question along the lines of 'How do you know you will get your CCT on such and such a date?' You need to be able to answer this question confidently and leave the panel in no mind that you will definitely get it. If you raise any doubt in their mind, your chances of success will be significantly reduced as they will be concerned about waiting 6 months for someone to join and then finding themselves back at square one if you can't. This is definitely an area to practise and, again, we advocate having a trusted colleague give you feedback on whether you have convinced them sufficiently that they would give you the job (not just because they like you!).

A good example might be 'I have completed each of my annual educational reviews successfully and have always been recorded as developing beyond expectation. I have recently met with my educational supervisor to review my portfolio and training and we both believe that I will be successful in my final educational review next week and will receive my CCT as planned at the end of my training in 2 months' time'.

Questions on courses attended

You most probably won't be asked a question directly about a course you have attended unless it is particularly unusual, e.g. Utilizing elephant training techniques to improve patient flow through outpatients. However, it is important to have considered the courses you have attended in order to be able to draw on these experiences to illustrate specific points. Ask yourself:

- What skills did I learn?
- How have I used these within the workplace?
- Which skills would be most useful to this employer?

This is best done with a firm grasp of the job requirements and the wishes and desires of the interview panel.

Five-year plan

You will almost certainly be asked a question about how you see the service developing in the future and your role in that development. To answer this effectively, you need to be aware of how your consultant colleagues see the service developing but also how the Chief Executive sees both the hospital and this service evolving over time. Regardless of your own wishes and desires, your answer must fit with the general direction of travel and be consistent with what all services in that specialty are facing. Beyond the expectations of colleagues and senior managers, you need to have a strong awareness of how the evolving healthcare structure, any pertinent National Service Frameworks (NSFs) and specific local constraints will influence a service. For example, your desire to create the world's most prominent hospital-based dermatology department in a DGH ignores the increasing trend that dermatology will move to the community. More appropriate would be to recognize this as a risk to funding and suggest how you would adapt the service to mitigate this risk by evolving its delivery model.

The most common mistake in answering this question is that the candidate just tells the panel what they already know and what they were told at the pre-interview visit. It is important to talk about how you personally see the service evolving and link that to the specific expertise or experience you bring to the group.

Example

'Over the next 5 years, I see A&E becoming an increasingly consultant-delivered service with an increasing focus on reducing admissions. I see my role well beyond just delivering the right treatment to the patient at the right time. It will become increasingly important to ensure effective working with my acute medical and surgical colleagues. In this regard, I will be able to build on the experience I gained as Locum Consultant at St Joseph's, where I undertook a project working with MAU and SAU [Medical/Surgical Admissions Units] to ensure all patients were triaged by a senior doctor to ensure right treatment first time without unnecessarily bouncing around the system. This project resulted in a significant reduction in acute admissions but more importantly a significant reduction in time to treatment for those patients needing admission, as well as a reduction in the overall workload for the staff involved.'

Questions on your added value

It is quite common to be asked about the added value you will bring to the job. It is important to appreciate that your general experience in the specialty is not 'added value'. Every candidate will have that, or they wouldn't have been short-listed. It is a good idea to think about aspects of your experience that are uniquely you. Ensure you have three areas of added value, other than your excellent general training in your speciality. This might include training in a specific area of interest, teaching skills, leadership skills or the ability to work well in a team. As always, think about what would be important to this panel or Trust specifically, for instance by enhancing their ability to

eve something specified in their annual report. It will only be of added value, of
…e, if that is what they want!

Questions regarding being a team player

At consultant interview it is absolutely essential that you demonstrate you will be a good team player because the expectation is that they will be 'stuck' with you for life, even though that is increasingly unusual. The last thing most organizations want is someone who will dysfunction a well-functioning team or department. There are a number of ways you can demonstrate this:

- By giving specific examples of team working (not just in questions about team working)
- By demonstrating through your answers that you are a solution-focused not problem-focused individual
- By developing rapport with the committee (see Chapter 4)
- By showing that you can manage conflict and differences of opinion constructively and effectively
- By demonstrating a tendency to give as well as sticking to you guns

Candidates find this area difficult to cover. However, there is no better example than where you have been a member of a team tasked with achieving something very difficult, with high potential for fallout and where ultimately the team was successful. A story about what the team went through and your (supportive, balanced, collaborative) role in that is a powerful illustration of your propensity to be successful in a team.

Questions on your strengths

The panel will be looking for certain strengths from the ultimately successful candidate and as part of their questions they may ask you what your strengths are. It is important to consider what was asked for in the job advert, job description and essential/desirable criteria, as well as at the pre-interview visit, when answering this question. Too many candidates trawl out a generic set of attributes for the 'perfect' colleague and fail to differentiate themselves from the crowd. Equally, if you are the last of six candidates, you have to ask yourself how much attention span the panel has when you open with 'good team player', after hearing it five times already. It is far more important to demonstrate the right strengths than fall into this typical trap.

For example, if the key message that came through all your meetings was that this service really needed a team player, you need to consider what words you can use to convey this message powerfully in both the answer to this question and other answers where your response involves describing a role you played. How can you deliver this in a fresh manner, given the lateness of the hour? What examples would the panel find genuinely interesting in answer to a question they are now bored of?

If the key message was they needed someone to lead and develop a service, what specific strengths would be important and what words could you use to describe your strengths in these areas? Use of the correct words conveys much, regardless of the quality of your answers. Strong candidates have great examples of strengths that match up directly to a department's needs and deliver those examples using language rich in words that have direct resonance with those strengths.

Examine Table 5.3 to see how specific words can be adopted to convey certain strengths.

Table 5.3 Words to convey character strengths

Proactive, goal-driven	Team player and supportive	Methodical and organized
Driven	Friendly	Detail orientated
Motivated	Harmony	Methodical
Passionate	Fair	Planned
Enthusiastic	Ethical	Structured
Goal-orientated	Considerate	Meticulous
Action-orientated	Helpful	Thorough
Successful	Flexible	Precise
Determined	Adaptable	Objective
Hard working	Inclusive	Patient
Innovative	Sincere	Considered
Persevering	Sensitive	Attention to detail
Results-driven	Loyal	
	Honest	
	Diplomatic	
	Empathetic	

As always, be sure you have sufficient evidence to back up the words you decide to use and avoid just trotting out a long list of generally 'important' qualities. It is particularly important in this question to appreciate the differing psychology of the panel members in relation to you. If you are a definite team player, you are more likely to place being sincere and loyal towards the top of the list. However, to an Island of Opportunity person that may come across as a weakness when they are looking for a go-getting, business developer with a strong sense of competition. In this regard, you need to pay particular attention to understanding different psychologies (islands, in our case) as outlined in a whole chapter on people (see Chapter 4).

Questions on your weaknesses

This is a particularly common question to be asked at consultant interview, often by the Chair and often feared by candidates. Many ask 'How far should I go?' If you portray no weaknesses you might be seen as arrogant and even dangerous, whereas if you portray too many of the wrong ones they start to wonder how you got this far and wonder if you might be dangerous! It is important to be aware that we all have weaknesses, so 'none' is rarely the right answer. However, be very careful what you do describe as a weakness and how you phrase your answer. The devil, as usual, is in the detailed use of language. For example, saying 'My *major* weakness is . . .' may raise immediate red flags to the panel, especially those members from the Island of Opportunity who will only be looking for minor ones, and may suggest that there are more you aren't raising, i.e. this is just the biggest one. Clearly, do not describe as a weakness anything that is fundamental to the job, e.g. attention to detail as a radiologist, poor eyesight as a keyhole surgeon or empathy as a palliative care specialist!

It can be helpful to give an example or story to help describe your weakness whilst also giving the panel greater insight and reassurance into what this means. Another strategy to use is to describe your weakness with reflection on what difficulties this might cause you and with a plan for improving in this area. The best result is to demonstrate self-awareness and already have a plan in motion to improve this aspect of self.

When describing your weakness, de-emphasize its frequency. Let's say you have been described as a bit of a bulldog when you want something. You could describe this as 'I never give in when I want something and this sometimes upsets people', or you could say 'When I feel strongly about something I can come across as a little passionate. However, I have learned to carefully consider the impact of this on colleagues, although I am still practising' (delivered with a smile at the end). You have been perfectly honest, but we guarantee that half the panel will see this as a strength, whilst the other half chalk it up as decent self-awareness and honesty—a win—win all round. Let's look at some more examples.

Example 1

'I am aware that my natural strengths can also be seen as weaknesses when used in the wrong circumstances or without regard to their impact on others. As I am sure you recognize from my CV, I am someone who likes to achieve to a very high level and get things done. As a result of this, in my ideal world I would like everything done yesterday. However, I have come to recognize in the last 6 months working as a locum consultant that, although some people are just like me, not everyone responds well to being driven along. I have learned to recognize people and circumstances where actually I will achieve some things more quickly by slowing down. I have also been fortunate enough to be able to observe one of my consultant colleagues who is extremely well respected and as a result I have started taking time to clearly explain to people why things have to change and what I am trying to achieve.'

Example 2

'I do have a strong sense of wanting things to be right. Whereas this is undoubtedly a strength as a histopathologist, I have come to recognize through multisource feedback that in certain circumstances my desire for certainty can hold up a diagnosis and prevent the surgeons from intervening early. I have met with my surgeons at St Elsewhere's to learn about the specific circumstances where speed is important to them and together we have developed a tagging system for requests to ensure speedy throughput of the most important ones.'

Gap questions

If you have gaps in your CV, someone is likely to notice them and ask, especially the Royal College or University Representatives. The most common gap question is an open one as follows:

'Tell me about any gaps or deficiencies in your training or experience.'

It is important to remember that all candidates have to be asked the same question and therefore you shouldn't just assume that this is directed at you specifically, or that you have to identify a specific gap. However, if there is a significant gap in your experience, e.g. 6 months without a post, you do need to be able to address it confidently or the panel may assume that you are worried or embarrassed about it and hiding something.

A useful strategy to use is this:

- Describe a point sometime in your last couple of years of training where you realized additional training or experience would be useful (ideally choose something that is important to this job)
- Describe what you did
- Explain the benefit to the department

This demonstrates to the panel that:

- You are reflective
- You are proactive and take action
- You have benefits and skills that they want

An example of this might be 'Last year I recognized that with increasing pressure on services' finances, clinical improvement expertise would become more important to prevent quality issues creeping in to services. So, I have attended courses on both clinical governance and audit and subsequently led two significant audit projects to enhance my experience. This area will become more important and I'd like to enhance these skills further'.

Let's look at some other examples.

Example 1

'Last year, as part of reflection for my annual review, I realized that it would be extremely useful to have additional training and experience in cardiology. As a result, I have spent 1 day a week for the last 9 months doing cardiology at St Mary's Hospital. On these days I participate actively in the echocardiography department, I attend the general cardiac clinic and I am involved in CCU and Cardiac ITU ward rounds. I know this experience will be extremely useful in care of the elderly at St Elsewhere's, where the appointment of a consultant with a cardiac interest would not only complement the existing skills well but also reduce the need for cardiac referrals to St Mary's.'

Even if you have a physical gap, we would encourage you to use the strategy above. Many people have gaps and not all short-listed candidates will fully match the specification. It is important to recognize this and have a positive response that demonstrates you have done something about it. If the panel really want to explore this physical gap they will ask you a supplementary question. You may feel compelled to highlight or address your physical gap despite our advice or because you are asked a supplementary question. In which case, it is important to be able to explain this succinctly and in a positive way, describing any benefit you got from the 'time out'. Clearly, where the career break or gap is massive, it cannot be ignored and must be appropriately addressed.

Example 2

'I took a 6-month break to study for my PLAB and establish my family in England. This was extremely beneficial in both developing my present excellent standard of English and ensuring my family stability living in a foreign country.'

Example 3

'I had a 10-year career break to raise my son with learning difficulties. This proved to be the ultimate leadership challenge and there is very little now that phases me as a result. I am sure this will be useful as we enter a period of huge uncertainty and change, with ever-decreasing finance.'

Example 4 (how not to do it)

'I applied for 76 different jobs but in the end nobody would take me, so I took the opportunity to study knitting.'

This will definitely raise doubts in the mind of panel members such as 'Why not? Do you have secrets we should know about?' Of course, if you are now applying for a job specializing in difficult wound closures, that knitting experience could be an asset! A better way of handling this would be:

'At that point there was a considerable imbalance of posts to trainees and so when I realized that I was going to be one of many who might have to sit it out for 6 months, I concentrated on self-study, developing an interest in XYZ and preparing myself for the next round to ensure that I got selected. That preparation paid off and I had no problem with subsequent appointment. The experience was an important lesson in foreseeing potential problems ahead of time, which is becoming an increasingly valuable skill in today's NHS.'

Negative questions

Negative questions are quite common. Examples include:

- Tell me a time when you failed to communicate successfully
- Tell me about a time when you were in conflict with a colleague or patient

You must have thought about examples to illustrate these types of questions before the interview. Saying 'I have never had a communication problem' or 'I cannot think of anything' will not serve you well and helps create a view that you have little self-awareness.

If you do not prepare these answers you are likely to think of something that only happened recently. This risks putting doubt into the mind of panel members that you have a real problem in this area. If unprepared it is often difficult to fully utilize your response to a maximum and turn a negative into a positive. Indeed, it is absolutely essential that despite being asked to describe something potentially negative about yourself that you leave the panel feeling positive about you.

> **USEFUL TIP**: Whatever the type of question, always start your answer with something positive, preferably involving some actual behaviour.

Strategy

Adoption of three simple principles will keep you on the straight and narrow:

- Use an example from some time ago—you do not want the panel to think you still have these types of problem
- Keep the example short and factual—do not embellish it or overdramatize what you did wrong
- Ensure you highlight what you learned from the experience and, more importantly, what you do differently today

Let's examine how that might look in an example.

> **Example**
> 'Four years ago, I was in an upper GI rotation at St Elsewhere's and a fellow StR and I fell out during a joint audit project we were leading. It delayed the project and we didn't resolve the issues, which led to a very unpleasant working relationship. That reinforced to me just how important constructive working relationships are and, if differences do develop, how vital it is to resolve them early. Since then, I've always watched when colleagues get stressed with others so that I can recognize the early signs and avoid the same triggers.'

Where problems involve others, which is quite common, it is very important not to criticize the other party as this can reinforce to the panel that, rather than learning, you actually felt you were right. Whereas you could have been, it will raise doubts about self-awareness and a lack of willingness to accept responsibility for problems. In the answer above, we focus on what you learned, not on who was to blame.

> **USEFUL TIP**: When asked about problems with colleagues, always describe the events factually and never attach blame.

Questions on your research

If there is a University Representative on the interview committee you will be asked about both teaching and research. As part of your interview preparation it is important to have a comprehensive understanding of not only what you did, factually, but also what it meant to you, the service and patients. Consider all of the following:

- What research have you done? Can you explain it in lay terms?
- If you have not done your own research, have you been involved in any multi-centre trials? If so, what was the trial about, what was your role and have the results been published?
- What piece of research has most influenced you? How has it influenced you, e.g. did it influence you to do further research/the project you conducted or did it change your practice?
- What are the research interests of the University Representative?
- What important key research has been published recently in your area (including electronic publications)?

If you are asked about recent publications these will be on key research likely to cause significant debate in your area of medicine or to change practice. We know of several candidates who have been asked about electronically published research. These cases have fallen into two main areas:

- Key area of practice and controversy explored in a large multicentre trial (in these cases the research was also reported in major newspapers, e.g. the *Times*)
- Very specific research relevant to specific senior lecturer posts

Remember, at interview all candidates have to be asked the same question. If everyone has done research you may be asked directly about it or to describe your hypothesis. The majority of the panel will not be specialists in your field and it is important to describe your research in terms that the entire panel will understand. Can you explain the benefits of your research for you, for further research and for patients?

If not all the candidates have done research, you may be asked 'What piece of research has influenced you most?' If you have done research, you must use this question as a springboard for describing what you have done. Did you read a specific scientific paper or papers before your research which influenced your hypothesis? Has your own research influenced your practice?

It's important to remember that the purpose of these questions is not to factually examine what you have done but to test out a range of abilities including thought process, reasoning, propensity to change when appropriate and proactivity, as well as any research ability that you have. This is what you need to demonstrate through the answers.

Other common questions

- Should all doctors do research?
- What research should we be doing in our department?

For each of the above, have an answer formed in your mind. In the first question, it is important to demonstrate the reasoning, as well as acknowledge and recognize that there might be other viewpoints. You won't earn Brownie points for sitting on the fence, but, equally, you might not be perceived in the best light if you appear to be completely rigid. The trick is to have a definite conclusion, with solid reasoning, but at least acknowledge alternatives. For the second question, again we need to understand the department's strategy and plans in order to answer in the best possible way. Ask yourself questions like:

- What research is aligned with their status, e.g. DGH?
- What research would help their desired positioning as a provider?
- What would enhance their reputation?
- What would help attract the sorts of patients they might want?

Behavioural questions

If you were being interviewed outside medicine you would find that most of the questions you were being asked were behavioural. It is well known that past behaviour is the best predictor of how someone may behave in the future. As an interviewer, if I can examine what someone did when faced with certain circumstances, this gives a very rich insight into how they might behave in similar circumstances in the future, as well as how they thought. This is also the reason why we are teaching you to adopt this approach as much as possible when answering each question as, by inference, you are saying to your interviewers 'I have faced this before and either succeeded (and I am therefore likely to do it again) or learned and adapted, which I am likely to do again!'

Increasingly, direct questions about your behaviour are playing a prominent role in the consultant interview. At this moment in time though, you are most likely to be asked behavioural questions by managers or the Chief Executive rather than from your future consultant colleagues.

Examples of questions asked

- Tell me about the last time you broke bad news to a patient
- Tell me about a time you disagreed with a colleague
- Give me an example that demonstrates your ability to lead; what exactly did you do?
- Tell me about how you teach medical students
- Tell me about a situation when a patient was demanding care you did not think was appropriate

Answering these questions takes discipline and practice. Skilled interviewers will also be looking for signs of authenticity. One of the reasons for asking these types of questions is that the answers are real and not semantic (what you think is the right answer or what you think someone needs to hear) and therefore are more reliable. It is important to ensure that answers do contain a factual description of the time, circumstances and who was involved so that the interviewer develops a sense of authenticity. However, you also need to demonstrate the qualities and skills you have and the behaviours you use, always with what they are looking for in mind. Consequently, it is useful to practise setting the scene sufficiently that you can do so succinctly and swiftly. Let's look at some examples.

Example 1

Tell me about a time you disagreed with a colleague.

Candidate 1	Candidate 2
In my previous job in St Elsewhere's I was one of four registrars working on the respiratory unit. The respiratory unit is spread over two wards and there is also a bronchoscopy suite and respiratory HDU (High Dependency Unit). The four StRs are expected to cover all of these areas, but on most days there are only two registrars available. On this particular day there had been a large number of admissions, four patients needed non-invasive ventilation and there was also a bronchoscopy list. It was my day to be rostered to the bronchoscopy unit. I had come in early to review all of the patients and we were about to see the first case on the list. (*We are 30 seconds*	I have always tried to work constructively and supportively with colleagues and I have been lucky enough not to have had many disagreements which are not easily resolvable. Six months ago, an StR colleague and I disagreed on the appropriate management plan for one of our patients with COPD (*8 seconds and the candidate is ready to discuss what he did*). The first thing I did, when he raised his concern, was to give him time to air his view fully. . . .

in and the scene is still being set.) I had just scrubbed up when one of my StR colleagues came in to the bronchoscopy suite to say he was concerned about my management plan for one of the patients on non-invasive ventilation. The patient, a 60-year-old ex-miner with COPD and a history of smoking for 44 years, had been admitted 3 days previously and I had been looking after him until the day before. This was the first time he had received non-invasive ventilation (*45 seconds and still the scene is being set and we are yet to find out what the candidate actually did*).

Clearly, Candidate 2 is much more focused. Remember, you are not being marked on your ability to tell a story, you are being marked on how you dealt with the problem. In my experience, when candidates get too involved in the story they frequently fail to answer the actual question, i.e. they skim over what they actually did because the story has assumed its own level of importance.

A useful structure to adopt in these situations is STAR:

- **Situation**
  - e.g. 'As a final-year StR . . .'
- **Task**
  - e.g. 'I had to lead the SHO audit programme . . .'
- **Actions**
  - e.g. 'My first action was . . .'
- **Result**
  - e.g. 'As a result of this project I improved my organizational skills and learned how to motivate junior colleagues to achieve good quality audits within tight timescales like a 4-month rotation'

USEFUL TIP: It is always a good idea to include reference points like time in the description of 'situation' as it demonstrates authenticity and allows the interviewer to understand how this relates to your career stage.

Example 2

Explain a situation when a patient was not happy with your care. What did you do?

> **Situation**
> In June this year, Mrs Jones, a patient with abnormal liver function tests, had been complaining to the nurses about the care she was receiving from the whole medical team.
>
> **Task**
> We needed to resolve this by better understanding Mrs Jones's concerns and how they related to her care.
>
> **Action**
> Firstly, I discussed Mrs Jones with the nursing team and reviewed the notes to see what had been said to Mrs Jones recently and to get a clear picture of the situation. I took a nurse with me and sat down with Mrs Jones and her husband and actively listened to her concerns. It quickly became clear she was frightened and thought we were hiding a diagnosis from her. I was able to explain where we were with her investigations and what needed to be done next to get a clear diagnosis. I reassured her that we would not hide the diagnosis from her once it was clear what the problem was. Finally, I suggested I would sit down again with them both in 48 hours' time to give them an update.
>
> **Result**
> This appeared to work because Mrs Jones stopped complaining to all the staff. I learned the importance of keeping patients updated even when there is no real news and it reinforced to me that in many cases when patients are complaining the underlying reason is that they are frightened and just need someone to talk to.

Opinion questions

Opinion questions are common and often seem quite benign. They aren't particularly effective because the interviewer tends to receive an answer that the candidate believes the interviewer wants to hear. These essentially come in two forms:

- Questions where there is essentially only one or two possible, often opposing, positions, i.e. agreement or disagreement, e.g. 'What is your view on revalidation?'
- Questions where there could be many different opinions of what constitutes the right answer, e.g. 'What makes an effective leader?'

Each of these types of question needs a different strategy. In the first type, the key is to come off the fence and give a confident opinion but without denigrating the opposing opinion, i.e. have strong reasoning why you hold a view but acknowledge an alternative view too. You almost certainly will not have the agreement of the whole panel, but you will have demonstrated you can develop opinions and make decisions whilst remaining open-minded. Having drawn a conclusion, you need to back it up with the reasoning *before* reflecting on the counter argument.

Example 1
What is your view on revalidation?
I think revalidation is a good thing. I believe the general public has a right to expect its doctors to keep up-to-date in their knowledge and skills, to demonstrate their compliance with Good Medical Practice and that this be reviewed by the GMC on a regular basis. However, I do not believe it will prevent another Harold Shipman. I am also aware that a number of my colleagues are concerned that the process is at risk of becoming too bureaucratic and time consuming and that appropriate clinical governance data systems and reporting mechanisms need to be in place for it to be effective.

In the second type of opinion question it is important to recognize that if you asked 10 different people you might get 10 different answers, none of which may be fundamentally flawed. In these questions, rather than just state your opinion it is much better to turn the question around to yourself and give an experiential answer where you describe how what you have learned makes you good at something. It is almost impossible with this approach for the panel to disagree with you and you have successfully created a further opportunity to promote yourself.

Example 2
What makes a good leader?
Last year I led a multidisciplinary audit on prescribing and drug errors. As a result of this experience, I learned how important it is to have a clear vision for projects that very different groups can understand, provide clear and regular direction, as well as keep people updated on how it is progressing. I also learned how important it is to keep people motivated, as well as the impact of leading by example, for instance in being diligent in the data collection to ensure no holes. Lastly, we had a lot of different characters in the project and although I had strong views about how best to achieve the aim, I also learned that you need to be a bit flexible in this as long as it delivers the right results.

Example 3
What makes a good undergraduate teacher?
I have been fortunate to have taught the undergraduates in psychiatry for the last 3 years and to play a key role in redeveloping their curriculum and training over the last year. I have always asked for feedback from my teaching sessions and from this I have learned that three things are essential if you are to be thought of as a good teacher: making teaching responsive to the undergraduate's needs, basing it on real patients and cases and making it interactive. I do this by. . . .

> **USEFUL TIP**: When answering opinion questions, always have one (an opinion!) with sound reasoning, but avoid alienating other opinions.

Questions regarding conflict resolution

A question on resolving conflict is a frequent component of a consultant interview. The panel want to assure themselves that you are not frequently in conflict with your colleagues, that you will be receptive to other points of view and that you will make a good team player. This is driven in part by too many experiences of entrenched conflict between consultants getting in the way of moving services forward.

You may be asked 'How will you deal with conflict between you and a consultant colleague (or a relative or a nurse)?' or a more behavioural type of question such as 'Tell me about a time you were in conflict with someone; what did you actually do?'

Whatever the question it is useful to use an experiential answer. As you answer the question you may want to change the word 'conflict' to 'disagreement' as it carries less emotion. You may also want to use an event that occurred a few months ago rather than last week. If you choose too recent an example the inference the panel might take is that you are always in conflict.

It is important to avoid saying that you have never been in conflict. As a consultant, you will have times when colleagues, patients or their relatives will disagree with you and you need to show that you have had experience at managing these types of situation.

Someone who manages or deals with conflict in a constructive manner will most likely adopt the following approach, which you can demonstrate through your answer by breaking it into three stages:

- Step 1 – Understand the problem by listening to the other party's point of view. If their position is not easily understandable, ask them what makes their position so important to them, i.e. what underpins it
- Step 2 – Define what the disagreement is actually about
- Step 3 – Work to achieve a solution that seems like a win for all parties concerned

Example

I do believe that I am someone who can work constructively within a team but recognize that it is only natural to disagree with colleagues about certain things from time to time. I also recognize that most conflict arises because of differences in personality and the key is to recognize that we actually need these differences within a team to achieve. Let me give you an example of how I manage conflict. Six months ago, I and another registrar were asked to write a guideline together. Not long after we started the project it became clear that we were both somewhat frustrated with each other as to how the guideline was developing. Recognizing that we were not going to be successful if we allowed our individual frustrations to grow I asked my colleague to meet with me over lunch. During lunch I explained very briefly that I was feeling frustrated as to how the project was developing and I suspected he felt the same way. I asked him to tell me his views on the project, what he felt was going right and what he felt were the issues. As he told me this I listened very carefully, making sure I didn't interrupt. What became clear as he spoke was that he was someone who liked to carefully plan things out and then systematically and methodically work through the plan. Also he was very worried that he had not written a guideline before and if he did not do this successfully it might impact on the assessment he received from his clinical supervisor. By contrast, I am someone who prefers a more flexible approach to projects and find a too rigid plan can stifle my creativity. I like to synthesize information and ideas in my head, but I can then sit down and write a well-constructed powerful argument relatively close to a deadline. As a result of our discussions we could both instantly see why each of us was frustrating the other, but we were able to also work out a plan together for achieving the guideline within the deadline. My colleague was keen to review the literature and evidence base, whilst it was agreed we would both brainstorm how this could be translated into everyday practice in our unit, and I would be responsible for the final writing of the practical aspects of the guideline.

So, in summary, I think that most conflict arises because people aren't all the same. The key to preventing this is to recognize it and watch for differences in thoughts and practices. When I do think conflict is developing between me and a colleague, I take time to listen to their point of view and then work towards a solution that represents a win for both of us.

USEFUL TIP: Make sure you have a conflict example with a positive outcome and clear learning points. Always avoid saying you've never been in conflict.

Communication questions

Communication questions are more common in some specialities than others, related heavily to the work itself or the consequence of poor communications, for instance in surgery. They are usually based around common communication issues relevant to the speciality and follow a number of formats:

- Giving a new diagnosis
- Breaking bad news
- Counselling, where there are a number of views as to what might be the right approach for future management (especially common in obstetrics and neonatology)

Typical examples include:

- Tell me how you would explain to a new patient they had *x* (e.g. breast cancer)
- How would you counsel parents whose baby was likely to be born at 23 weeks gestation?

- How do you tell relatives that their loved one has just died (usually A&E)?
- How would you counsel parents whose unborn baby was found to have *x* on antenatal scan (obstetrics)?
- How do you break bad news?

With all of these questions, the approach you use will be very discriminating. If you use the third person and the future you will rapidly give the panel the impression that you have just read about this topic in a textbook but have never done it yourself. If you use the first person and describe an event you were actually involved in the answer will flow much better, you are less likely to leave key things out and most importantly you will come across as empathetic and someone who can do the job.

How would you counsel parents whose baby is likely to be born at 23 weeks gestation?

Candidate 1	Candidate 2
I would follow the guidance of both the Nuffield Council on Bioethics and that published by Wilkinson et al. on behalf of the British Association of Perinatal Medicine. These guidelines state that it is inappropriate to offer resuscitation to babies of 22+6 days and less. From 23 weeks, we know some babies will survive but that it is very difficult to predict future outcome. At 24 weeks, babies should be offered full invasive neonatal intensive care. In these situations at 23 weeks gestation we would therefore want to make sure both parents were present for any discussion. We would need to read through the notes carefully to ensure we were aware of the following key pieces of information: the previous obstetric history, the accuracy of the dates, the present history, whether any antenatal steroids have been given and the estimated weight of the fetus from a recent scan.	Working in a busy, level 3 NICU I have had to counsel a number of families in this situation. I am always mindful of the ethical guidance in this area and that it is very difficult to predict the outcome for any one baby born between 23+0 and 23+6 weeks. This means in reality every conversation I have will be different. To give you a feel of what I typically do, let me describe what I did last week when I was asked to see Mr and Mrs Smith. The information I was given was that Mrs Smith was 23+2 by dates and in early labour. This was her second pregnancy, her first baby having died at 23+0 weeks 1 year previously. The first thing I did was review the antenatal notes and talk to the midwife. I particularly wanted to know more about mum's first baby, how sure we were of her dates, what was happening now, had mum had any antenatal steroids and was there a scan giving the present estimated weight of the baby.

Although the answers are essentially the same with Candidate 1, you are definitely thinking has this person ever done this or has he/she just revised from a textbook? With Candidate 2 you absolutely know he/she has done this and that he/she really recognizes how difficult these situations can be.

Clinical questions

Clinical questions are unusual in the consultant interview as the expectation is that you would not have your CCT/passed your exit exam without having good clinical knowledge. Taking this aside, they are not unheard of in surgical interviews where you may be asked how you would approach a patient with a specific problem. In our experience, these questions are either about very difficult procedures where there may be ethical debate as to what it is appropriate to do and if something is to be done who should do it, or about procedures where there are new or innovative ways to resolve the problem. In the latter, where there is more than one clinical approach, the panel will be expecting you to explain why you prefer your approach over others and the pros and cons of each intervention. Remember, the vast majority of the panel will be from the Island of Opportunity and so they will not be expecting a detailed step-by-step approach to the procedure itself.

Leadership and management questions

You will be asked some sort of leadership or management question at the consultant interview. This question is more likely to be asked by a manager or director and therefore more likely to be a behavioural question. It is vital, therefore, that you have examples of being a leader and a manager. For each, you need to be clear what behaviours you actually displayed and what benefits this gave at the time, as well as what benefits they will give your future employer. Sadly, many people answer leadership or management questions by demonstrating that they have attended a course. It is highly unlikely that you would even be short-listed without having done that and so this just places you in the pack. Really good candidates want to demonstrate the application of learning in this area and have a range of examples to use.

To answer leadership and management questions effectively it is important to be clear on the difference between leadership and management. Leadership is about people and direction, with a long-term time horizon, whereas management is about implementing and organizing based on that direction, with a more immediate time horizon.

Examples of each might include:

Leadership
- Leading a multidisciplinary team in an audit, e.g. leading the determination of its strategy and ensuring that everybody is on board
- Leading a clinical service improvement, e.g. prioritizing improvements based on service strategy and then spearheading an important initiative
- Leading a change in how the junior doctors work, requiring engagement and influencing aspects of leadership
- Leading a redesign of the junior doctors' teaching programme, focusing on its purpose and how this has changed over time

Management

- Managing the junior doctor audit programme, e.g. making sure audits are completed on time and fully written up
- Managing the rota
- Working within the risk management team to define and quantify risks
- Managing the junior doctor education programme, i.e. organizing venues, making sure speakers turn up, ensuring that everybody has the right materials, etc.

Consider what skills and qualities are useful in each role and how you can demonstrate these skills in your answer. Examples include:

Leadership

- Influencing, communication and engagement skills
- Ability to inspire
- Being visionary
- Leading by example
- Being open to ideas
- Being focused on improvement

What behaviours demonstrate these skills and qualities, e.g. being visible or organizing a motivation launch event for a major project?

Management

- Organizational skills
- Delegation skills
- Time management skills
- Project planning
- Communication skills
- Having a methodical and systematic approach

What behaviours demonstrate these skills and qualities, e.g. organizing an elective to a remote part of the globe or running a newsletter for a clinical trial?

In truth, leadership and management often sit hand-in-hand in medicine and those asking you the questions may not understand the difference themselves. They are also heavily influenced by an individual's psychology, for instance, someone wired to have acute attention to detail and a methodical planned approach to things may not recognize the importance of walking the floor amongst the people, i.e. visibility. Where the question permits, it is best to answer the question specifically about leadership or management but recognise the value of the 'other side' too. Let's look at an example:

> **How would we recognize that you are a good leader?**
> 'Two years ago, I led the setup of an exchange medicine programme with Botswana, in which individuals would join us for training and we would assist them in setting up a more robust medical programme back home. Firstly, I ensured that everybody understood what the vision was for the project, why we were doing this and how it would benefit us, by organizing

a series of launch events and spending time talking to key individuals. I ran a series of brainstorming sessions to ensure that everybody had the opportunity to contribute and then synthesized the best ideas to improve the overall programme. I took this approach because when I thought about what would make it successful, I realized that buy-in and involvement were critical and so this was where I put my efforts. Obviously, once I'd achieved this, there was a huge amount of management involved too, from organizing governance arrangements to detailed planning of trips. It was a great opportunity to apply some of the most important leadership principles that I had learned from courses, but in truth, leadership is also a frame of mind and I believe you never stop learning.'

This candidate has successfully delivered a clear message that he/she has developed leadership knowledge and applied that learning, using some of the most important transformational leadership skills, whilst also differentiating leadership from management in a way that tells someone with a 'management' view of leadership that he/she has the experience and the ability to apply those skills too.

> **USEFUL TIP**: Avoid simply saying you've been on a course—always have examples of the application of knowledge and skills acquired. If it's interesting they'll remember it too!

Questions regarding clinical Governance

It is highly probable that you will be asked a question on clinical governance as part of your interview. These questions are often asked by the Medical Director, who may be from either the Island of Opportunity or the Island of Intellect (or a combination of the two). Consequently, it would be useful to consider the Medical Director's island when forming your answer. Juniors tend to think of clinical governance as being audit, but it is important to remember that it is an umbrella term for a whole variety of activities which together improve the quality of care that we give to our patients.

Activities that make up clinical governance

- Clinical effectiveness
- Audit
- Evidence-based guidelines
- Care pathways
- Research and development
- Benchmarking
- Risk management
- Patient, public and carer involvement
- Education, training and continuous professional development (CPD)
- Strategic capacity and capability
- Staff management and performance

- Information management
- *Communication*
- *Leadership*
- *Team working*

> **USEFUL TIP**: Be careful not to show your naivety by confusing clinical governance with audit (a part of an effective clinical governance effort) or falling into the trap of suggesting that clinical governance is just about safety.

As always, consider what evidence you have that illustrates your full engagement in the spirit of clinical governance across the key areas of audit, risk management, patient and public involvement and your future CPD. When considering audit, always choose a project that was indeed genuinely an audit (and not a mini research project) and which followed the audit cycle.

You may not have any direct experience in risk management, but you must be clear in your own mind what the key risks are for your service. It is important to understand the key clinical risks, e.g. hospital-associated infection, venothrombo embolism and speciality-specific clinical risks, as well as non-clinical risks and risks associated with the larger political agenda. For example, in neonatal medicine the risks you might want to highlight, depending on the exact question asked, might include:

- Infection control
- Equipment management
- Appropriate training and development
- Nursing and medical staffing
- Demand management working within a network

Recognize that patient and public involvement is very high on most organizations' agendas, so you must have thought about this area in advance. How have you or how could you involve patients and the public in your specialty?

Examples

- Patient surveys (including real-time feedback)
- Patient feedback, e.g. as part of multisource feedback
- Patient comment cards
- Using patient diaries to make service improvements
- Involvement of patients in user groups to look at a specific area of service development or care pathway
- Working closely with charity groups
- Developing expert patients to help teach other patients and staff about their conditions
- Taking time to educate the patients you see in your clinic about their problems so they can predominantly self-manage their disease

With increasing financial austerity requiring greater attention to innovation and improvement, as well as increasing clinical risk if cost cutting is not intelligently designed, clinical governance has taken on a new life and many services are keen to ensure that their consultants demonstrate understanding and skill in this area. If you haven't already done so, we advocate attending a clinical governance or clinical effectiveness course and then seeking opportunities to apply the principles. This provides a compelling benefit for many services that find themselves weak in this area.

Questions regarding professional dilemmas

Professional dilemmas frequently feature in the collection of questions asked at interview. They are designed to test out a variety of skills including reasoning, clinical governance, approach to conflict, sensitive issues and proactivity. They tend to follow a few key themes:

- The drunken colleague
- The bullied junior
- The poorly performing colleague

We will deal with each of them in turn, although there are broad principles covering all of them. It is useful to remember that you have absolute control as to where your answer goes. If you end up talking about the GMC, dismissal, etc. it is because you took the answer there and so you had better be sure of your facts!

The drunken colleague

A typical question would be 'You have been working for our organization as a consultant for 1 year when one of your consultant colleagues arrives for work clearly the worse for alcohol. What would you do?'

The key issues that need to be considered in your answer are as follows:

- Patient safety is your number one consideration, i.e. you must check all clinical work done by your consultant colleague this morning and ensure appropriate cover for his on-going clinical work that morning. If necessary this will need to be you
- You need to get the consultant home. Do not let him drive; be proactive and get him a taxi
- You need to consider why this consultant has behaved in this way. Is this a one off? Is it a sign of a more chronic problem? Are you an appropriate person to talk with your colleague and explore the precipitators of this event in more detail or would it be better coming from a more senior colleague?
- Do not immediately refer to the Clinical Director/Medical Director. You are a consultant now and you need to manage these problems initially yourself. Do not immediately refer to the GMC! This may be a one off; maybe something dreadful happened to him the night before, e.g. his wife died last night. However, you do need to be clear on your future course of action, e.g. monitor for other signs of stress
- If you decide to make this a case of chronic alcohol abuse, consider what type of support the consultant could access, e.g. the BMA counselling service, occupational health, Alcoholics Anonymous. What would you say to your colleague with respect to your obligations concerning patient safety, referral, escalation, etc?

The key is to demonstrate a clear knowledge of your responsibilities as well as a considered and supportive approach to handling the situation.

The bullied junior

A typical question would be 'You have been working for our organization as a consultant for 1 year when one of the juniors comes to tell you in confidence that they are being bullied by one of your consultant colleagues. What would you do?'

The key issues that need to be considered in your answer are as follows:

- Get a full understanding of the situation. This involves sitting down with the trainee and exploring the issues. What actually happened, has it occurred more than once, does she think it is just happening to her or is it happening to others?
- If appropriate, explore with the junior in a very supportive way whether this is in fact bullying or has arisen out of a difference in personality and expectations
- Ensure you have a good understanding of what the junior is asking for—formal grievance/complaint or simply some quiet help resolving it?
- Employ possible discrete questioning of other staff to see if others have noticed a problem or are subject to the same behaviour. Reflect on whether similar allegations have been made about this consultant in the past or is this new
- If you feel you have a good relationship with the consultant, sit down with him/her and discuss the issue, after you have carefully considered what you know so far, non-judgementally
- If you do not know the consultant well and you feel there are real issues, you will need to raise your concerns with the Clinical Service Lead and, depending on the seriousness of the alleged behaviour, HR may need to be involved
- If you feel there has definitely been a case of bullying you will need to make the junior aware of the Trust bullying and intimidation policy, which will probably stipulate who to contact and how to have it resolved

In this instance, again being aware of your responsibilities and a calm approach are required. It is important to acknowledge that you are aware there may be malicious reasons for these accusations, e.g. the junior being given a poor report, but that you would remain open-minded until you had explored the issues sufficiently to draw a conclusion. You are expected to demonstrate a neutral position, supportive to all, but clear in your professional responsibility.

> **USEFUL TIP**: Always remember that complaints about one person from another person may have unseen reasons, e.g. a poor reference had been written.

The poorly performing colleague

A typical question might be 'How would you deal with a colleague whose performance you were concerned about?'

The key issues that need to be considered in your answer are as follows:

- Poor performance can be very subjective, i.e. we may perceive colleagues as performing poorly because they are not like us

- If you are going to deal with an issue of poor performance you first have to have objective evidence that this is the case. You will get nowhere with a subjective view of the situation. Do you have outcome data or workload data that suggest there is an issue, are their results significant outliers from their peers, have there been lots of written complaints, etc?
- You need to consider if you are the correct person to deal with this issue. Is this something that an informal chat between two colleagues might reasonably resolve or is this something that needs a more formal approach? Do you have any sort of line management over this doctor or should you be referring your objective concerns to the Clinical Service Lead?
- If asked what you will do as the Clinical Service Lead, consider the following:
  - Collecting objective evidence
  - Reflecting on what you think might be the cause of this performance issue (these are just hypotheses at the present)
  - Sitting down with the individual and explaining your concerns in the first person so as not to cause additional conflict and resistance, e.g. 'I am concerned that the waiting list for your clinics is now more than 18 weeks'
  - Asking the individual if he has ideas for improving performance or removing blocks
  - Agreeing SMART (Specific, Measurable, Agreed, Realistic, Timed) written objectives for improving performance
- You may want to consider the role of the National Clinical Assessment Service (NCAS) if your initial strategies do not result in improvement in your colleague's performance, but this should not be your first choice or the first thing you say in your answer. If involving NCAS you would need to have discussed the situation first with the Trust Medical Director

In common with previous answers, you need to demonstrate a sense of responsibility to the service and patients, with a supportive attitude to the colleague. It is always worth remembering that performance issues are almost always multifactorial and the individual is only one component in a series of interrelated issues or events that add up to a certain level of performance. You must consider the wider influences.

Ethical questions

Some specialities lend themselves to ethical questions more than others. Remember, there will always be more than one point of view when answering the question (otherwise it is hardly an ethical issue!); however, you do need to have a view that you can justify whilst potentially seeing (and presenting) the other point of view too, if appropriate.

There are a few classic questions:

- Should we offer surgery to smokers?
- Should we offer elective surgery to obese patients?
- A 22-year-old man has been involved in a severe RTA. He is comatose and urgently needs blood. Without this he will almost certainly die. His girlfriend says he is a practising Jehovah's Witness and would not want blood. What would you do?

- A woman is in labour at 25 weeks gestation. She tells you that she is aware that babies born at this age are likely to be very handicapped. She asks you not to resuscitate her baby
- A woman has fetal distress at term. She wants a natural birth and is refusing a Caesarean section

It can be useful to acknowledge, certainly for the latter three questions, that this is a very difficult area for you as a doctor and that the key is to handle the situation extremely sensitively. For each question appropriate to your specialty you need to consider:

- Is there any legal basis to your answer?
- Is there a strong view among the specific professionals in your area? For example, vascular surgeons often answer the question about smoking and surgery with a 'NO' where most general surgeons will say 'YES'
- What is your view and how can you justify it? For example:

Example 1

'As a doctor I took an oath to give all of my patients the best care I could. I personally could not withhold a life-saving treatment especially where the patient himself could not tell me his wishes and where there was no apparent advanced directive. In this situation I would seek the support and consensus of my colleagues and if we were all in agreement I would give the patient blood.'

Example 2

Alternatively, 'I think it is very important to respect the religious views of others. I would immediately commence resuscitation with non-blood products and would organize urgent cross-match in case it became clear giving blood was a possibility. I would ask the girlfriend if she or the young man's family knew if he had a written advanced directive. If this was available I would follow the instructions contained within it. If not available, I would need to communicate rapidly with the next of kin, which may not be the girlfriend, carefully explaining that the young man will die if not given blood, and assess their reaction to that information. If it was clear that the next of kin understood this and remained persistent he would not want blood, I would ask them to sign to that effect in the presence of myself and a senior colleague.'

USEFUL TIP: Ethical questions are also opinion questions, so we'd like to remind you that you need to have one, or at least a mechanism for arriving at one.

The NHS and political agenda

This is an increasingly common area to be asked one or more questions in and you need to ensure that you are fully conversant with the latest strategies and how they will impact clinical services. Because this area is of such importance, we have devoted significant attention to it in Chapter 9. It is always worth remembering that the sands of NHS policy shift frequently and you must be up-to-date at the time of your interview.

Meeting the needs of more than one interviewer

On occasions you may be asked a question where you know there are very different views around the table and also very different sets of internal wiring. You may well have discovered this from your pre-interview visit. Often questions are asked on issues that are topical to or causing distress to services and individuals at that time. Consequently, these may well be the same issues expressed to you when you probe on your pre-interview visit. The key in these situations is to be clear of who the key players are and to try to satisfy their needs. Who carries most weight and what is their view? The most likely area of difference in opinion is between the Management/Directors and the consultants in your speciality over future service development.

It is important to present a balanced view without appearing to sit on the fence. That's not always easy. We actually need to use a psychological approach to ensure that the right people hear the right things for them. Let's use an example to show how you can approach this best.

Example

You are a neurologist (Island of Intellect). The Chief Executive (Island of Opportunity) asks you about service development in your field. You are aware that he thinks that the consultants are not being proactive enough and his words at the pre-interview visit were a lighter version of 'behaving like dinosaurs'.

You turn to face the Chief Executive and with very good eye contact and a strong confident posture you talk dynamically about the opportunities there are in your field and the benefits you will personally bring the organization by attracting new patients in your area of interest. When you have finished you actively drop eye contact with the Chief Executive turn your body towards your consultant colleague and make eye contact. In a quieter more even-toned voice talk about the difficulties and problems that will need to be overcome to pursue this service development and the importance of ensuring robust, safe practice.

In this scenario, the Chief Executive, with a relatively short attention span, only hears the first part of your answer full of opportunity and benefits to him and the organization. When you drop your eye contact with him he stops listening. Your consultant colleague, who by his nature listens to your whole answer, is reassured by you having a conversation directly with him over the problems and difficulties that have to be overcome.

If the key players are from the Island of Opportunity and the Island of Intellect, deal with the Island of Opportunity dweller first. If they are from the Island of Team Spirit and the Island of Intellect, deal with the Island of Team Spirit dweller first. If they are from the Island of Team Spirit and the Island of Opportunity, reassure the Island of Team Spirit dweller in your first sentence that patients and the team are at the heart of everything you do and then deal with the Island of Opportunity dweller's needs before returning to the Island of Team Spirit. If all of that sounds complicated and you're worried you might get it wrong, the two general principles to consider are the need to address the Island of Opportunity dwellers first, otherwise they lose interest, and to deal with the Island of Intellect dwellers last, as they are the most patient and will listen to everything anyway. The Island of Team Spirit dwellers are most likely to develop an early emotional reaction and this needs considering early in sensitive issues.

In summary:

- Work out the two key players and their islands
- Make sure you maintain good eye contact with each individually when discussing the points that are important to them
- Very definitely drop eye contact when you swap between the two
- Deal with the islands in this order:
  - Team Spirit (but only for a single sentence if an Island of Opportunity dweller is one of your key players in relation to this specific question)
  - Opportunity
  - Intellect

Interview question dynamic

When answering questions it is useful to consider the interrelationship between (Figure 5.2):

- Your island
- The interviewer's island
- The interviewer's purpose

This can have a profound impact on the manner in which you answer questions, the reasoning you choose and whether you avoid falling into an island trap that doesn't serve you well. This will undoubtedly mean you need to modify your answers. Given the importance of people and their differences in the interview scenario, we have devoted a whole chapter to this subject and so this brief insertion needs to be supplemented by a deep read of Chapter 4.

                    Your wiring

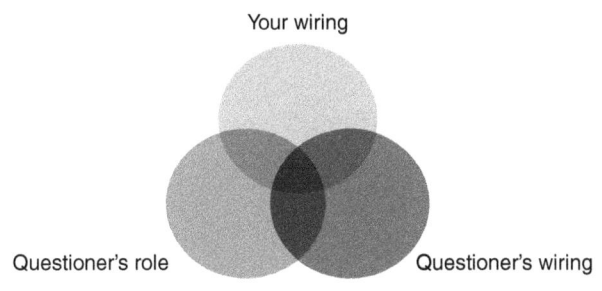

Questioner's role   Questioner's wiring

Figure 5.2 Interview question dynamic.

Let us imagine for a moment you are applying for a consultant post in a prestigious Teaching Hospital. You are from the Island of Intellect and the Professor representing the University is from the Island of Opportunity; he is on the interview panel to assess your research worth. What would be important to him and what meaning do you want him to take from your answer?

Without considering the Professor specifically, as an Island of Intellect dweller you would most naturally talk about an Island of Intellect topic from an Island of Intellect perspective, e.g. discussing your ability to fully evaluate the literature, develop clear hypotheses and design experiments or studies. There is nothing specifically wrong with this answer and the skills are undoubtedly valuable, but the goal here is to get the job and so you need to ask yourself whether this answer will appeal to the Island of Opportunity Professor? Well, bluntly, the answer is no. He would be more excited to hear that the research you did previously was funded by a large MRC grant that you wrote the application for, resulted in eight publications in highly ranked journals and has been presented at the most prestigious international meeting in your field in a prominent spot.

This tailored approach, choosing distinct aspects to focus on, needs to be underpinned by the understanding that interviews are emotion-driven events and emotions are predominantly driven by *meaning*. As a result of your response, the Professor will draw certain meanings. These meanings will either resonate with him and excite him or turn him off. You always need to ask yourself 'What meaning do I think he might draw from this answer?' Additionally, if I want him to recommend me, what *meaning* would it be most helpful for him to have? Taking our example of the prominent Professor, it might be that you are a high producer, are successful in obtaining grants, want to do further research and will bring large wodges of cash into the department!

Whenever you are considering an answer to a question, consider what meaning you want the panel to take away from your answer. You will have a good understanding of the meanings you need to portray if you reflect back on the job description and your pre-interview visit.

Chapter 6
The interview

Introduction

However much preparation you have done, for most candidates the interview day itself can be somewhat daunting or even downright frightening. The first part of this chapter focuses on how you can reduce any anxiety through both careful planning and a few simple exercises and tips. The second part of the chapter deals at a practical level with what happens in the interview itself so you will know exactly what to expect.

This chapter does not deal with how to respond to interview questions (with the exception of where you do not understand what has been asked). Preparation and answering of interview questions has been discussed in great detail in Chapter 5.

On the day—developing the right frame of mind and reducing anxiety

Pre-interview nerves

Most candidates will have a degree of interview nerves and it can be helpful to remember that other interviewees are likely to be feeling similar to you. A little bit of anxiety, as opposed to complacency, is often useful to fuel the desire to achieve and ensure you go the extra mile to get the job. However, if anxiety really takes hold and a candidate appears dysfunctional to the panel it can be viewed disadvantageously, with panel members questioning (internally, at least) whether you would be equally dysfunctional in a stressful clinical situation or when leading something important. Much of what we are about to cover deals with controlling those nerves and giving you the best shot at a confident performance on the day.

Practical preparation

There is much that can be done to reduce nerves and although a significant amount of this is practical and common sense, it is worth reminding ourselves of the following:

- The more prepared you are, the calmer you will feel, so start your interview preparation early
- When you go to the pre-interview visit, physically find out where the interview room is so that you can find it more easily on the day of the interview (it's one less thing to worry about and we all know how one part of a hospital can look much like another and even the best signage isn't going to direct you to room F1238B)
- Decide what you are going to wear a few days before the interview
  - Try everything on:
    - Do you feel comfortable?
    - Is it pressed, clean and odour free?
    - When you look at yourself in the mirror do you look like a serious candidate for the post? Do you look like a consultant? If not, do you need to wear something different?
    - Guys—take your new shirt out of the packet, remove all the pins, wash and iron it

- Girls—make sure you have at least three pairs of new tights and that you pack a spare pair on the day
- If you are going to wear new shoes, start breaking them in early (remember to take the label off the bottom of them too!)
* If HR has insisted on you bringing lots of paperwork to the interview, e.g. birth certificates, passports, GMC certificate, licence to practice, degree certificates, then collect them all together a few days before your interview (the last thing you want to be doing the night before your interview is frantically looking for these)
* The evening before
  - Lay out your clothes and polish your shoes
  - Make sure you have the exact venue details and timings for your interview
  - Print off a map suitable to get you to the hospital and a plan of the hospital too if you are in any doubt where you are going
  - Make sure you have more than one electronic copy of your presentation (e.g. on a laptop, CD and a USB stick) as well as a hard copy. Make sure you save your presentation in PowerPoint 97–2003 as well as in your normal version of PowerPoint; this is because many hospital computer systems only recognize the 97–2003 version of PowerPoint and not the more modern versions
  - Pack a bag with an umbrella or rain coat, a hairbrush or comb, plenty of change in case the car park is pay & display and, if you are wearing tights or stockings, a spare pair (essentially, leave nothing to chance)
* Ensure that you are in the best possible condition and position to perform well
  - Do not work the night before your interview (although it may sound unbelievable, I have met candidates who, not wanting to let their existing, temporary organization down, have had little or no sleep and then wondered why they could not function effectively and answer questions well)
  - Do not offer to work the morning of your interview, even if you are an internal candidate (your focus and your goal must be the interview)
  - The night before your interview remind yourself of your unique selling points, personal examples that you have identified and the benefits these will bring the organization
  - Consider practising some of the more likely key questions, for example:
    - Your CCT date
    - Your CV
    - The added value you bring
    - Five-year plan
    - Your leadership qualities
    - Your weaknesses
* The night before your interview, get an early night and do not drink too much alcohol (Dutch courage is no help if it results in you talking double Dutch on the day!)
* Give yourself plenty of time to get to your interview and remember that parking at peak times can be very difficult in many hospitals and that public transport can be late (it is much better to arrive an hour early and relax than at the last minute,

having struggled to find a parking spot and consequently having sprinted from a distance, causing you to feel very stressed out)
- Make sure you take a bottle of water with you and a complex carbohydrate snack of some kind, e.g. a muesli bar (having a snack is particularly important if your interview is scheduled around lunchtime because if you are hungry or dehydrated you will not be able to answer the questions as effectively)

If you do arrive at the interview very early, consider going away again as it can become very anxiety stimulating listening to other candidates tell you how wonderful they are or what experience they have, let alone how difficult the questions were or how horrible the panel are. Additionally, the waiting rooms for interview candidates are often small, stuffy internal rooms with no natural light. These rooms have the ability to dull your senses long before you enter the interview room. If you decide not to stay, go and have a walk, and get some fresh air and a drink of water.

> **USEFUL TIP:** If you feel the need to consume food or liquids beforehand, ensure they are not vivid in colour—a blackcurrant spill on a white shirt is hard to conceal!

What is anxiety?

Despite careful preparation, it is still possible, even normal, to feel anxious and nervous. Understanding what anxiety is and its common causes makes it possible to develop strategies to deal with it. Firstly, it is important to recognize that fear is mostly perceptual and that anxiety is simply the output of distinct neural processing caused by:

- Focusing on what might go wrong
- Poor preparation
- Not managing your physiology

Consequently, it is important to understand the behavioural triad of

- Focus
- Meaning
- Physiology or behaviour

These three factors are related and all can cause us anxiety and yet all are within our control if we choose to exercise it. At a simple level, we need to recognize that what we focus on and the meaning we give it drives our physiological responses and our behaviour. If we focus on what might go wrong at the interview and attach a meaning such as 'this will mean that I fail to get the job I have always wanted' then this will immediately set in motion a specific physiological response of anxiety and fear (fast breathing, sweaty palms, darting eyes, etc.), along with certain behaviours or body language, e.g. head bent, eyes down.

The reverse works too—we can induce a feeling of anxiety if we start breathing slightly faster and shallower, not that we recommend this! However, it is important to appreciate that there is a link between these physical and mental factors. By understanding how we can become anxious, we can use these same factors of focus, meaning and physiology to not only reduce feelings of anxiety but also induce a sense of calm confidence. The techniques most beneficial for controlling these parameters are:

- Visualization (focus and meaning)
- Repeating mantras (focus and meaning)
- Asking positive questions (focus and meaning)
- Breathing (physiology)
- Centring our energy (physiology)

You may want to consider one or more of the above techniques both before and on the day. All are proven to work for some people, but it is possible that not everything will work for any one individual in particular. If nothing else, we strongly recommend you practise the breathing technique as it can be done anywhere (and works on just about everybody) and mentally check yourself if you begin to adopt a negative focus, as this can undermine all your pre-interview preparation.

Strategies for building confidence and reducing or preventing anxiety

Mantras and positive messages

Remember that you tend to get what you think. If you keep telling your subconscious brain that you will not get the job, you are not good enough, you are going to make a mess of things, etc. then you will most likely not get the job, be good enough and make a mess. Spend the time before the interview (ideally starting several weeks before) giving yourself some positive messages by developing a series of positive phrases that mean something to you.

A mantra is a phrase that reinforces your status, success or achievement of a specific goal. It needs to be repeated over and over until subconsciously it has become reality, thus driving you to behave in that manner without really thinking about it. It can also act as a gentle reminder to you of your purpose and strengths at that moment in time. The best mantra is one you have specifically and meaningfully designed for yourself, but examples could include:

- I am ready, I am ready, I am ready to be an excellent consultant
- All the strength I need is within me now (Anthony Robbins)
- I am the best, the best I can be
- I am the best, the best for this job
- I have the most to bring of any candidate
- I am successful
- I am a consultant
- I am a great consultant
- The job is mine

When choosing your own mantra it is important that it includes positive words only and includes what you want to come true or achieve. For example, 'I will not fail' is not a good mantra as it contains the word 'fail' and subconsciously your brain, unfortunately, will focus on this.

It is also important to assume that what you want to achieve has already happened. For example, a mantra such as 'I want the job' puts you at risk of still wanting the job after the interview, whereas 'The job is mine' focuses your brain on believing you have achieved it. Remember, it is designed to induce both mental and physiological states that are helpful, so that the last thing you need is one that leaves you 'wanting'.

Try to make your mantra rhythmical, e.g. 'I am a consultant' may become 'I am a consultant, I am a consultant, I am, I am, I am a consultant'. If your mantra is to be truly effective then it needs to be chanted out loud, ideally when doing some exercise such as brisk walking or running. Rhythmical mantras are therefore great when doing rhythmical exercise!

Finally, a great mantra that remains unspoken is unlikely to deliver its benefits. Many great achievers combine mantras with other beneficial activity. For instance, going out for a brisk walk really early in the morning gives you exercise and the perfect opportunity to 'chant' your mantra whilst nobody is about!

In summary, the most important things to remember are:

- Choose something that resonates or works for you
- Make sure it contains only positive words
- Make sure it assumes you have achieved your goal
- Start using it at least 2 weeks before the interview
- Chant it repeatedly, ideally whilst exercising
- Say it positively, with strength or conviction
- Most importantly, believe it!

Visualization

Visualization can be a very powerful tool for putting you in a successful frame of mind and is utilized by almost all of the most successful sports men and women. Visualization works on the premise that our subconscious brain cannot differentiate between something vividly imagined which has not yet happened and the same situation in reality. By visualizing, you imprint on the subconscious brain something that it believes has already happened or been experienced. Then, when the event comes along for real, it already has the blueprint for what should happen (in the way you would like it to happen). Assuming you have visualized something positive, then the outcome is likely to be positive. We do hope, however, you can see that it is important to visualize the right things. If you spend the time before the interview focusing on failing or focusing on why someone else is going to get the job then you will most likely not get the job.

The key to visualization is to spend just a few minutes each day visualizing yourself in the interview itself, performing really well and ultimately being successful. Visualization depends on you being able to see pictures in your mind and not everyone can do this. If you fall into this latter category you can adapt the technique by trying to imagine voices or feelings associated with a successful interview. Assuming you can make these voices and feelings rich, this adapted technique can be equally successful.

If you are able to visualize, the clearer (e.g. seeing actual people known to be on the panel), the brighter and more colorful you can make your visualization the better. If you can then add voices and feelings too, your visualization will be the more powerful for it. Ultimately, the power of visualization depends on how real you can make it.

Practicalities of visualization

- Picture a fantastic interview
- Picture the panel asking you questions
- Picture yourself confidently responding to their questions
- See yourself smiling
- Hear yourself speaking with confidence and passion
- Imagine yourself in a calm state
- Feel the rapport between you and the panel
- Care about the panel and in helping them achieve the best consultant (you!)
- Tell yourself you will do well

Asking positive questions

Asking yourself positive questions works in much the same way as mantras and visualization—it gets you to focus on success, not failure. Many successful people have trained themselves to ask carefully worded, positive questions at key moments. Learn to ask yourself questions such as:

- How can I demonstrate that I am the best candidate for the job?
- What will I do first when I get the job?

Conversely, each time you spot yourself asking a negative question, make sure that you immediately change your focus and return to positive questioning or another positive technique. Again, the wrong, negative focus can bring the wrong results and so questions like 'How can I prevent messing up?' or 'What will I do if I don't get the job?' can result in your brain focusing on messing up and failing to be appointed.

Breathing

When we become anxious our breathing becomes faster and shallower. This can make us feel light-headed and more anxious. Consequently, we then breathe even faster, feel even more light-headed and before we know it we are in a vicious cycle. Controlling breathing, therefore, is a very powerful technique, quite literally at our disposal in any moment, which can induce a sense of calm and negate nerves.

The breathing exercise below works well for me and everyone I have shared it with. You do need to practise it in advance so do not leave your first attempt to the day of the interview.

Firstly, you need to learn to breathe from your diaphragm and not your rib cage. Take several deep breaths in front of a mirror so that you notice what happens.

Did your shoulders move? If so then you were breathing from your rib cage and not from your diaphragm and were only using the upper part of your lungs to breathe. To breathe using your diaphragm you must push your abdomen out as you breathe in and pull your abdomen in as you breathe out (this is the exact opposite to what you will have done if you were breathing from your upper chest and moving your shoulders when you took a large breath before).

Initially just practise breathing from your diaphragm. As you inspire, push your abdomen out as far as possible. It is worth wearing loose clothes when first practising this and putting your hand on your abdomen to check you are doing it properly. Remember, do not allow your shoulders to move.

Once you are happy with the action, practise breathing in through your nose and out through your mouth or nose. You need to breathe out for twice as long as you breathe in. To help you practise this, count slowly as you breathe in and double the count as you breathe out, e.g. if you breathe in for 4 seconds you need to breathe out for 8 seconds. Do this slowly 5–10 times, with your eyes closed if you prefer. As you breathe out try to relax your shoulders, upper chest, face and jaw. If the exercise is working you will literally feel as if oxygen is rushing to your brain and then a great sense of calmness descending over you.

Breathing exercise summary

- Use diaphragmatic breathing
- Breathe in through your nose for a count of 1 (which should be a few seconds)
- Take a brief natural pause
- Breathe out through your mouth or nose for a count of 2, i.e. double the length of inspiration
- Repeat 5–10 times each session

On the day of the interview you can literally do this exercise anywhere and it will take less than 2 minutes to do whilst significantly enhancing your calmness.

Centring energy

This exercise is particularly useful if you are feeling a little shaky and wobbly as it helps give you strength again, especially in your lower body, enhancing your sense of being in control. The technique involves the following:

- Stand with your feet about shoulder width apart
- Close your eyes
- Imagine a rod of steel passing through your body from head to floor
- This rod is now being screwed to the floor and is then being pulled slowly upwards
- As the rod is pulled upwards feel your chin and head lifting upwards
- Feel your neck lengthening
- Feel your shoulders been pulled back
- Feel your spine straightening throughout its length
- Feel your legs straighten and the muscles contract so that your legs feel stronger

When done well your whole body will feel much stronger and poised. You will no longer have jelly legs and your posture should demonstrate an appearance of confidence. Like all of these exercises not everything works for everyone. If this does not work for you, try one of the other strategies.

The interview

What actually happens at the interview?

For many candidates the consultant interview may be the first formal interview that they have had for many years so it is useful to spend a few minutes considering what actually happens.

It is rare for the interview panel to meet before the interview process. Usually, a short period of time will have been set aside (e.g. 15–30 minutes) for the Chair to lay out the format of the interview to the panel and for the panel to agree on what questions will be asked. With the exception of the work around behavioural questions, there has been almost no work on standardization of interview questions for consultant interviews or which questions are best at discriminating the ideal candidate. As a result, most panel members will come to the interview with an idea of two to three questions they would like to ask. Depending on their role, e.g. Royal College Representative, these questions may have a clear focus. The individual panel members will sometimes test their questions out on the rest of the panel and a decision will be made regarding which questions should be used. In this period, any ambiguities within questions will be ironed out.

In general, your interview will last between 30 and 45 minutes, although add another 15 minutes if you have been asked to do a presentation within the interview itself. If you have not been told the exact length and this is important to you, ask Medical Staffing. The panel will usually be sat in a U-shape around a board-room table with the Chair at the top and the panel around the sides. You will be expected to sit at the bottom of the table. You should be provided with a glass of water but, if not, do ask for one. If offered a drink always say 'yes' even if you are not thirsty. It gives you something to hold to keep your nervous hands under control and it is common for a candidate's voice to become dry as the interview progresses.

> **USEFUL TIP:** Always accept a glass of water. You will be doing a lot of talking and are likely to get a dry throat. If you start coughing it can appear as if you are nervous. If nothing else it gives you something to do with your hands!

Either a member of the panel (usually the Chair) or a representative from Medical Staffing will come and collect you from the waiting room. They will take you into the room where a good chairperson will introduce you to all the panel members. If you have been asked to do a presentation as part of your interview, this will likely come next. The chairperson will usually say something along the lines of 'Dr Smith, we would like you to start with your presentation. You have 10 minutes to do this and after that the panel will ask you any questions arising from your presentation. We will then go immediately into the interview itself'.

The interview will usually start with the Royal College Representative. Very occasionally the Chair may ask you an opening question with the idea of relaxing you. After the Royal College Representative has questioned you it is usual for the questions to go round the table in a clock-like manner. All members of the panel will ask you questions except for the Medical Staffing Representative, who is only there to ensure that the interview is conducted in an appropriate and fair manner. Because each panel member will ask you questions, it is usual for each member to ask no more than one or two questions. The Chair or Medical Staffing Representative must ensure that each panel member asks each candidate the same questions.

The interview has to be seen to be objective, not subjective. As such, each panel member will mark you on the answers to all of your questions. Usually Medical Staffing has produced some sort of sheet for each panel member to record notes, but it is very rare for the panel to agree a formal structured marking process. Each panel member will usually decide whether they are going to give you a mark for each question or for each panel member's questions. Remember, if you don't attempt to answer the question then you will get no marks.

It is quite rare for your CV to be taken into account at this stage. If it is, it is likely to carry no more weight than a single panel member's questions.

The last person to ask questions is usually the Chair. There will be an opportunity for you to ask any questions you may have and possibly an opportunity for you to tell the panel any additional information you would like them to hear (more of this later). The Chair will then say something along the lines of 'Dr Smith, as you are aware, we are interviewing six candidates for this post today. We do not envisage finishing interviewing until 4.30 pm and hope to have made a decision by 5.30 pm. You are very welcome to stay, but we understand if you have to leave before that time. This will not in any way affect the decision made by the panel. We have a mobile number here for you of 07.... Is that a number we can contact you on?'.

Once all the candidates have been interviewed, the Chair will then lead the process to agree which candidate should be appointed. Different Chairs will approach this differently, but often each panel member is asked to state their preferred candidate. If everyone has chosen the same candidate then the process is complete, the references will be read and assuming there is nothing untoward, e.g. the candidate has been referred to the GMC, the candidate will be offered the post.

If there isn't universal agreement then the process of negotiation begins. Each panel member then states why they believe their preferred-choice candidate should be appointed and, if appropriate, raises their concerns about the other panel members' choice of candidates. A process of negotiation then takes place until consensus is reached, ideally as a whole or if not as a majority. If no consensus can be reached or if the panel feels that no candidate was suitable then they do not have to appoint.

It is rare for the references to be used as part of the decision-making process. If this was an interview for a senior post outside the NHS or for a senior management or director post within the NHS, the candidates might not provide the names of referees until after the interview process and certainly would not want their referees approached prior to interview. The appointment, therefore, would always be subject to references and the role of references is to ensure that there is nothing that would prevent the candidate being appointed, not to judge suitability or desirability. The Chair of the panel and a number of panel members will be used to this system of appointing. Additionally, the quality of references varies considerably, with much depending on the quality of the writing. Some referees are much more articulate than others, providing an unfair advantage for some candidates. In general, therefore, the references are only read after a decision has been made and then only for the candidate who has been appointed.

If the candidates have stayed behind to await the outcome, the successful candidate will be invited back into the room and offered the post. You will be asked immediately whether you accept. Hesitation at this stage or a request to await the outcome of a different interview in say a week's time will probably be met with a 'no', especially if there was another suitable candidate. The other candidates will then be told that they have unfortunately been unsuccessful on this occasion. They should be offered immediate feedback or feedback with a specific panel member within a few days (see Chapter 14).

The panel

Hopefully you will have been told in advance who will be on your interview panel and the role they play, e.g. Mr Brown, Chief Operations Officer (representing the Chief Executive). If you have not been told, ask Medical Staffing who is likely to be on the panel, as they must tell you.

A typical panel comprises the following individuals:

- Chairperson (often Chairperson of the Trust or a Non-Executive Director)
- Royal College Representative
- Chief Executive or their representative (usually a Director of the Trust or a senior, non-medical manager)
- Medical Director or representative (usually a directorate or divisional medical director not in the same speciality as the post)
- Clinical Director (this may or may not be someone in your speciality)
- Consultant in your speciality (often only one)
- University Representative (ideally in your speciality)
- (Senior Manager)
- (Lay Member or patient representative)

Panels are usually kept relatively small as every member has to ask questions. The larger they are the more unwieldy the process. A patient representative is most likely to be found on a Consultant Psychiatrist interview, but their presence will increase with the increasing health agenda for patient and public involvement. You are more likely to find a senior manager, e.g. a divisional Business Manager, where there is a significant service development remit to the new role.

The role of individual panel members

Some members of the interview committee will have a very specific remit that determines the questions they will ask you. For others, there may be no clear remit and their questions may cover a broader variety of subjects.

Royal College Representative

After the Chair has put you at ease, the first person to ask you questions will be the Royal College Representative. Their role is to ensure you will get your CCT when you say you will and that you have the correct specialist training for this post. After that, the order in which questions are asked will vary from panel to panel.

University Representative

The University Representative is there to ensure you will contribute to the teaching and training of undergraduates and to ask you questions on research.

Chief Executive

The Chief Executive or his/her representative is likely to ask you questions on service development and the added value you bring to the organization. He may ask you questions related to the NHS political agenda. Your understanding in this area is becoming increasingly important.

Medical Director

The Medical Director will ask you questions relative to his or her role. Topics are likely to include clinical governance, revalidation and professional issues, e.g. the poorly performing doctor.

Chairperson

The Chair is likely to ask you more personal questions. These might include your hobbies, how you relax and questions about your weaknesses.

Other panel members

The consultant representing your specialty might ask you about how your areas of expertise will fit with the other members of the department.

The other panel members will ask questions around the key subject areas described in Chapter 5.

Ensuring the best chance of appointment

Building on both the first part of this chapter and the book as a whole, it is important to ensure you create the best chance of appointment. There is no doubt your chances of selection will depend heavily on how well you have prepared (see Chapter 5). However, 'how' you perform on the day, not just what you say, will also contribute.

In this section, we will cover some of the on-the-day elements that can help you succeed, including the following:

- Demonstrating confidence
- Building rapport
- Behaviour in the interview
- Dealing with different types of interviewer
- Answering all questions
- Answering the difficult question
- Feedback on your answers
- Answering the 'Have you any other questions?' question
- Using 'Is there anything else you would like to tell the panel?' as a final opportunity to promote yourself

Box 6.1 is a reminder of the key things you need to do at the interview if you want to be seen in the best possible light by the interview panel.

Demonstrating confidence

Grooming, posture and a confident, non-anxious body language all contribute in demonstrating to the panel that you are confident. It is important to use all the strategies described in the practical preparation section and have developed some of the tools, e.g. breathing and visualization as described in the section on 'Strategies for building confidence and reducing and preventing anxiety'.

Grooming

It is really important that you dress like a consultant. What you wear does not necessarily matter to all panel members but it does matter to the Island of Opportunity inhabitants and they will want to see you dressed how they would dress, in a smart suit or as a lady in a smart dress. These are people who will also notice if your shoes are not clean or if things are not well ironed and will subconsciously mark you down as a result. Remember, the more you dress like a consultant, the more confident you will feel and the more others will see you as both a consultant and a colleague.

Posture

Before you go into the interview spend time developing a confident posture, stand tall, shoulders back, chin up. Consider using the energy centring exercise to help you. I am sure these are all things your mother used to say when you were younger, but it is true; developing a confident posture makes you feel confident and drives away fear. It helps you speak with authority as a peer to these fellow senior people.

Initial impressions

Unfortunately, you have very little time to ensure the panel members make the right first impression of you, raising the importance of getting this right first time. It is said that people make judgements of other people within the first 30 seconds of meeting

> **Box 6.1 The interview—a summary of the key points**
>
> - Make eye contact with each panel member as they are introduced to you. Ideally exchange some pleasantry
> - Always say yes when offered a drink
>   - Your voice will get dry
>   - If nothing else, it gives you something to fiddle with if you are feeling nervous
> - Watch your posture:
>   - Keep your head up
>   - Lean slightly inwards towards your interviewer
>   - Keep arms and hands open
>   - Maintain *good eye contact* with your interviewer but occasionally scan the room to look at the other panel members
> - Answer every question
>   - No answer means no marks
> - Use the strategies described in Chapter 5 for answering questions:
>   - Pause for 10 seconds to organize your thoughts
>   - Tell the panel what you are going to tell them, i.e. answer the question
>   - Tell the panel the answer, raising three key points that help to promote you
>   - Summarize your answer, focusing on the benefits to the department
>   - Take no more than 2 minutes
> - If you do not understand the question, respond 'If I understand you correctly...'
>   - This will get better clarification of what is expected of you than just asking the interviewer to repeat the question
> - If asked in the interview about whether you will accept the job if offered, always respond without pausing with a resounding 'YES'
> - Do not rely on your CV or references to get you the job
>   - You need to get the job through the interview itself

them and many will be familiar with the phrase 'you never get a second chance to make a first impression'. Having made those judgements in the first 30 seconds, they then spend the rest of the time looking for the evidence to back up this idea, often overlooking other realities. If the panel's initial impression is that you are someone who is confident, amicable and looks ready to be a consultant they will be searching out the evidence within your interview that supports this idea. If their initial impression is that you are nervous, will struggle to take control in an emergency or are not ready to be a consultant, they will proactively be looking for evidence within your interview that supports this idea. The first few seconds and minutes of your interview are therefore critical.

> **USEFUL TIP:** First impressions do matter at the consultant interview. Make sure you dress the part and exude confidence as you enter the room.

Entrance

Considering the importance of getting the first impression right, it is essential your entrance to the interview room creates the right impression. You may want to practise this in advance.

- Walk tall when you enter
- Smile
- (Firm hand shake if appropriate*)
- Introduce yourself

*Because of the layout of the interview room, it may not be possible or appropriate to shake hands with each member of the panel. If it is appropriate to shake hands the key is to consider whose hand you are shaking and if all else fails to try to mirror their handshake. Remember (Chapter 4) that not all people are the same. The 'typical' surgeon or Chief Executive will have a firm dominating handshake but the HR professional may be softer and less dominant. A weak handshake to a typical cardiologist can be taken as a sign of lack of confidence while a firm handshake to a softer person can seem overpowering.

A good Chair will introduce you to each panel member. If this happens, you can immediately start building rapport by adopting the following technique; as each member is introduced turn towards them, make eye contact and exchange a pleasantry, e.g. 'Nice to meet you again', 'Good afternoon', 'Pleased to meet you'.

> **USEFUL TIP**: One of the easiest ways to develop rapport is to slowly rotate in your chair as you are introduced to each panel member. Make sure you make strong eye contact with each member in turn as you do this and ideally exchange some pleasantry.

Posture and body language to convey confidence and build rapport

Clearly, your entrance is very important in conveying confidence and building rapport. However, it is also essential that your posture and body language continues to convey confidence throughout the rest of your interview, as well as ensuring that rapport with the panel members is not broken. A good posture to adopt is that of 'immediacy'. The master of this was Bill Clinton and you may want to watch some old footage of him to see how it works. Done well, you can engender huge rapport with individuals.

Immediacy

With immediacy you need to sit leaning slightly forward. Keep your arms and your hands open, maintain good eye contact without staring the other person out and smile! We cannot emphasize the importance of smiling enough. Smiling makes you appear more relaxed and more confident.

Controlling your hands

If you are very nervous and feel it will show in your hands consider putting them on the table, loosely joining your hands together. If you are very worried about what your hands are conveying, consider sitting on them. It is important never to fold your arms as it tends to looks as if you are bored and disinterested in the job. On a similar theme never put your elbows on the table—it can be seen as both rude and threatening.

Some of us like to use our hands when speaking and if this is natural to you, you will certainly come across as passionate. However, try to ensure that your arm and hand movements do not distract from your answers. A simple rule is to keep your hands below your face and within the width of your body.

Eye contact

To ensure maximum rapport, slowly rotate your seating position as you move from one panel member to another so that you develop maximum eye contact. For example, as the Royal College Representative is questioning you, turn to face them. When the questions move onto the next panel member, change your sitting position slightly so you are now facing them. Make this slight change in position every time the questions move on, but do make sure that you turn occasionally to scan the whole panel and engage with the other panel members. If not you could spend almost 40 minutes with your back to a panel member. This will not help rapport at all.

Smiling

There's a huge volume written about body language in interviews and not all of it is helpful. Indeed, for some of you this may be a consideration too far. However, if body language is not your thing and you decide to ignore the majority of this section, then we strongly encourage you to remember the importance of smiling. Smiling is a very powerful, simple tool that you don't need to be an actor to use. When you smile, your face relaxes and you immediately appear more confident to the panel members. Smiling makes the interviewer think you are interested in the subject you are talking about. Try smiling before each answer, at least once in the middle and at the end of your answer.

Other techniques for developing rapport

This has been discussed in detail in Chapter 4. If all of this appears to be going out of the window on the day, remember people like people who are like themselves. Try to mirror key aspects of your interviewer's behaviour. If they are confident and direct in their questioning, try to be confident and direct in your response. If their question asking is slow and considered, try to be slower and more considered in your response, perhaps outlining the structure you will use to answer the question and ensuring you refer to the evidence base within the body of your answer.

Mirroring the other person's body language to develop increased rapport is well described in books and scientific (psychology) literature. It is something that happens naturally when we have rapport with someone. Many doctors will do this subconsciously through years of practice at developing rapport with patients. In general, it is a good approach to *subtly* adopt. However, if you don't feel confident in adopting it and feel it is just one more thing to worry about, then we would recommend concentrating on delivering the right responses to the questions and not adjusting your body posture as we have described.

Behaviour during the interview

It is obviously important to behave in a professional manner throughout the interview. However, unfortunately, whether consciously or subconsciously, panel members may behave in certain ways that you might find challenging, especially if you do not recognize these events or episodes for what they are. We will concentrate on three scenarios:

- The angry or aggressive interviewer
- The unprepared interviewer
- The nervous interviewer

The angry or aggressive interviewer

Some authors talk about how different interviewers are assigned different 'characters' or roles in the interview, but, in our experience, interviewers naturally play certain roles by just being themselves. For instance, let's consider when an interviewer might become angry or aggressive. This will usually occur in an opinion-type question when the interviewee has come off the fence with a distinct answer and the interviewer will disagree with their point of view. The key to handling this scenario is not to rise to the bait and in particular not to become angry or aggressive back, nor to concede to the interviewer's point of view. By now, the rest of the panel will not be judging you on the content of your answer but how you deal with the subsequent conversation.

At a practical level you have two strategies. The first is to simply say 'I think at this moment we will simply have to agree to disagree. I think this is a really important area which needs strong debate and I very much welcome the opportunity to do this further if I am appointed to the post'.

The other strategy is to take the debate a little further whilst remaining calm and confident. This takes practice, as it will be very easy for you to become emotional (which can be an automatic response, if you are not careful). In this situation, ask your interviewer to explain more about their point of view, e.g. 'You obviously feel very strongly about your point of view. Can you help me understand why you feel that way?' The angry or aggressive interviewer is most likely to come from the Island of Opportunity and giving them the opportunity to hear their own voice will actually gain you points rather than lose you points. Additionally, you are now having a proper conversation which is the key to a good interview. When your angry, aggressive interviewer has explained their point of view, respond with 'You are clearly raising some very important points and ideas which obviously need further debate with a wider audience. At this moment in time I stick by my opinion, but I look forward to the opportunity for a lively and positive discussion together if I am appointed' (with a smile!).

It is important not to suggest or tell the interviewer that they are wrong (even if they are). Remember that they are in front of colleagues and losing face will *definitely* lose you their support and Island of Opportunity inhabitants will fight strongly for their point of view. It can be useful practising phrases like 'My position stems from x piece of research . . .', which demonstrates that it is a considered opinion, that you know your stuff, but that it is simply an opinion to be adapted according to what else you learn. This shows you to be a balanced, sensible individual, who values others' opinions too.

> **USEFUL TIP:** If you feel yourself getting angry during the interview take some slow abdominal breaths before responding.

The unprepared interviewer

You may notice during your interview that one (sometimes more than one!) of the panel members seems somewhat unprepared. Maybe they have spent the whole interview process reading through your CV and still seem to be doing this when it is their turn to ask questions. How would you feel in this situation? There is no right or wrong answer. The important point is to know how you would feel so that you can recognize what is happening and then manage your emotions. It can be useful to ask yourself the following helpful question: 'I wonder what important issue has prevented them from preparing and therefore I wonder how I can help them discover the right information'. This approach reminds you that it isn't just laziness that prevents preparation and they may have been up all night resuscitating and managing a difficult patient or dealing with a Trust crisis.

If you come from the Island of Intellect you are likely to feel somewhat aggrieved, as you personally would never come to the most important day of someone's life unprepared and disorganized. Others may be worried that the interviewer has found a significant mistake or something he or she does not like. Once you know how this will make you feel you will be able to recognize these feelings in the interview. In the interview, if you find yourself putting these types of meaning to an interviewer's behaviour you need to change your focus. Try thinking 'this is a fantastic opportunity to use everything that is on my CV to impress this interviewer'.

The nervous interviewer

It is worth considering for a moment why an interviewer might appear as nervous as you. If this is the first time they have been an interviewer it might also be the first time they have sat in a room with the Chief Executive and the Medical Director since the day they got their consultant post. This can be nerve-racking for a new interviewer, they want to impress their peers just as much as you and the only experience they have of what is expected of them is the interview or interviews they went through to get their own consultant post.

When people are nervous the quality of their questions may be poor and they may ask them in away that is not only difficult for you to understand but also difficult for the rest of the panel to understand. If you are asked a question and do not understand what is being asked of you, use the techniques described below. Besides this, it is also important to treat these interviewers gently. Think about how you would want to be communicated with if you were feeling nervous and under stress. Smiling is particularly valuable as it relaxes the recipient and calms their nerves.

Feedback on your answers

Do not expect to receive feedback on any of your responses to the questions asked. Similarly, do not try to read anything into the facial expressions or body language of your interviewers. Many look quite stony-faced and it isn't you who has caused this. Interviewing is tiring and although it's a stressful 60 minutes for you, it could be a mind-numbing 6 hours for them. You'd look stony-faced if you had to ask and listen to the same questions six times in a row!

Worrying about the non-verbal feedback after each question will simply distract you from listening to and answering properly the next question. Once you have given an answer, essentially its impact is now out of your hands. You can't undo it or influence its effect and so it is much better to move on and put your energies into getting the next question right.

Answering all questions

It is really important in the interview that you answer all of the questions you are asked. All candidates are asked the same questions and all candidates are marked on all questions, so, at a simple level, if you make no attempt to answer a question you will lose marks unnecessarily. However, it is also really important that you do not come across as someone who is simply spouting on about something you clearly know nothing about, as this is generally frowned upon in medicine. This is most likely to happen if you are ill-prepared or when facing a particularly difficult question. Consequently, you need to develop your techniques for addressing questions where the answer isn't immediately obvious, something we will deal with in subsequent sections of this chapter.

Answering the difficult question

When facing a particularly difficult question, your goal is to ensure that you answer it competently without spouting rubbish. Difficult questions can put people into a panic and hijack your ability to think clearly—just when you need it. The same is true of questions that you haven't understood clearly. To help avoid the adverse effects of these scenarios, adopt the following three steps, known as CPA:

- Clarify, to ensure you fully understand
- Pause for longer than normal
- Answer the question asked

It is important to avoid ever saying only 'I do not know' and the above technique provides you with breathing and thinking space. Let's examine the steps more closely.

Clarify

When you do not fully understand a question or where you think the question is ambiguous or difficult, always get the interviewer to clarify it for you. Done in the correct way, it may cause the interviewer to reveal more information about the question, providing you with important clues about what they are looking for in your answer. Avoid the trap of simply getting the interviewer to repeat the question, as that is exactly what they will do and you will learn nothing new. Instead use phrases such as:

- 'If I understand you correctly . . .'
- 'If I heard you correctly . . .'

As you do this, speak more slowly than normal and speak very clearly. The more slowly you speak, the more likely the interviewer is to add some additional information to their original question.

> **USEFUL TIP:** Never just ask an interviewer to repeat a question. Always ask for clarification.

Pause for longer than normal

Say to the panel 'Can I just have a minute to think about my answer?' It is obviously important that you do not then take several minutes, but recognize that within medicine doctors do not always know the answers to everything and we do naturally pause for longer than 10 seconds, on occasion, to consider our answers. During your pause, think logically what this question could mean. If it contained terms you have not heard of, would there be a sensible explanation of what the words might mean? Consider who is asking the question and therefore what the question is most likely to be on coming from them. In most cases, we can come to some logical conclusions and even if we are slightly off, a considered answer, well thought through and delivered, will definitely earn more points than either no answer or one where it is clear that no thought has gone into it.

Answer the question

In an ideal world you will now have a clear answer in your mind and confidence that it successfully addresses the question being asked. If you are still unsure, attempt to answer the question but preface it with something along the lines of 'I am not 100% sure I fully grasp the question at this point, but assuming you are referring to XXX then my answer is . . .'. If you are barking up the wrong tree, this lets them know so that they can see the reasoning in your answer, i.e. how it relates to what you have understood as the question.

If you do not preface the answer, then it simply looks like a poor answer to the question or that you don't know the answer at all. If you simply appear to have misunderstood the question but give a highly competent answer to your interpretation of the question, clearly stated to them, then they won't necessarily assume you don't know the answer to the original question, i.e. they'll probably give you the benefit of the doubt. It is worth remembering that the question itself may only be the vehicle for assessing your powers of reasoning and so a well-reasoned answer to a different question can be pretty successful!

Answering the 'Have you any other questions?' question

This question is quite common at the end of interviews, but be very careful how you respond. In general, at consultant interview, if you have done your homework correctly and made best use of your pre-interview visit, you really shouldn't have any questions. In which case, by far the safest answer is 'Thank you but all my questions were answered at the pre-interview visit'. Asking further questions at this point not only is unhelpful but also runs the risk of being detrimental to the overall impression you give.

Some authors suggest being clever and asking the panel's view on something political. However, unless this something political is ground-breaking news, highly pertinent to the service and something you could not reasonably have discussed at the pre-interview visit I would avoid asking it. The risk here is that your attempt to be clever actually backfires on you and the panel members think 'Shouldn't he have asked this before?' or 'Shouldn't he have made sure he knew the answer to this before the interview?'. Worse still, it could show them up and make them uncomfortable and you have to ask whether that is a helpful last impression. The goal is to leave them with a feeling of certainty about you, not with nagging questions about whether you are committed or have thoroughly investigated the job that they may be considering offering you. Never at this stage (unless of course you do not want the job!) ask questions about:

- Salary
- Job plans
- Part-time working

If you get the job you can negotiate all of these things later from a much stronger position. It's amazing how flexible people become when they are certain they want you. Certainty first, negotiation second! Finally, remember you do not have to ask what will happen next, as the Chair will tell you this at the end of the interview anyway.

Answering the 'Is there anything else you would like to tell the panel?' question

It is increasingly common for the Chair to ask something along the lines of the following, at the end of the interview:

- 'Is there anything else you would like to tell the panel?'
- 'Is there anything else you would like the panel to know about you?'
- 'Would you like to add anything to what you have already said?'
- 'Are there any final comments you would like to make?'
- 'Is there anything you would like to add to any of the questions you have been asked today?'

You could just say 'no' and many candidates do just this. However, this could also be seen as an opportunity to leave the interview panel on a high, remembering the positive things that you want them to hear about you. By telling the panel why you absolutely want the job and why you believe you are the best candidate for the job at this stage, you are essentially summarizing in your own words what you want them to believe your interview has shown. Remember, just as interviewer concentration is strongest at the beginning and end of each question, it is also strongest at the beginning and end of each interview. Consequently, any final points you make are likely to have increased prominence in their thoughts when they deliberate who to appoint. Remember that 30-second statement you developed as part of the getting to know yourself exercise? This is the time to use it.

Our one word of caution here is against regurgitating things you have already said, in the way that you have already said them. This is not a useful use of your final words and could serve to irritate panel members. The best close is punchy, to the point and emphasizes your unique selling points matched perfectly to their most important requirements.

The locum interview

In days gone past, the locum consultant post was sometimes seen as something to be frowned upon. However, times have changed. You only have to review the *British Medical Journal* to know that there are more locum posts than substantive ones. There is an increasing trend by Trusts to appoint consultants on a fixed-term contract—a locum post by any other name—and it is likely this trend will increase with increasing uncertainty arising out of a dynamic healthcare marketplace. Choosing a locum post today, especially if it is the right type of locum, e.g. one where a substantial post is likely in the near future, can provide the opening you need so that you are the favoured internal candidate when the permanent job is advertised.

With reducing substantive posts there comes increasing competition in the job market. So, even with a locum post it is important to talk in advance of the interview date to the named consultant on the job advert. This will help you understand what the department is really wanting from this post and will ensure you use each of your answers to promote those things about yourself that are important to the panel. It is often not possible to do a pre-interview visit except perhaps immediately before the interview itself. This does vary with length of locum post, though, and if it is a substantial, fixed-term appointment then you should always ask if you can visit.

It is important to recognize that locum job interviews are very different from a substantive post interview. There is no requirement for the formal interview panel structure and there will be no Royal College Representative. The panel usually comprises no more than two to three people, often all working in the department concerned but not always all consultants. These individuals may never have sat on a formal consultant interview committee before. The interview is likely to be much more informal and to concentrate on why you are capable of doing the job at that moment in time. Our experience is that the quality of questioning may not be as good as that in a substantive post interview.

For most locum posts the two key requirements are:

- Someone who can hit the ground running and get on with the job with little support
- Someone who is easy to get on with and will not rock the boat

Bearing this in mind, the questions are much more likely to focus on your CV and your clinical experience. You are more likely to be asked questions around managing specific everyday scenarios, e.g. angry relatives, breaking bad news or getting the multidisciplinary team on your side.

You may well be asked what added value you will bring. In this situation, focus predominantly on the immediate and short-term added value you can bring within the duration of the post. For instance, if there is a teaching element to the role and you have lots of teaching experience, this would be good to bring out. Are you a life support course instructor? Do you have specific expertise that would be of immediate clinical value?

The panel are much less likely to be looking for someone who will come in and lead service development, although that should not stop you getting involved if you get the post! Indeed, if you want the permanent post at the end of the locum, you must do this to demonstrate just how valuable a colleague you would be. Although there is no such thing as indispensable, you can certainly embed yourself sufficiently so as to make it a gut-wrenching experience to let you go!

You are unlikely to be asked questions about NHS politics, but you should still make sure that you are aware of key initiatives within your speciality, especially structural and National Service Framework-driven changes, as well as having a view of what they mean to staff, services and Trusts.

Accepting a job when you really want another one

Jobs are often like buses—they appear to be very scarce and then three turn up at once. For many trainees, a number of potential jobs will come up simultaneously and it is possible, even likely, that the interview dates do not necessarily match your order of preference for the jobs. What should you do in this case? This section considers both the legal and the moral perspective, but only you can decide what the right thing is for you to do. It is important to remember that substantive posts are becoming scarcer but also a job doesn't have to be for life as it used to be.

Legally, having accepted a job there is nothing to stop you getting another job as long as you give the appropriate amount of notice (usually 3 months) to the first employer. Even if you have not signed a written contract by accepting the post at interview, you have entered into a verbal contract and notice will need to be given. Unless you were days from actually starting, it is relatively rare for someone to be held to commencing a new job that they are leaving shortly after starting. This is just pragmatic, as the early days and weeks are often filled with induction—pointless if you are not going to be there. If the jobs have truly come at the same time, then 3 months' notice will probably expire before you were due to start anyway.

Morally, the stakes are much greater. It takes time to go to advert, short-list and appoint a colleague. If you do pull out of a job after accepting it, the first Trust is likely to be at least 3 months behind where it really wanted to be and this may have implications for patient care and safety. You cannot let the first employer know the night before you should be turning up that you won't be coming, even if you have seen others, especially junior doctors, do that in the past. To do so could be putting patient safety at risk, which is contrary to the GMC's principles of 'Good Medical Practice'.

More than this, most specialties are their own small world. Do not be surprised if the first hospital contacts not only your referees but also your new employer. How will that make you feel and how might that affect your future career progression? Certainly, if you want to take on regional or college roles in the future, you will find memories of being let down run deep and long. Additionally, what about the other candidates who desperately wanted the job in that hospital? You certainly won't be making any friends with this course of action. It is also worth considering just how influential the people in the original Trust are. Could they make your life difficult going forwards? Lots of considerations—very few of them legal but all of them difficult.

Ultimately it is your decision and it has to be taken in the context of your life as a whole, not in the moment. Personally, assuming I thought the risk was worth it, I would either make a decision not to go to the first interview or, if I went to the first interview, to accept the job if I got it. You could try negotiating for some extra time after the post has been offered, but my experience is that this will be refused unless the first post is a locum post or there are no other suitable candidates to appoint. To accept and then resign would be seen in an even worse light.

Chapter 7
Interview candidates

Introduction

In this chapter, we focus on the dynamic brought by different combinations of candidate, looking at three specific scenarios. Firstly, we look at the implications of there being an internal candidate, from the perspective of being both the internal candidate and the competing external candidate. We then examine the implications of being either the only candidate or a head-hunted candidate, two scenarios where it is easy to 'undo' being offered the job.

The internal candidate

There is no doubt that being an internal candidate can put you at a considerable advantage. Some of the interview committee may well:

- Know your past, your good points and bad points and will be better able to judge your likely future contribution
- Have already developed a relationship with you, including a sense of whether they feel comfortable working with you for the next 30 years

However, this familiarity or perceived familiarity can also be the internal candidate's downfall. It is not infrequent that we come across internal candidates who believe the job is in the bag and so fail to prepare or engage in the activity that ensures they are likely to be offered the job, e.g. undertaking pre-interview visits. Sometimes it is because they think it is embarrassing to do something like a pre-interview visit if they are already employed in the Trust and know the staff well. We also find internal candidates who are reluctant to really sell themselves at interview when already known, again out of embarrassment.

The advice is clear—prepare as though you were an external candidate whilst making best use or advantage of your internal status. Take nothing for granted and ensure you do your homework as thoroughly as any good external candidate. When experiencing your efforts to prepare, your colleagues, far from thinking it is weird, are likely to view this as the sort of commitment they would want from a future colleague. Box 7.1 explores the internal candidate's 'must do' list if you are to be successful.

Being an external candidate when there is an internal candidate

It is very easy as an external candidate to subconsciously give up when there is an internal candidate, wrongly assuming that they will automatically get the job. If you start telling yourself that you will not get the job because there is an internal candidate, you can probably be rest assured that you won't, but neither might the internal candidate. We know of many doctors who got jobs even when there was an internal candidate. A common point that is fed back to internal candidates when they do not get the job is something along the lines of 'Dr X sold himself/promoted himself so much better'. What's being reflected here is that the external candidate really tried, whilst the internal candidate did not.

Box 7.1 Internal candidate must-do's and don'ts

- Do undertake pre-interview meetings with all key players. Remember, although you know about the day-to-day running of the service, you are less likely to know about the strategic direction for both the service and the organization
- Do not assume the job is yours (if you do you will not prepare)
- Do prepare in as much detail as if you were applying for an external post
- Do remember you will only be judged on your performance in the interview
- Do remember that not everyone around the interview table will have met you before or be aware of your achievements within the service already. Unless you tell people of your achievements, they will not be able to take them into account when deciding who to offer the post to
- Do not be embarrassed about discussing what you have done. Just because Dr X knows you did an audit project with him does not mean that the Medical Director and Chief Executive know
- Do not be too casual/laid back

> **USEFUL TIP**: If you convince yourself you won't get the job because of an internal candidate, it becomes the most likely outcome, even though the internal candidate might not get the job either. Approach the interview with the right mindset!

If you are still struggling with this then we encourage you to consider the following. If the internal candidate is a locum, the reasons they were chosen (often to do with operational, clinical delivery) may be very different to the key criteria being used for a substantive post. Equally, the internal candidate just approaching CCT may well have special interests that are different from the preferred interests being sought. If you need more convincing, try reading the advice to internal candidates above, so that you understand just how easy it can be to mess things up from this perspective.

As an external candidate with an internal candidate in the running too, good preparation is absolutely key. Take time to think about what it is that makes you stand out from other candidates and why these skills, qualities or areas of expertise will benefit this organization. If you work diligently through Chapter 5 you will put yourself in a very good place to compete on at least a level playing field at the interview.

Becoming an internal candidate

Having made the case that you can succeed as an external candidate against an internal one, there is no doubt that being an internal candidate can improve your chances of getting the job, as long as you don't presume or fail to prepare appropriately. For existing teams, one of the most important considerations when choosing a new consultant is will they fit in to the team? Doing a locum consultant post, especially where there is the possibility of a future substantive post, is one way of demonstrating this. It also gives *you* the opportunity to see if you will fit in with the team and be happy working there permanently.

Strategically, if you have a select number of Trusts that you would like to work for, you might consider making a proactive approach to the team, ahead of a job being advertised, to let them know that you are particularly keen to work with them and would like to be thought of if they are considering either a locum or a substantive post. Many services worry that they won't be able to appoint when they finally get approval for a job, so knowing that there are keen candidates out there can be very helpful. If they know when you could be available for a locum, they may just align their timing with yours!

> **USEFUL TIP:** If you know there will be a permanent post in the relatively near future, consider applying for the locum post in the same organization.

The only candidate

Occasionally, you may find that you are the only candidate who has been short-listed for interview. Again, it is very easy in this case to assume the job is yours. Remember that an interview panel does not have to make an appointment and sometimes will not make an appointment in this situation deliberately. Failing to be appointed when you are the only candidate can be a big psychological knock because you can't fall back on 'the other person must have performed better'. Consequently, your brain is going to tell you that it is because you were not strong enough and that could affect your confidence in subsequent interviews. With this in mind, it is even more vital to maximize your chances of being appointed.

To be successful you will again need to drop the assumption of automatic offer and really try as though you were up against strong competition. In many respects you are—the perception of who else is out there. You will need to prepare for the interview following all the advice in Chapter 5 and keep asking yourself the question 'What would give them the confidence to appoint me, knowing I am the best candidate there is?'

The head-hunted candidate

It is not uncommon for doctors to be head-hunted to consultant posts, especially in specialties where it can be difficult to find good candidates or where specific skill sets are required. If you are being head-hunted it is important not to get lost in the warm, fuzzy feelings that come from having your self-esteem boosted by knowing that someone apparently wants you specifically. This can lead to poor career choices and a lax approach to interview preparation. If you find yourself in this position, ask yourself the question 'Do I really want this job or am I only applying because I feel flattered?'

It is important to remember that head-hunters have many reasons for head-hunting and not all of them are completely altruistic. Our own experience is that when head-hunting is happening, usually more than one consultant in a department is head-hunting and there may be several head-hunted candidates who apply for the post.

Many of the 'rules' that apply for the internal candidate also apply to the head-hunted candidate. In particular, do not assume the job is yours as this will put you at risk of not preparing effectively. It is always worth asking why you are being head-hunted as you will be able to use that information to successfully sell yourself during the interview. If the department is using an external head-hunter, you can ask them directly what sort of person they are looking for specifically. Briefs to agencies will cover everything from must-have skills to ideal profiles. Knowing this information allows you to think about how your skills, attributes and experience would benefit the department or organization.

Chapter 8

Interview questions

Introduction

This chapter outlines typical interview questions only. It does not tell you how to prepare yourself so you can answer these questions effectively or give you model answers. We strongly recommend, regardless of how late you have left your interview preparation, that you do not start by reading this chapter. Instead, start by working through Chapter 5. The questions in this chapter are best used to supplement the preparation you will undertake in Chapter 5.

These questions are all real questions collected from previous interviewees. As such, you may think some are very similar in content, and indeed they are, but we have included them all to give you a feel for how different individuals word questions slightly differently. In Chapter 10, which looks at specialty-specific interviews, there are examples of specialty-specific general and ethical questions.

All that said, if you decide to ignore the advice on where to start and go straight to question practice, remember these key points:

- Practise your answers out loud (most of us waffle when we go through answers in our head)
- Pause before answering the question and think about what you want to say, in particular how you will use this answer to promote yourself as the best candidate for the post
- Divide your answer into three parts:
  - Start with a short, sharp answer during which you tell the panel what you are going to tell them
  - Back the answer up with your evidence and examples
  - Tell the panel what you have just told them and why it will benefit their organization
- Spend no more than 2–3 minutes answering any one question
- When asked for an opinion, recognize both sides of any debate/discussion, but ultimately come off the fence with a distinct answer, backed up by sensible reasoning
- Talk in the first person and in the present tense, i.e. use 'I do' rather then 'We should'

Questions about your CV

- Tell me about your CV
- Tell us about yourself
- Describe your clinical training
- Tell me about the gaps in your CV
- Tell me about the gaps in your training
- What are the gaps in your training and knowledge? How will you fill these gaps?
- Summarize your qualities and attributes in five (three) sentences
- How do you know you are ready to be a consultant?
- Where did you develop the qualities to be a consultant?
- What qualities do you need to be a consultant? How do you know that you have got them?

- Where did you acquire the maturity to be a consultant?
- Will you get your CCT when you say you will?
- How do you know you will get your CCT on . . .?
- How sure are you that you will get your CCT?
- I am concerned you do not have the appropriate training to get your CCT in 3 months time
- Have you had enough training to become a consultant?
- Do you think the duration of training you have had is sufficient?
- Do you think your training has been good enough for you to be a consultant?
- There are five excellent candidates outside. Why should we appoint you?
- Briefly reassure me that you have the correct training and experience for this post
- Why should we give you this job?
- What added value do you bring to this post?
- What are you most proud of on your CV and why?
- What are the three key messages I should take away from your CV?
- What do you think are essential skills for being a consultant? How does your CV demonstrate you have them?
- Do you think a CV is helpful in short-listing candidates?
- Do you think a standard application form is a good way to short-list candidates?
- What will you bring to this post?
- Is there anything we should know about you that is not on your CV?
- If we give you this job, will anything come back to haunt us?
- How will you complement the other members of the team?
- We already have experts in x and y which are your strengths on your CV. What else can you add to our service?
- Getting a consultant post is like getting married. What do you bring to the marriage?
- Highlight an area of your CV (training) that you wish to bring to our attention
- What have you learned from working at a tertiary/specialist centre?
- What would you do differently if you had your training again?
- What do you think are essential skills for a consultant in speciality x? How does your CV demonstrate you have them?

Questions about self

- What do you have to offer St Elsewhere's?
- What does this post offer you?
- What attracted you to this post?
- Why do you want to relocate to x?
- What will be the personal challenges in this role?
- What do you think the key challenges will be for you as you make the transition from junior doctor to consultant?
- What would be the first thing you would do if you became a consultant in this hospital?
- What do you think will be the key challenges of this post?
- What has made you the person you are?

- How would you describe yourself?
- How would your patients describe you?
- What would your patients say about you?
- How would your colleagues describe you?
- What are your strengths?
- What are your weaknesses? What do you do to address these?
- What makes you angry?
- How do you know you are successful?
- What drives you personally?
- How do you know your colleagues trust you?
- How can we know we can trust you?
- How do you respond to criticism?
- What do you do when someone gets angry with you?
- What do you do when someone disagrees with your decision?
- How do you deal with colleagues who do not agree with your point of view?
- What will you bring to this hospital?
- What difference will you make to St Elsewhere's?
- What experiences outside medicine contribute to the type of consultant you will be?
- How would you describe your personality? What would others say?
- How do you behave in meetings?
- Is work—life balance important? How do you keep balance in your life?
- What is most important to you outside work?
- It is important for this hospital to know its staff lead healthy, balanced lives. How can you reassure me?
- Medicine is stressful. How do you deal with it?
- How do you cope with stress?
- Do you think NHS doctors should be allowed to do private practice?
- How do you keep up-to-date?
- Should CPD (Continuous Professional Development) be for the benefit of the doctor or the hospital?
- How do you identify your deficiencies or areas of development?
- Is it okay for consultants to ask for help?
- What will you do as a consultant when you encounter a situation you have not encountered before?
- What was the most difficult clinical situation you have had to face?
- We have advertised this job as one with a specialty that would 'complement the current department'. What specialty do you offer and why does this 'complement the current department'?

Questions about service development

- What do you want to achieve in your first year as a consultant?
- Where do you see yourself in 3 (5, 10) years' time?
- What would you like to be doing in 3 (5, 10) years' time?

- What would you change about this service in this hospital?
- How would you develop our service?
- Where would you like to see this service in 5 (10, 15) years' time? What role would you play in that development?
- What are the key aspects of the hospital's strategic plan which relate to your discipline? How would you deliver this?
- What will be the key challenges for the service over the next 5 years and how would you address them?
- What do you think will be the key challenges for this Trust over the next 3 (5, 10) years?
- What do you think will be the key challenges for healthcare over the next 3 (5, 10) years? If you were in my shoes (usually Chief Executive or MD) what would you be doing about it?
- What would you do to change/improve this service if you became consultant?
- How would you go about setting up a new service offering this specialty?

Behavioural questions

These questions are becoming more and more common in consultant interviews. Behavioural questions are used widely outside medicine where it is recognized that your past behaviour is the best predictor of your future behaviour.

- Tell me about a time when you had to make a difficult clinical decision
- Tell me about a time when you had to counsel a patient about x
- Tell me about a time when you had to break bad news
- Tell me about a time when you were in disagreement with a colleague
- Tell me about a time when you failed to communicate effectively
- Tell me about a time when you had to lead a team
- Give me an example of why you are a good team player
- Tell me about the occasion where you are most proud of your leadership
- Tell me about your worst day in medicine
- Tell us about the last time you had to break bad news to a patient. What happened?
- Tell me about an incident where you completed a risk management form
- Is it important to control your emotions at work? Tell me more. Tell me about a situation when you felt emotional
- Describe an occasion when you have had to assimilate a range of different information in order to produce a tangible argument
- Tell me about an occasion where you were in disagreement with either a patient or a colleague
- Describe an occasion when you had to lead the multidisciplinary team. What did you actually do?
- How do you teach the multidisciplinary team?

Questions about communication

- Which are more important: good communication skills or good clinical skills?
- Is it okay to say sorry? Tell me about the last time you had to say sorry to a patient
- What makes good communication? Tell me about a time recently when you think your communication was good
- What do you think about communication in the health service? What would you do differently?
- Staff always complain about a lack of or poor communication. How would you improve it?
- How do you ensure you communicate effectively with patients?
- Tell me about a situation when you failed to communicate effectively. What did you learn?
- What do you think are the three most important aspects of communicating effectively with patients?

Questions about teaching and training

- Tell me about your teaching experience
- How do you know you are a good teacher?
- How have you developed your teaching skills?
- Tell us how you have used feedback to develop your teaching
- Tell me about negative feedback you have had about your teaching
- How would you deliver postgraduate training in this department if you could start with a clean sheet?
- How would you organize postgraduate teaching in this service?
- What do you think undergraduates should know about our speciality? How would you go about delivering training?
- If we could only give five tutorials to medical students in this speciality, what would they be on?
- How would you teach medical students?
- If you could change training in this speciality, what would you do?
- Do you think external training is necessary for doctors or can it be all learned on the job?
- What are your views of speciality training in the independent sector?
- If you were an educational supervisor, what would you do?
- Do you think as a busy DGH we should be educating medical students or should we leave it to the teaching hospitals?
- Do you think DGHs should teach medical students? Why?
- What would be the advantages and disadvantage of increasing medical students in our hospital? What would you do?
- Do you think the present training system produces better doctors than the old?
- What teaching methods do you prefer?
- What types of teaching do you like? What do you find the most difficult and why?

- Tell us about a teaching experience that went wrong for you as the teacher. What did you learn?
- Which of the training courses that you have attended taught you the most?
- What are the pros and cons of problem-based learning?
- Give me examples of problem-based learning you have undertaken and the outcomes
- How would you propose to maintain high teaching levels whilst adhering to the EWTD (European Working Time Directive)?
- What do you find the most difficult to teach?
- What is the difference between a good and a brilliant teacher? How do I know which you are?
- Is it right to raid training budgets when hospitals are over-spent?
- How would you develop the registrar teaching programme?
- How would you use the internet to set up a teaching programme?

General questions

- Do you think it is good for consultants to move?
- Do you think consultant jobs should be for life?
- Do you think interviews are a good way for appointing consultants?
- Was the old-fashioned way of trial by sherry a good way of appointing consultants?
- In the old days we had trial by sherry. Do you think it would be a good idea to go back to this?
- How should we appoint consultants?
- What would be the best way of finding out if you were the best colleague for us?
- Do you think a sub-consultant/junior consultant grade is a good idea?
- What is your view on the sub-consultant grade?
- Do you think all doctors should do locum consultant work before becoming a consultant?
- Do you think consultants should have SPAs (supporting professional activities)?
- Is 1 PA (anything up to 2.5 PAs) enough for supporting professional activity?
- What will you do in your SPA time?
- How would you ensure we had high-quality junior doctors?
- Is it right for hospitals to market their services?
- How will you market yourself as a new consultant?
- What are your views on revalidation?
- Do you think revalidation is practical?
- What is your view on competency-based assessments for consultants?
- What do you think is the difference between lack of fitness to practice and underperforming?
- What do you think the role of NCAS is?
- How would you manage sickness and absence?
- Why do we need consultants?
- What is the most difficult clinical aspect of this job?
- What will be the hardest clinical aspect to deal with as a consultant?

- How will you contribute clinically to the department?
- What skills do you bring to our service that other consultants do not have?
- How do your skills and areas of expertise complement this department?
- How should a hospital like ours go about improving the care for x?
- If you were appointed consultant here, what is the first thing you would change?
- In August it is likely we will have insufficient numbers of doctors to run a middle-grade rota. How would you go about resolving this issue?

Professional dilemmas

- I want you to imagine that you have been a consultant now for 1 year. Your consultant colleague comes to work this morning clearly the worse the wear for alcohol. What do you do?
- As a consultant you have reason to believe that a consultant colleague drinks excessively when on call and may on occasion have both driven to the hospital and seen patients when over the legal alcohol limit and clearly under the influence of alcohol. What would you do?
- Six months into the consultant role you find that you are taking twice as long to do procedure x (or see patients in clinic) compared to one of your consultant colleagues. What would you do?
- The nurses are asking you to speak to the relatives of a patient. The relatives are very angry with the apparent care they have received from one of your colleagues. What would you do?
- A colleague happens to mention to you in confidence that one of your juniors has now been to A&E twice after a brawl, following drinking heavily. What would you do?
- A colleague appears to you to have significant personal issues (his marriage is breaking up and his ex-partner wishes to move away with the children) which are affecting the way he does his job. What would you do?
- You are concerned about a colleague's performance and explain this to your Clinical Director. What would you expect the CD to do?
- Your very-conscientious colleague is working up to 14 hours per day. You are concerned for her mental health. What would you do?
- One of your trainees tells you that she is being bullied by one of your consultant colleagues. What would you do?
- One of your trainees comes to tell you that she feels she is being sexually harassed by the Clinical Service Lead. What would you do?
- A junior nurse tells you that she overheard one of the new doctors bragging about the drugs he takes on a Friday night. What would you do?
- Your registrar brings it to your attention that one of her more junior colleagues has been late for work every day this week. What would you do?
- Your registrar comes to tell you that the SHO (Senior House Officer) she is doing nights with is not safe. She is not confident when dealing with sick patients and cannot do basic procedures. If you were the consultant, what would you do?

- One of your SHOs is clearly not up to the mark. His clinical decisions are weak and, although there have been no formal complaints, you have heard grumblings from patients. What would you do?
- How would you manage a junior colleague where concerns have been raised by the nursing staff regarding her safety?
- A junior doctor appears to be struggling to reach the standards required. What would you do?
- What would you do if it was clear you were developing a mental health issue?

Questions about leadership and management ability

- What makes a good leader?
- Why will you make a good leader?
- What type of leader are you?
- Are you a leader or a follower?
- Would you rather lead or follow?
- Do you think leaders are born or made? What were you?
- What is the difference between management and leadership?
- Does the NHS need more managers, leaders, both or neither?
- Is there a role in the NHS for non-clinical managers? Why?
- What is your opinion of managers within the health service?
- Tell me about a time when you demonstrated good leadership
- What has been your biggest leadership challenge? What did you do and what skills did you display?
- Tell me about the leadership project you are most proud of
- Can you learn leadership and management on a course?
- How have you developed your management skills? Give me an example of how you have used these skills as a junior doctor
- What skills do you demonstrate as a leader? What skills are you working on and how?
- How will you develop leadership within this service?
- How will you develop your leadership within this directorate?
- How would you engage the clinical team in one of your ideas?
- If you had to pick a team to introduce a major change in service, how would you choose the team members?
- What makes a good team? How will you develop a high-performing team?
- How will you ensure a high-quality team?
- Tell me about a time when you implemented a significant change
- What changes would you want to make to this service? How would you do this?
- If you got this post, what ideas do you have for developing the service and role?
- What do you do when you have an idea and you think others will or do show resistance towards it?
- Tell me about a time when you had to deal with a conflict situation
- How would you try to resolve conflict between your consultant colleagues?

- What influencing skills do you have?
- Give an example of when you have shown initiative
- Is it okay to break rules?
- Tell me about a time when you had to influence others
- Tell me about a time when you have had to negotiate your position
- Is it possible to motivate junior doctors in the present climate? How would you do it?
- How do you motivate people?
- How do you motivate yourself?
- What would you do if one of your team was not performing to the level you like?
- When was the last time you disagreed with a colleague?
- When was the last time you argued with a colleague?
- What do you think of MDT (multidisciplinary team) meetings? How would you run an MDT meeting?
- What advice would you give to managers during reorganization/merger of this service?
- How would you approach developing a business case?
- What is 'demand management'?
- How would you ration your resources?
- How would you go about introducing a new piece of equipment and procedure to the hospital?
- How are you going to cope working in a department with well-established colleagues?
- How would you deal with a failing colleague?
- How do you act as a leader in a multidisciplinary team?
- Give an example of when you have been a good leader
- Give an example of when you have challenged your organization's practice to achieve a goal
- Tell me about KPIs (Key Performance Indicators). What KPIs do you think we should have in this speciality?
- How do you ensure accuracy of coding?
- How would you go about empowering the senior nursing staff on the ward?
- What outcomes should we be measuring in this service?
- What is your view on patient-reported outcome measures (PROMs)?
- What are your views on the target of 18-week waits? Do you think it is realistic to decrease it to 6 weeks?
- What are your views on the target for 4-hour treatment in A&E?
- On a daily basis our hospital struggles for beds. How would you manage hospital beds?

Questions about being a team player

- What team-building skills do you bring?
- How do we know you will be a good team player?
- What is your natural role within a team?
- Tell us about a time you worked effectively as part of a team

- Can you be both a team player and a leader?
- What qualities do you bring to any team?

Questions about clinical governance

- Do you see clinical governance as an opportunity or a threat?
- If you were the Medical Director how would you ensure continued enthusiasm for clinical governance?
- How would you go about setting up clinical governance in a service that had previously played lip service only to it?
- How would you develop clinical governance in speciality x?
- How will you contribute to clinical governance in your consultant role?
- Do you think clinical governance makes a difference?
- What is your experience of clinical governance?
- What roles have you played in clinical governance as a junior doctor?
- What do you think of clinical audits? How would you run an audit programme in your service?
- Should junior doctors do audit?
- Can audits ever be multidisciplinary?
- What makes a good audit? Tell me about a good audit that you have done
- Tell me how you have used audit to change practice
- Tell me about your last audit. What action plan did you develop? How did you ensure the actions were taken?
- How does audit contribute to the business function of the Trust?
- What are the main risks in this speciality?
- What do you think are the five key risks in x? How would you go about managing these?
- How would you go about developing a risk strategy for the service?
- How can you contribute to risk prevention?
- How do you contribute to risk prevention?
- Tell me about the last critical incident form you completed
- How will you encourage your colleagues to complete clinical incident forms?
- What are your views on root cause analysis?
- How do I know you are a safe doctor?
- How do we know you are practicing in line with the GMC standards of good medical practice?
- Tell me about the biggest mistake you made in medicine
- Tell me about the last time you made a medical error
- Can you truly have a blame-free culture? How would you develop it?
- If you prescribed the wrong dose of a drug and a nurse then gave it, what would you do?
- Tell me about a complaint you have received. How did you handle it?
- How would you encourage patient and public involvement in our hospital?
- How would you encourage patient and public involvement in this service?
- How would you involve patients in developing this service?

- Do you think patient and public involvement is just a government fad?
- Should patients have choice?
- How would you develop patient and public involvement?
- How does patient feedback influence your practice?
- How would you measure patient feedback in an effective way?
- How can patient feedback be used to change services?
- How do we know that you are responsive to patient needs?
- Can patient choice be the main driver for improvements in the NHS?
- What do you feel is the real role of the NPSA (National Patient Safety Agency)?
- Do you think the consultant on the ground can benefit from the work of the NPSA?
- Do you think rationing of care is appropriate?
- If you had to ration care in this speciality, how would you go about doing it?
- Is revalidation a good thing?
- How do you think we should revalidate consultants?
- How do audit and research contribute to the business function of the Trust?
- What is your view on whistle blowing?
- Give an example of when you have challenged current practice in order to improve a service
- How do you assess that you are delivering a high-quality service?

Questions about research

- Tell me about the research you have done
- What research are you most proud of?
- Which piece of research has most influenced you?
- Why should doctors do research?
- Should doctors do research?
- Should all doctors do research?
- Do you think it is possible to be a consultant without having done research?
- Why did you do research? What did you gain? Should everyone do it? What are the alternatives to a higher degree?
- What did you learn by doing research?
- What was your null hypothesis for x?
- Which piece of research that you have read in the last year has had the biggest impact on you?
- How will you go about seeking funding for research?
- Do you think you will be able to combine research and a consultant's commitment?
- What research would you like to do as a consultant?
- Do you think there is any role for individual research in the new junior doctors training?
- What do you think about the latest research in x? Is it applicable to us in a DGH?
- What is the best publication/paper you have read and why?
- Do DGHs have a role in research?
- What should we learn from the major published research in x? (Usually something new or close to the heart of the University Representative)

Consider looking at the electronically published research in your area. Two candidates we know were asked about papers published electronically only 2–3 days before their interviews. In both cases the research was pivotal.

Political and hot topics

Please read Chapter 9 before addressing these questions. Political questions go rapidly out of date. However, what follows will give you a flavour of the types of political questions being asked in the period up to this book being written. The new questions come first and the older last.

- Where do you see the NHS in 5 years time?
- What do you think are the opportunities and risks associated with clinical commissioning of this service?
- Do you think GPs should be commissioning secondary care services?
- What three key messages did you take away from the NHS White Paper? What will they mean to this organization?
- Do you think it is possible for an organization like ours to become a Foundation Trust?
- How do we need to adapt as a service to remain viable?
- What will competition mean to a service like ours?
- Is it possible for NHS services to compete with the independent sector?
- Why do you think this government is so interested in patient choice?
- What will the effects of increasing patient choice be on a service like ours?
- Is it possible to have both competition and collaboration in the NHS?
- What do you think will be the benefits to this organization of merging with the provider arm of the PCT?
- How would you go about making a cost improvement in speciality x of at least 4% per annum for the next 3 years?
- What are your views on CQUIN (Commissioning Quality and Innovation)? How would you get your colleagues to buy into this?
- What is CQUIN and how does it affect our service?
- What is QIPP (Quality, Improvement, Productivity and Prevention)?
- If you could develop a QIPP project that would make the biggest difference to service x, what would it be?
- What did you think was most important when you read our quality accounts?
- What is your view on what is happening to our health service?
- Are SHAs useful?
- What functions currently conducted by SHAs do we need in the health service?
- Is a market economy compatible with a free NHS?
- What is CQC (Care Quality Commission)? What is your view on its standards of quality and safety?
- What is your view on the BMA 'Save our NHS' campaign?
- Do you think we should be rationing healthcare?
- What are the latest government initiatives that you are aware of? How might these impact this hospital?

- What are the latest government initiatives that you are aware of? How might these impact on speciality *x*?
- Is it possible for a Foundation Trust to work with community providers?
- What did you take away from the Darzi report?
- Should we be worried about Darzi?
- What should this service be doing in response to Darzi?
- How will the Darzi report affect this service?
- How would you tackle the EWTD?
- Do you think Commissioning a World Class Service will really make a difference to patient care?
- Do you think there is a place for practice-based commissioning?
- How could we make our service more community based?
- How would you proactively move services into the community?
- What do you think of the concept of polyclinics? Should we be worried about these?
- The PCT has to find alternative providers or provision in different settings for more services. What do you think we should be doing?
- What are your views on patient choice?
- What do you think of the 18-week wait?
- What do you think of the 4-hour targets in A&E?
- How could A&E and other services work more effectively together?
- Is it a good or a bad thing not having an A&E department in this hospital?
- What do you think will be the effects of the Tooke report on this speciality?
- How would you develop appraisals to improve performance?

Clinical dilemmas and ethics

Clinical management at consultant interviews is often discussed in the context of a clinical dilemma, an ethical issue or the breaking of bad news. A number of general examples are given below. It is important to consider the areas of controversy or dilemma in your own speciality and to have a clear strategy for answering these questions. Specialty-specific ethical questions can be found in Chapter 10.

- How would you counsel a patient who was found to have *x*?
- How do you discuss risk with your patients?
- Should we offer intensive care to patients over the age of 85?
- How would you ration heathcare?
- When did you last have to break bad news to a patient? What happened?
- How would you explain *x* to a patient with no medical knowledge?
- Should we offer surgery for *x* to patients who smoke?
- Should we offer surgery for *x* to patients who are obese?
- One of your patients is a Jehovah's Witness. He needs urgent blood products or he will die. He is unconscious and you are unable to discuss the issue with him. What would you do?

Chapter 9
Political and hot topics in the NHS

Introduction

In so many cases, it is a lack of understanding of the political agenda that gives most trainees (and existing consultants) their greatest cause for concern when applying for a consultant post. As a result, many invest the majority of their interview preparation time trying to develop a significant knowledge of the evolving healthcare landscape but without any clear direction. In this short chapter, we'll provide guidance on how to go about preparation sensibly, with a clear focus.

It is perhaps important at this stage to re-emphasize that the majority of your time should be invested in reflecting on how you can best demonstrate that you have the qualities, skills, abilities and interests to succeed in the post you are applying for, i.e. the benefit you bring to the Trust you are applying to. In general, unless the job specifically concerns the strategic development of a service, spend no more than 20% of your preparation time thinking about the political agenda. Any more and we are starting to worry that you are not focusing on other important areas sufficiently.

> **USEFUL TIP:** Spend no longer than 20% of your preparation time on the political agenda, concentrating more on you and how you bring benefit with your knowledge, skills and interests.

It will not have escaped you that this chapter is only short and does not appear to mention a single political agenda or hot potato in any depth. This is purposeful. The political agenda is constantly changing and what was 'hot' at interview this month will not be 'hot' in 6 months' time. There is no substitute for getting up-to-date at the time and we want to avoid the natural temptation for you to use the book as gospel when in fact you need to be seeing what is current. This chapter will, however, help you work out what you need to know for your specific interview and how to obtain that knowledge.

The importance of understanding the political agenda

Having made the case for not overly focusing on the political agenda, as you have lots of preparation to do and not just this, it is still imperative that you understand just how important an area this is. Trusts need consultants who understand the environment in which they operate and what it takes to be successful today. Someone who is 'market savvy', as well as a solid clinician or surgeon, has the potential to take services forward and deliver stability and growth. The alternative is inertia in services, with a very high cost of being on the wrong side of financial balance.

Your interview panel will contain at least one senior manager. Part of their remit, in a good Trust, will be to ascertain what you might bring to their Trust from a business perspective. They are going to be interested in things such as:

- Do you understand what it takes to be successful today?
- Is your focus entirely clinical, or do you have a balanced clinical—business focus?
- Do you have any insight into financial effectiveness in a service?

Trust management tends to feel at odds with or in competition with its clinical workforce at a time when clinical and non-clinical staff need to be pulling together to adapt and evolve services to be fit for practice today. Someone who appears to know what health is about today, is sympathetic to the need for a business focus and is still a great clinical choice for the post could find themselves in hot demand.

How to get a clear understanding of what might come up

When it comes to the political agenda, interviewers tend to ask questions that are both relevant and topical. They can no more remember what the 2000 NHS Plan said than you can and it is not relevant anyway, having subsequently been superseded by Darzi, the 2010 White Paper, the Future Forum and possibly more by the time you read this.

You will meet people who have lists of political documents and policies going back 10–12 years, which they have been reviewing for their interview. Do not do this. Instead, a better strategy is to decide on the topics you are going to investigate as a result of your pre-interview visit:

- What did the Medical Director and Chief Executive talk about?
- What was causing the Clinical Director sleepless nights?
- When you asked about the political issues concerning them, what did they answer?

These are the topics you must know about and where they are most likely to ask questions. Additionally, devote the remaining allocation of 'political research' time to our 'be familiar with this' list, which is relatively current today (2011) and likely to be important generally (see Box 9.1).

It is important to know, politically and strategically, what is going on in the Trust and so some key reading includes the following documents:

- Strategic Plan
- Annual Plan
- Quality Accounts
- Annual Report

Usually these are available on the Trust website (Quality Accounts are available on www.nhs.uk—the NHS Choices website) but, if not, you can ask for a copy through the Freedom of Information officer.

> **USEFUL TIP:** Review the notes you made at the pre-interview visit. What political topics were discussed? You must be up-to-date in these areas. These are the topics you are most likely to be questioned upon in the interview itself.

> **Box 9.1 Important political topics to be familiar with**
>
> The following have proved to be important topic areas politically, each standing the test of time. Make sure you are at least aware of the key principles and information in each. In each case, always ask yourself 'What does this mean in my specialty or to this Trust?'
>
> - Key points in the latest White Paper (there's always a current one!)
>   - What it means, not just what it says
> - Commissioning of provider services
>   - How?
>   - Implications for your specialty
> - Progression of a healthcare marketplace
>   - Where is this in your specialty?
>   - Examples of impact
> - What financial systems and principles affect your strategy?
>   - How is funding/remuneration provided?
>   - What indicators or measures affect funding in your specialty?
>   - Where have there been funding issues in your specialty?
> - What's happening in Primary Care?
>   - How does this affect GPs?
>   - What, in turn, does that mean for your specialty?
> - Major health challenges under government spotlight
>   - For example, obesity or alcohol abuse
>   - How might they affect your specialty?

If you have time, it can be useful to review:

- The latest Trust Board minutes (these will be available on the internet)
- The 'in-hospital' glossy magazine (you can pick one of these up from the waiting areas during your pre-interview visits. These can be a valuable source of information on future developments, what the organization is proud of and the general direction the Trust is going in)

Besides being up-to-date in health as a whole, you need to know what is hot in your specialty and how this is affecting your type of service. The quickest way to find this out is by networking with your present:

- Consultant
- Clinical Service Lead
- Clinical or Divisional Director
- Business Manager

Ask them:

- What is relevant now?
- What is causing them to stop, think or take action?

- What do they find worrying to their specialty?
- What does everybody seem to be talking about?

How to keep up-to-date

It is very easy to become overwhelmed as you attempt to keep up-to-date. A good starting point is to get into the habit of reading a few key documents each day or week in the period leading up to applying for consultant posts. It is better to absorb in some depth and consider what something really means than to have a superficial and arguably less valuable list of facts that you can regurgitate. To be seen as a consultant, you will need to demonstrate critical appraisal and the ability to develop a considered point of view. Consider using the following:

The *Times* (www.thetimes.co.uk/tto/news/) or other good-quality newspaper

This is a very good source of healthcare news and can be read both as a hard copy and electronically.

Health Service Journal (www.hsj.co.uk)

This is a weekly magazine (similar in style to the *BMJ*) produced for health service managers. The journal is usually available in all medical libraries and there may also be a copy somewhere in your department. There is an online version where daily health news can be accessed. The full journal, more detailed articles and back articles can only be accessed electronically through subscription, but this can be done in 3-month blocks and is worth the investment.

British Medical Journal (www.bmj.com)

There are a number of areas worth reviewing in the *BMJ* each week, although in fairness the *Health Service Journal* and the *Times* are often better. The sections worth reviewing are the newspaper section, the news section within the journal itself and any relevant editorials.

Doctors.net.uk (www.doctors.net.uk)

This website collects daily medical news together in one place but often has a more clinical, rather than political, slant. To access the news you must join the organization.

Other important sources of information.

Networking

Talk to your present consultant, Clinical Service Lead and Clinical Director and ask them what is topical. Can you attend a directorate business meeting to get a greater understanding of the key areas of interest?

BMA electronic newsletters

If you are a member of the BMA it produces electronic newsletters for different staff groups. These will keep you up-to-date on some of the NHS initiatives, especially those that directly affect doctors.

eMedicus (www.emedicus.co.uk)

This website has a detailed, political and service-focused programme entitled 'INSIGHTS—Understanding the Evolving Healthcare Landscape' in e-learning form, which is regularly updated to keep in line with the current political agenda and latest White Papers.

Royal College and Society websites

These can be a very useful source of major political initiatives, especially those affecting your own specialty specifically. In response to major political changes or initiatives, each Royal College and learned society will produce a response and possibly even establish sub committees. Read these responses and then review the original documentation (see below for further details on how to go about doing this).

Department of Health website (www.dh.gov.uk)

Ultimately the DH website is the best source of information about the NHS. However, this website is absolutely massive. It is therefore very easy to get 'lost' within it, waste endless hours and become deviated from your true purpose. It is an excellent resource if you know what you are looking for. In particular, if there is a National Service Framework affecting your speciality, the DH website is often the place where the information and supporting data are pulled together. The best examples of this are in:

- Cardiology
- Cancer
- Long-term conditions

Because of it size, it is very easy to find a document on the DH website the first time around and then not be able to find it again later. Either use bookmarks to prevent this happening or save all relevant documents to your computer as you go along. Saving the links is best done if you want to go back soon, but they do move things around somewhat and so if you wish to preserve something, download it.

Other websites

There are, of course, a number of other organizations with websites which might have relevant information at any one stage, e.g. the GMC, NHS Institute for Innovation and Improvement, and National Patient Safety Agency. Again, rather than just dipping in to these, use a good search engine such as Google and access them if they appear to have a view or input in to the specific agenda you are researching.

Courses

A number of organizations offer consultant interview courses. All of them (good ones, anyway) will spend a short period of time on the political agenda. Medicology (www.medicology.co.uk) is an organization that runs both one-day open courses and e-learning courses on Consultant Interview Skills and on The Evolving Healthcare Landscape, keeping both firmly up-to-date with the current political agenda.

Publications

The NHS Confederation produces an annual handbook which has to be purchased but contains relatively up to date articles about the structure of the NHS, current developments and emphasis.

Researching and reading political documents

Once you are clear what areas to research, how do you go about it? We would advise using Google and the Department of Health website. Aim to read articles from key sources, including the Department of Health, GMC, NHS organizations and Royal Colleges. Try to use trusted and learned sources rather than those that peddle frivolous opinion. As many documents go through a system of revision and change, make sure you look at the most up-to-date first and only review older documents if these are clearly referenced in the latest version.

Even if you vow only to review documents that are up-to-date and relevant, it is still incredibly easy to become overwhelmed. The most important thing to recognize is that the interview is not an exam. It is not a knowledge test of what was written in paragraph 3 on page 57. What the panel want to know is how you think a particular aspect of the political agenda or direction will affect the Trust, the department, the specialty, consultants and the workforce generally. They will want to know that you understand both sides of the argument, but also that you are able to come off the fence with an opinion or a view which you can justify with some substance.

How to prepare

- Start by reading the executive summary of the latest documents or papers you have found. In most cases this will be sufficient depth of knowledge for the interview. Alternatively, the executive summary will point you to key areas of the document that you should read (especially if you are asking that all-important question of 'What does this mean to me and my specialty?')
- Consider having some debate with other senior trainees or your current consultant colleagues on some of the issues, so that you develop your arguments, can see the benefits but can also consider the difficulties any proposal may have

- Remember, at the interview there will predominantly be people in managerial roles. These people will generally see the opportunity in any government initiative and will want to see a consultant who can make government initiatives work, not obstruct their implementation
- Think about why an interview committee might ask you about any political agenda. What would be important to them to hear when you answer this question?

In Box 9.2 we have used the example of revalidation to show you how you should prepare for answering political questions.

Box 9.2 How to prepare for answering political questions (using revalidation as an example)

How not to prepare

As I write this chapter, 'revalidation' has been 10 years in development. There have been three White Papers and 'millions' of man-hours invested. There has been a consultation exercise which has not yet reported fully. Most Royal Colleges have detailed responses on their websites on revalidation. I could spend a week reading about this one subject alone. Much of what I read will be outdated and will have been superseded by newer information or thinking.

How to prepare

I tend to 'Google' revalidation and note the key information on the GMC website. There have been major changes to proposals over recent weeks.

- I read these
- I review my Royal College website to see if there has been a formal response to this new information
- I consider what revalidation means to the Medical Director and the Trust and what it will mean to doctors in my service
- I consider what revalidation means to patients and the public
- I debate with my colleagues the opportunities that revalidation brings but also some of the difficulties and issues it raises
- I consider questions I might be asked
  - Do I think revalidation is either necessary or good?
  - How will I go about ensuring I get revalidated?
  - How would I ensure effective revalidation in speciality x?

Chapter 10
Specialty-specific interviews

Introduction

This chapter is designed to provide a brief insight into the differences between specialties and how they approach the interview process. It should be read in conjunction with Chapters 4 and 6. The specialties covered are:

- Anaesthesia
- Emergency medicine
- Medicine
- Psychiatry
- Obstetrics and gynaecology
- Paediatrics and neonatal specialities
- Pathology and laboratory-based specialities
- Radiology
- Surgery

Author contributions

Each of these sections has been written by a guest author from within that specialty. Across the board, they are all experienced, senior clinicians with many years' experience in interviewing for consultants. However, it is also important to remember that they are individuals and each individual has their own unique way of thinking too.

We have done comparatively little editing and given relatively free rein to those individuals in deciding what's important. Each was provided with the broad section titles for some consistency. The content is very much their own and we have left it largely untouched so that you may get a feeling for style, psychology and focus, accepting that they are also unique too. As a consequence, although the section structure is consistent, you will find a considerable variation in what authors have chosen to focus on.

Psychology of the specialties

In each specialty, we have provided a perspective on the likely psychology of the individuals you may come across. This is written by us, not the guest authors, who we can't expect to have sufficient understanding of psychological difference. However, what we have written must never be taken as gospel. There is no substitute for being a good detective and finding out exactly who is on your panel and exactly how they are wired as individuals.

The anaesthetic consultant interview

Dr Helga Becker, Consultant Anaesthetist, Dudley Group of Hospitals NHS Foundation Trust.

The interview panel

In terms of number of consultants, anaesthetics is often the single largest department in a Trust and so the interview panel will not be particularly representative of the department as a whole. Besides the usual suspects like Chief Executive and Medical Director, the panel will probably have the Clinical Director and maybe another consultant from the department. Given the importance of surgery to an average Trust, the non-clinical members of the panel will be most interested in how well theatre runs.

Psychology of the specialty

Anaesthetics tends to be a risk-adverse profession where safety trumps heroics. An attitude of problem prevention through effective preparation prevails over having to sort things out in the moment and so anaesthetists like to be assured and aware of what they are dealing with. Although anaesthetists have to work with the predominantly Island of Opportunity surgeons, the nature of the work draws predominantly Island of Intellect individuals who are cautious, evidence-based, considered in their thoughts and actions and who like a sense of certainty. This needs considering when answering questions during the interview, especially when managing the differences between management and anaesthetists. See Chapter 4.

What do the panel want to see from a consultant anaesthetist colleague?

Anaesthetists tend to be structured, risk-adverse characters and so a good study of the job description and advertisement will be quite instructive regarding the skills, attitudes and other qualities that are desired from any successful candidate. Beyond the specifics of the job description and person specification, it is generally accepted that a good anaesthetist shows a considered, unflustered and structured approach to problems, difficult situations and tasks in general. The candidate also needs to show good, emphatic communication and team-working skills, technical abilities and a well-developed sense of responsibility and involvement. A high consideration for efficient theatre flow is also important.

What is a consultant anaesthetist interview like and how does this differ from other specialty interviews?

The interview tends to be a structured series of questions in a fairly traditional format with representatives from both the department and the wider Trust management and senior management teams. Besides questions around clinical competency and safety, questions also focus on the role of anaesthetics today, improving theatre efficiency and relationships, given that anaesthetists interact with many.

The best preparation is the visit to the prospective department prior to short-listing. This provides the opportunity to look at the local facilities and speak to as many colleagues as possible. It is strongly advisable to initially ask for a meeting with the Clinical Director or Service Head. A proactive approach in this respect is usually appreciated and welcome. These visits can be extremely helpful in gauging the character of the department and in providing an opportunity to gain an insight into likely topics affecting the department or Trust which may come up at interview.

After short-listing, a second visit to the department is necessary. At this visit, if possible, a meeting with the Chief Executive and Medical Director should also be sought to more deeply explore the Trust and to show keen interest.

What else might I commonly need to do as part of the interview process?

Presentations are an unusual component of a consultant anaesthetist interview and the interview tends to follow a fairly traditional, interview panel-based approach.

Questions about the wider NHS in general and current hot topics are common. Form your own opinion and understand how your future in the secondary care sector, for example, may be affected. The recent Care Quality Commission reports and the Business Plan for the hospital are good documents to start with. Be prepared!

Helpful hints

A major part of the interview will revolve around clinical governance and quality issues, other management issues and the pressures facing the Trust and the wider NHS.

Questions to do with team-working and working relations with colleagues from different specialties and the handling of difficult interpersonal situations are almost guaranteed in the anaesthetic consultant interview. Team-working is extremely important in everyday clinical practice and also for the development and maintenance of a well-functioning, flexible and cohesive anaesthetic department. Self-reflection and some rehearsal before the interview for these predictable questions are important components of sensible preparation.

Critical factors leading to success

When applying for a new job, the first hurdle is overcome when the candidate is invited for an interview! Given the risk-adverse nature of anaesthetists, clearly laying out your skills, experience and track record in your CV is vital, with the aim of giving the short-listing team a sense of security and reassurance.

It is helpful to see the interview as another viva, where not just clinical skills are under scrutiny (that aspect has also been dealt with along the way but will usually be reassessed by the College Representative). Consequently, a major part of this 'viva' will revolve around issues currently facing the Trust and wider NHS, along with how they impact on anaesthetics, as well as clinical governance and quality issues, given the safety-conscious nature of the specialty.

Critical factors leading to people falling down at anaesthetic consultant interview

The two most important things that reduce chances of success when applying for a consultant anaesthetic position are an obvious lack of structured preparation for the interview and a failure to demonstrate those characteristics that make enthusiastic and sincere team-working likely.

Key questions asked at anaesthetic interviews

- Why are you applying for this job in particular?
- What are your plans for your professional future?
- What purpose does SPA time serve and how will you use it?
- Questions regarding current clinical developments, recent NICE Guidelines, National Standards relating to anaesthetics and relevant subspecialties
- Be ready for questions stemming from your CV and make sure you know it well

These questions can be uncomfortable to answer if you need to explain why you left a previous employer, why there was a gap in training, etc. The key is honesty and a good, structured explanation of the circumstances. The interviewers must not be left in doubt about your level of commitment.

Note: it is also useful for anaesthetists to review the questions asked at surgical interview as some of these can be common to both specialties.

Common specialty-specific questions

- A surgical consultant approaches you because he wants to do an extensive laparotomy on a patient with severely limited physiological reserve. You, after due consideration, think that surgery should not go ahead. How do you resolve this situation?
- Nationally published mortality statistics usually do not include any data specific for anaesthesia. What are your thoughts about this?
- The role of Physicians' Assistants in Anaesthesia and Intensive Care has recently been redebated/revived nationally. What are your thoughts on this topic?
- Many Trusts in this country are aiming to increase the number of same-day admissions for surgery and decrease length of stay for surgical patients whilst avoiding premature discharges and early readmissions. How can you as an anaesthetic consultant contribute to this process?
- How would you go about improving theatre utilization?
- What do you believe are the five key things required to ensure effective day-case surgery, not just from the anaesthetic perspective?
- How do you ensure effective risk management in anaesthetics?
- Should chronic pain services be provided in secondary care?

Typical ethical dilemmas

- A patient suffers from a carcinoma, which at the time of diagnosis is operable and for which surgery is the only curative treatment option. He also, has significant comorbidities which puts him in a high-risk category for 30-day mortality and significant incapacitation complications. Yes or no to surgery? Under which circumstances would you be prepared to support a decision to go ahead/anaesthetzse this patient?
- DNAR (do not resuscitate) orders and (palliative) surgical procedures

- Consent in labour or other situations of severe distress
- A patient with learning difficulties has had a cholecystecomy, to which he consented at the time, but he suffered complications which result in his need for invasive organ support on the Intensive Care Unit, including sedation. His elderly parents are alive but so frail that they are unable to care for him and his usual carers now raise the question of action under the Deprivation of Liberty Act. What are your thoughts on this?
- A 19-year-old boy has been involved in an RTA. You believe he is brain dead but you have not formally tested him yet. How would you approach the relatives in this case?
- Should anaesthetists be expected to anaesthetize high-risk patients for elective surgery?

The emergency medicine consultant interview

Dr Vikas Sodiwala, Consultant in Emergency Medicine, United Lincolnshire Hospitals NHS Trust.

The interview panel

The majority of the panel will be highly goal driven, looking for opportunities to excel and develop the Emergency Medicine (EM) service. They will be looking for 'quick wins' and opportunities to improve processes and protocols to make patients flow more effectively and efficiently through the service. This is to be expected, given the degree to which emergency care remains in the political spotlight.

Psychology of the specialty

EM is often a fast-paced environment where quick action is necessary. By definition, professionals are often called upon to make judgements in the absence of the ideal level of information. Consequently, professionals need to have a degree of risk tolerance and be able to act decisively even in the face of ambiguity. The leaders in EM need to provide decisive, directive instructions designed to elicit rapid action in others. Not surprisingly, EM tends to draw significant numbers of individuals from the Island of Opportunity and this needs considering when answering questions. See Chapter 4.

What do the panel want to see from a consultant emergency medicine colleague?

The Emergency Department (ED) is the hub for the delivery of emergency care. It interacts with virtually all other hospital specialities and with many stakeholders in the wider healthcare community. Any project, initiative or change involving emergency care of patients is likely to impact on the ED. Consultants in EM must therefore have not only exemplary clinical skills but also leadership and management expertise with excellent interpersonal skills. They must have an awareness of the multifactorial components that can affect the ED and have a regard for ethics and time management.

The consultant must be a dynamic and enthusiastic individual who will champion projects and push forward initiatives.

What is a consultant emergency medicine interview like and how does it differ from other specialty interviews?

The interview does not test clinical knowledge. It does test you on administrative, management and leadership issues. It is comparable to the management component of the Fellowship of College of Emergency Medicine (FCEM) exam but taken a step further, as you are required to think of real-life answers and not typical exam answers. With the ED being the hub of a hospital seeing the acutely unwell, questions regarding conduct and behaviour of other doctors and staff are frequent, as there is a possibility of staff coming through the ED with their own problems (see example below).

What else might I commonly need to do as part of the interview process?

Presentations are common in EM interviews. Common topics revolve around ED processes, service development and interactions with other stakeholders. Examples include:

- What service developments can you bring to the department/Trust?
- What is the impact of walk-in centres and urgent care centres on EDs?
- Can you use LEAN processes in the ED?
- What is the role of a modern consultant in EM?

Helpful hints

The College of Emergency Medicine (CEM) website is a definite read before the interview. The section titled 'Current issues and statements' can be found in the 'About the College' tab and contains the College's views on all aspects of emergency care. It will direct you to the 'hot' topics in EM and can direct further reading. Many of the questions asked by the Chief Executive, General Mangers and the Clinical Directors will be concerning these topics.

Other useful reads are the *EMJ* (*Emergency Medicine Journal*) (particularly the editorials and commentaries) and the *EMJ Supplement* which covers topical and political issues in emergency care.

Critical factors leading to success

EM is a relatively young specialty that is still developing at a phenomenal pace. At interview you must come across as someone who knows what is going on in the specialty and where the specialty wants to be. You must therefore know about the key college statements and documents such as 'The Way Ahead' document and what impacts this will have on patients, your department and the hospital.

Critical factors leading to people falling down at EM consultant interview

A fatal trap is a lack of enthusiasm and dynamism when talking to the panel. If you cannot show that you are passionate about your specialty and the changes that are occurring then you will not succeed.

Key questions asked at EM interviews

- How have you ensured you have enough knowledge about the smaller surgical specialties that you have not had training in?
- How do you balance service delivery with training in the ED?
- Tell us how you can teach effectively whilst working on the shop floor
- Should GPs be based in the ED?
- Can you think of ways to improve the ED patient journey?
- What will your special interest be?

Common specialty-specific questions

- Is the 4-hour standard helpful? Should it have decreased from 98% to 95%? Should it be abolished?
- Is there a place for allied health professionals working at the frontline in the ED?
- How would you deal with a consultant colleague from another specialty who is brought in to your department drunk/with an OD (overdose)?
- What would the impact of a walk-in centre, minor injuries unit, urgent care centre or out of hours service be if it opened its doors next door to the ED?
- What did the Mid-Staffordshire Enquiry highlight about emergency care in the ED?

Typical ethical dilemmas

- A patient has taken a lethal overdose of Paracetamol. She has presented to the ED, and a 4-hour blood test reveals that she is well above the treatment line. She is now refusing any further treatment and wants to leave. What is your course of action?
- A 16-year-old presents to the ED, accompanied by her mother, with a laceration to the arm after falling off a bike. The wound will need suturing. The patient refuses the treatment as she is scared of needles. What would you do?
- A patient is brought in with a non-fatal stab wound to the left arm whilst drinking at a pub. The police have not been informed yet and the patient does not want them involved. The charge nurse asks whether he should call the police and what information can be given out

The Medicine (consultant physician) interview

Dr Stuart Bloom, Consultant Gastroenterologist, University College London Hospitals NHS Foundation Trust.

The interview panel

This will involve a range of personality types depending on the makeup of the panel. There will be a Royal College of Physicians Representative (often rather senior, non-aggressive physicians), who will usually flesh out your professional qualifications and experience; these will generally be the least taxing of the questions, because they relate to your previous medical experience.

The key personnel will be your potential colleagues, who may be presented by a Clinical Director and perhaps one other Consultant. You should have had a chance to at least talk to these people on the telephone or preferably have met them and know something of their approach and their idea of the job. They will expect professional competence as a given and be more interested in what you can bring to the department and how you complement the existing skills. This may include an appetite for research or education and training. The panel will also include a representative of the Chief Executive and the Medical Director. The Medical Directors are often very driven, busy people, who will want to explore your knowledge of governance structures and the wider NHS. They will usually be of a different medical specialty to yours. Finally, there may well be an administrator or manager, who may ask you questions about finance or resource allocation.

Psychology of the specialty

Physicians in general come from all islands, given that the collection of specialties represented by this broad group is diverse. It is important to consider an individual's context to better predict which island they are from. However, physicians typically entered medicine to be of service to others and use their intellect positively. This combination of drivers or motivations means that adult medicine frequently draws individuals who are a combination of the Islands of Team Spirit and Intellect. See Chapter 4.

What do the panel want to see from a consultant physician colleague?

The traditional consultant physician appointment involves a commitment to clinical service, some aspect of research, or development and educational training, and the panel will want to explore these various components. It is now extremely rare to have a truly general medical appointment; the job will nearly always have a specialty interest and perhaps a commitment to the acute medical unit.

What is a consultant physician interview like and how does it differ from other specialty interviews?

The interviews are predictably stressful but can be fun—it depends on whether you can answer all the questions! You can expect the interview to be probing, but it is relatively rare to be asked questions about clinical scenarios, although you may well be expected to refer to professional experience in terms of number of catheters or number of endoscopies carried out. Generally you will be assessed for the expertise and special skills you bring to a team of people, rather than being appointable because of unique experience with the left nostril.

What else might I commonly need to do as part of the interview process?

Success depends on careful preparation, including often several visits to the hospital and discussions with as many of the interested parties as possible. You must know exactly what the job involves and have a clear idea of what you can bring to the team. You may well be required to make a presentation on, for instance, ensuring high quality in the endoscopy unit or another aspect of delivering a high quality service.

Helpful hints

If the job is a replacement one, talk to the outgoing post-holder. Try to find out what the priorities for the new post-holder are and whether you offer a good fit. Ask some colleagues for a dress-rehearsal interview. Read up on the proposals for the latest NHS reorganization and consider how this might affect your new department. Have a clear idea of what you would want to achieve in the first year or two.

Critical factors leading to success

Pre-interview preparation is the most important factor. The panel will assume clinical competence, unless you lead them to think otherwise. They will be more interested in assessing whether they will be able to work with you and whether you will be a committed colleague, often for very many years.

Critical factors leading to people falling down at consultant physician interview

- Inadequate preparation
- Woolly or waffling answers to questions (try to speak clearly and concisely and answer the question)

Key questions asked at physician interviews

- Tell us how your clinical experience fits you for this post
- What do you think you can bring to the department?
- What do you think are the current problems facing the department?
- Tell us about your attitude to the European Working Time Directive
- Questions on finance, e.g. what do you know about service line reporting?

Common specialty-specific questions

- What do you see as being the most important areas of development in the specialty over the next 10 years?
- How do you see the European Working Time Directive impacting on the acquisition of endoscopic experience?

- What are the problems in becoming involved in recruiting patients to clinical trials?

Typical ethical dilemmas

- What are your views on euthanasia?
- How do you address the issue of prescribing a drug that might not be NICE approved?
- An alcoholic patient is becoming violent and aggressive on the ward. The nursing staff want you to discharge him. What are the issues?

The psychiatry consultant interview

Dr Neelima Reddi, Consultant Psychiatrist, Surrey & Borders Partnership NHS Foundation Trust.

The interview panel

The interview panel will consist predominantly of two groups: psychiatrists, who have a deep commitment to their patients, a strong sense of ethics, right and wrong, and a longer-term view, as patients can be with them for extended durations, and managers, who typically are more concerned with what needs delivering and fixing in the short term. Even in the limited scenario of an interview panel, these differing outlooks can cause tension, which candidates need to learn to manage. Honing your skills in adapting answers in the moment will pay dividends in psychiatry.

Psychology of the specialty

Psychiatrists take a deeply analytical approach to the complex problems of mental health (MH), with seemingly small factors often playing a big part in the overall picture. Having taken the trouble to get deeply inside someone's life to understand what's going on, they are then required to demonstrate huge empathy and seek out solutions that are acceptable for their patients. Their objective detachment, coupled with this empathetic commitment to the patient's security and well-being, naturally draws individuals from the Islands of both Intellect and Team Spirit, or commonly a mixture of the two. This needs carefully considering when answering questions. See Chapter 4.

What do the panel want to see from a consultant psychiatrist colleague?

The panel will want to know that you can work as part of a multidisciplinary team. They are also keen to know that you understand both the business and NHS political agenda. Many MH Trusts are moving towards being business units, whether or not they are Foundation Trusts, and panels will be looking for candidates who can balance clinical and business agendas to create security and success for the Trust.

What is a consultant psychiatrist interview like and how does it differ from other specialty interviews?

Consultant interviews in psychiatry differ from other specialities in that there is a high likelihood that there will be a service user on your interview panel. The degree of influence this person has will vary from panel to panel but he/she particularly will want to see that you have empathy with patients with mental illness and that you will work with service users to help them manage their health.

What else might I commonly need to do as part of the interview process?

Presentations are common in psychiatry consultant interviews. If there is not a service user on the panel you may be asked to do a presentation to a group of service users. If you are asked to do a presentation separate from your interview, always ask Medical Staffing who is going to be in the audience. If the audience is predominantly service users, consider carefully how you can demonstrate that you are empathetic to your audience's needs.

Helpful hints

Psychiatry is undergoing lots of change. Care for MH patients has been delivered in MH institutions and hospitals, and by community and private providers, and each is currently trying to work out where it stands and what it must do in relation to competition, choice, payment systems and financial reform. Make sure you take time to do a pre-interview visit or indeed visits and listen carefully to the business and NHS issues that are affecting the service. You are likely to be asked questions about this. Think about your role and how you can be helpful to a service wrestling with these changes.

Critical factors leading to success

Take time to meet key members of the multidisciplinary team. Do not forget to meet with the Chief Executive and the Medical Director. Psychiatry interview panels seem keener than others to ask questions about your understanding of the business side of MH. Make sure you have read the Trust's strategic plan and consider talking to your present Team Manager and the Associate Medical Director in your present Trust.

Critical factors leading to people falling down at psychiatry consultant interview

The main reason individuals do not succeed at consultant psychiatrist interview is that they are uncomfortable with promoting themselves. As a result they fail to come across as motivated and excited by the job. For many psychiatrists, promoting yourself could seem arrogant, rude or unprofessional. As a result, there is a danger that they rely on people concluding or noticing their qualities and strengths but do not do anything towards helping themselves get the job. Psychiatrists also like to feel secure about their decisions and so candidates can sometimes fail to sufficiently convince an interview panel that they are strong enough. Being prepared and acutely familiar with your strengths and limitations, as well as the evidence that supports this, all helps.

Key questions asked at psychiatry interviews

- Have you had sufficient training to be a consultant in psychiatry?
- How do you cope with stress?
- How would you ensure patient and public involvement in MH?
- What should we teach medical students about MH?
- Is payment-by-results possible in psychiatry? What do you think are the key issues?
- What are the implications of patient choice in psychiatry?

Common specialty-specific questions

- Do you think supervision is sustainable? How will you provide supervision to trainees?
- I have schizophrenia. How can you reassure me that you are a good doctor for me?
- What are your views on specialty training, e.g. psychiatric intensive care, in the independent sector?
- Is the new Mental Health Act a good thing?
- What are your views on supervised treatment in the community (SCT)?
- What is your view of Mental Health Advocates?
- Is it right that psychiatric intensive care is often provided by the private sector?
- What are the implications of government healthcare policy on MH?
- What are your views on the recent MH advertising campaign?
- How do you assess that you are delivering a high quality service?
- Do you think business units are a good idea in MH?

Typical ethical dilemmas

- You have just seen a gentleman in A&E and have assessed him as being at high suicide risk. There are no in-patient beds available in the MH Trust, so what would you do?
- You have a patient on supervised community treatment. His family do not think this is acceptable and think he should still be an in-patient. What would you do?
- You believe a colleague may have alcohol addiction. You have noticed the smell of alcohol on his breath a number of times. What would you do?

The obstetric and gynaecology (obs & gynae) consultant interview

Dr Lucy Kean, Consultant Obstetrician, Nottingham University Hospitals NHS Trust.

The interview panel

The panel or advisory appointment committee (AAC) will consist of a number of set members and there may be additional members depending on the post for which you are being interviewed. There are six key individuals who must be present on the AAC, in common with most consultant interviews in many specialties. These include:

- Lay member, usually Chair of the AAC
  - (generally not medical but may ask about team working, etc.)
- Chief Executive
  - (examining how you add value to the Trust and its objectives)
- Medical Director
  - (may probe deeply into your understanding of and readiness for consultant-hood, including areas of weakness)
- College Representative
  - (concerned with fullness of training and relevance of experience)
- Clinical Director and/or another consultant
  - (in-depth questioning about suitability, fit and value to their service)
- Academic Representative
  - (in-depth questioning about education and teaching experience and value)

Psychology of the specialty

Obstetrics and gynaecology is a highly practical specialty or set of specialties where strong direction and rapid action is often a critical success factor to avoid problems. Whereas risk management is a vital aspect of successful services, care comes with an element of risk and so a degree of risk tolerance is important. These job characteristics tend to draw professionals from the Island of Opportunity or a mixture of Opportunity and Team Spirit. This needs to be considered when answering questions. See Chapter 4.

What do the panel want to see from a consultant obs & gynae colleague?

The panel will wish to explore your knowledge of all aspects of consultant work. Many of the questions asked will be standard and expected, but don't worry about giving answers that are different from other candidates. Showing flair is important, but you must demonstrate that you are safe and competent above all things.

Risk management is hugely important in maternity care and it will form a larger part of an interview for a consultant post that includes obstetrics than many other specialties.

What is a consultant obs & gynae interview like and how does this differ from other specialty interviews?

The interview is likely to be fairly direct and probing, focusing on areas that are particularly important in obstetrics and gynaecology and looking for certain aspects of thinking or experience. Some of these areas include the following.

Clinical skills

Answer fully and methodically. Think carefully before starting, as adding steps that should be covered earlier in the answer can give the impression of lack of clarity of thought. The panel will be observing your ability to think under stress.

Management and finance

Know how NHS finances works. Think about how you would help deliver a cost improvement plan or improve efficiency. Meet with the departmental finance director before the interview.

Team-working and interpersonal skills

Be able to discuss how you have team-worked and give examples, both as a team leader and as a team player. You might be asked to describe how you have managed situations of conflict. Think through a real scenario that you have been involved in recently. If your Trust offers conflict resolution training, try to attend; to be able to state that you have received formal training and to show how you have used this is particularly powerful.

Clinical governance and risk management

Find out at what level the department is currently assessed for the Clinical Negligence Scheme for Trusts (CNST). You will need to understand the risk management and clinical governance processes used in acute hospitals and show that you have been involved in these processes. It is useful to have attended risk management meetings so that you can talk knowledgeably.

What else might I commonly need to do as part of the interview process?

Most Trusts will ask you to present on a topic, usually about local service development, e.g.

- How would I develop a team in urogynaecology?
- What are the challenges facing the development of fetal medicine in this Trust?

The panel will be looking to ensure that your answer focuses on the question and the local issues. It is particularly important to provide a multidisciplinary answer. If possible, talk to members of both the medical and the nursing/midwifery teams when gathering your information.

Helpful hints

- Use active rather than passive language, e.g. 'In my role I was required to . . .' can be rephrased as 'My key tasks as . . .'
- Don't underplay or overstate your achievements

Getting the balance right is important and takes practice, so ask colleagues to watch you present.

Critical factors leading to success

Successful candidates have done their research into the job so that they understand the local pressures and problems. Knowledge brings confidence, which allows you to give concise answers.

Talk to key people including the managers and midwifery/nursing leads.

Critical factors leading to people falling down at obs & gynae consultant interview

Lack of insight into local problems and challenges, along with generalized and uncertain answers.

Appearing arrogant, e.g. assuming the role of team leader when asked about team-working, rather than discussing both leadership and team-player roles.

Key questions asked at obs & gynae interviews

- What would you do if you thought a colleague's performance was not of an acceptable standard?
- How would you manage a junior member of your team who is not making satisfactory progress?
- How should we balance the need for training our trainees with maintaining consultant competencies?
- What evidence can you give that you are an effective teacher?
- What are the main challenges in attaining the next level for CNST?
- How do you discuss risk with your patients?
- What are the main financial challenges facing the directorate and how would you help to meet them?
- How will you help us to deliver a 5% cost improvement programme?
- What are the relevant CQUINs for the directorate and where are the challenges in meeting these?
- What new innovations will we see in the next 5 years that will impact on obstetrics and gynaecology?
- How would you go about introducing a new technique into your clinical practice?
- What are your views on waiting targets? Do you think it is realistic to decrease the target to 6 weeks?
- How could we better organize gynaecology services in this Trust?

Common specialty-specific questions

- How should we respond to the changing practice of gynaecology?
- Should labour ward emergency training be entirely multidisciplinary and, if so, why?
- What do you see as the impact of GP-based commissioning on gynaecology in a secondary centre, and what services that are currently offered by secondary centres in gynaecology would be better allocated elsewhere?
- How will central commissioning affect our ability to offer a maternity service that reflects local needs?
- What is an ideal Caesarean section rate and should we reduce our Caesarean section rate? If so, how would you set about achieving this?
- What do you think are the five key risks in obstetrics? How would you go about managing these?
- Do you think there should be 24-hour consultant cover of labour wards?
- Is CNST 3 achievable in this hospital?
- How would you counsel a woman requesting a home birth?

Typical ethical dilemmas

- A woman declines blood and blood products with a signed advanced directive. She has a difficult Caesarean section and requires a general anaesthetic. Once anaesthetized her husband, who is of the same faith, begs you to do everything necessary to save her life, including giving blood if necessary
- A young woman with a needle phobia arrives in early labour. The fetus is clearly compromised and delivery by urgent Caesarean section is indicated. She is declining delivery as she knows it must involve either a spinal or a general anaesthetic, both of which require cannulation. She wants to have the baby delivered but cannot face the thought of the needles
- A very young woman whose first language is not English reveals to the midwife at an antenatal clinic appointment that she is regularly subjected to domestic violence. She begs the midwife not to say anything to anyone as she fears the violence will increase if her husband or his family discover she has confided in her midwife. The midwife comes to you for advice on what should happen now
- A primigravida lady is demanding an elective LSCS (lower segment caesarean section). There is no medical reason for requiring this. What would you do?
- Should patients be able to demand LSCS on request?
- How would you counsel parents whose fetus was found to have trisomy 18 following amniocentesis?
- How would you counsel parents whose fetus was found to have complex congenital fetal abnormalities on their detailed scan?
- Tell me about the last family you had to manage where the fetus had a major anomaly. How did you counsel the parents?
- How would you deal with the women in established labour who is refusing LSCS despite the baby being in fetal distress?

The paediatric or neonatal consultant interview

Dr Sara Watkin, Consultant Neonatologist, University College London Hospitals NHS Foundation Trust.

The interview panel

By and large, paediatricians are happy, friendly types who like nothing better than a chat with their future colleague. Although by nature a consultant interview is formal, they will try to make it as informal and relaxed as possible for you. The paediatricians on the panel will warm to you if you are relaxed and friendly and relate your answers to real families, their children and the teams and colleagues you work with. The panel will of course be balanced by a number of more goal-orientated individuals such as the Chief Executive, Clinical or Divisional Director and possibly the Medical Director, who will want to know what added value you will bring but without rocking the boat. It is almost unheard of to have an aggressive interviewer in a paediatric interview. Neonatologists are again very team-orientated, but there is a technical and analytical side to their work. They are fairly obsessive about attention to detail and reducing risk.

Psychology of the specialty

Paediatrics is a team-based specialty requiring empathy, patience and kindness. With considerable emotional, emotive and ethical dimensions to the specialty, paediatricians tend to be highly aware of their impact on others. Consequently, a great many paediatricians are from the Island of Team Spirit. Neonatal medicine adds an analytical dimension, with an acute focus on attention to detail. Neonatologists tend to come from the Island of Intellect or the Island of Team Spirit (or be a mixture of these two).

What do the panel want to see from a consultant paediatric colleague?

Without a doubt they want to know that you are a team player. They want to gain a strong sense that you are an empathetic individual and that you have excellent communication skills, especially with children and their families. Although they want a colleague who is dynamic and will make things happen, they want this colleague in a form that won't rock the boat or challenge the harmonious working environment they enjoy. Neonatologists will want someone who they consider safe, extremely hard-working and flexible in relation to working hours.

What is a consultant paediatric interview like and how does it differ from other specialty interviews?

A paediatric interview is probably the most friendly of all consultant interviews. This makes it a potential minefield for candidates, who can easily find themselves enjoying this friendly chat whilst failing to promote themselves as the best candidate for the job. Paradoxically, too much 'sell' can result in someone being seen as arrogant, which could bother paediatricians. The key is to achieve a balance. The neonatal interview can also feel quite 'interrogative', as panel members seek to examine weakness and risks.

What else might I commonly need to do as part of the interview process?

Presentations are very common in consultant paediatric and neonatal interviews. The topic might be related to a specific interest required by the panel, e.g. safeguarding children, an issue relevant to the specialty or the added value you will bring to the service.

Helpful hints

You must do a pre-interview visit. Make sure you spend time talking to the nurses and other members of the multidisciplinary team. Be extra nice to the secretaries. Paediatrics is very much about team-working and the consultants on your interview committee will almost certainly have sought feedback from wider team members. They will take it poorly if you have appeared rude or cold to anyone. By the same token, in a small department make sure you see all the consultants, whether they are on the interview panel or not. Paediatricians have their feelings hurt easily.

In general, your pre-interview visit will feel very laid-back and friendly. This can lure candidates into a false sense of security. You still have to prepare and you absolutely still have to promote yourself.

Critical factors leading to success

- Make sure you take time to do a pre-interview visit
- Remember, the panel members are on your side
- Ensure your examples have a strong emphasis on children, their families or the team
- Do not come across as too boastful, whilst still promoting your examples with passion
- Do not come across as pushy

Critical factors leading to people falling down at paediatric or neonatal consultant interview

- Appearing arrogant, aggressive or too pushy
- Appearing cold and insincere
- Not relating your examples to real people
- Being impolite or showing poor manners
- Appearing not to listen

Key questions asked at paediatric interviews

- Summarize the key aspects of your training and experience relevant to this post
- How do your special interests complement those of the department?

- How do you know you are a good team player?
- Tell me about the last time you failed to communicate effectively?
- How would you deal with conflict between you and some parents?
- How would you go about teaching medical students?
- What are your strengths?
- What are your weaknesses?
- How do you cope with stress? What do you do to relieve your own stress?

Common specialty-specific questions

Paediatrics

- Your registrar comes to tell you that the SHO she is doing nights with is not safe. She is very unconfident to go to labour suite and cannot do basic procedures on the ward. What would you do?
- What are your views on the RCPCH (Royal College of Paediatrics and Child Health) document 'Modelling the Future'? What should this service be doing? How do you think children's services should be delivered?
- Have you had level 3 safeguarding training?
- I have been struggling to appoint a designated paediatrician for child protection in our hospital. What would you advise?
- How would you deliver the designated Paediatrician in Child Protection role in a busy DGH such as ours?
- Should paediatrics be a consultant-delivered service?
- Should paediatricians ever be part of Hospital-at-Night?
- What should Trusts be doing to better protect children?
- How would you deliver medical services for the detection of NAI (non-accidental injury) in a busy town like ours?
- What have you taken away from the report on *x* [usually to do with child protection, e.g. New Laming Report (13/03/09)]?

Neonatal

- What are the challenges facing neonatal medicine in the next 10 years?
- What are the key issues affecting neonatal networks?
- What constitutes good medical practice in neonatal medicine and how will you ensure your practice is up to standard?
- What are the key risks within neonatal intensive care? How would you go about reducing them?
- How would you ensure safe induction for neonatal trainees?
- How can we improve working relationships between neonatologists and obstetricians?
- What constitutes good medical practice in neonatal medicine and how will you ensure your practice is up to standard?

Typical ethical dilemmas

Paediatrics

- A 14-year-old child under your care is refusing further treatment for his life-threatening disease. Without treatment he will almost certainly die. His parents want him to have everything done. How would you handle the situation?
- Your nurses have raised concerns that a 3-year-old child under your care might be suffering emotional neglect. What would you do?
- As a paediatric consultant you are called by A&E for your advice. A 4-year-old boy is being resuscitated in A&E following a collision with a motor bike. He has decreasing neuro-obs and needs urgent imaging and probable neurosurgery. He is accompanied by his au-pair whose English is poor. His parents are out of the country on business and both uncontactable until late tonight. What are the issues and what would you do?
- A 7-year-old boy is ventilated on ITU following a severe head injury in an RTA. It is likely that he is not going to recover. How would you go about considering and withdrawing intensive care treatment?

Neonatal medicine

- Should we resuscitate babies at 23 weeks' gestation? How would you counsel a woman in labour at 23 weeks' gestation?
- How would you counsel a couple who have just been told by the obstetricians that their 18- week-gestation baby has Edward's syndrome?
- A 24-week-gestation baby has recently been born to parents who are both Jehovah's Witnesses. The baby is very sick and it is likely that he will require blood products at some time. How would you manage this child and his family?
- A lady presents at 23 weeks' gestation in preterm labour. The obstetricians believe she is likely to deliver within the next 3 hours. How would you mange this?

The pathology and laboratory-based specialty consultant interview

Dr Deepti Radia, Consultant Haematologist, Guy's and St Thomas' NHS Foundation Trust.

The interview panel

The interview panel conforms closely to the generic description in earlier chapters, including:

- The Royal College of Pathology Representative to ensure you have obtained the required qualifications and to give you a chance to go through your CV
- Management Representative, who may be from the laboratory aspect so could be a Senior Biomedical Scientist (BMS) or Lead Clinician in the specialty

- Consultant with specialist interest and your likely colleague-to-be, who will be looking to see if you will 'fit into the team'
- In a teaching hospital, a University Representative, who will be interested in your potential to contribute to academia including research, translational research in the laboratory, and development of new investigative tools
- Medical Director Representative, who will be looking at issues around managing and working in teams, as well as leadership qualities
- Chief Executive Representative, who will be looking to see what you can contribute to the Trust
- Lay Chair, who is usually the friendly face and there to ensure you are comfortable and the process is fair. They are on the candidate's side!

Psychology of the specialty

Laboratories tend to be structured, orderly environments where strict adherence to protocols and procedures ensures accuracy and lower error rates. Besides working with a team, there are fairly considerable elements of the work that are conducted in isolation, requiring concentration and attention to detail. Consequently, this environment draws significant numbers from the Island of Intellect and this should be taken into account when answering the questions. See Chapter 4.

What do the panel want to see from a consultant pathologist/laboratory-based colleague?

The panel as a whole will be looking to explore the candidate in relation to four basic areas by asking the following questions. Does the candidate/will the candidate.

- Have the appropriate skill set for the job, i.e. are you a competent doctor?
- Have the drive and enthusiasm to make a difference to the post/department or Trust?
- Fit into and enhance the current team structure, i.e. your personality and communication skills?
- Demonstrate that he/she has the potential to learn and adapt to a changing environment?

What is a consultant pathology and laboratory-based specialty interview like and how does it differ from other specialty interviews?

The structure and format of a typical pathology and laboratory-based specialty interview tends to be somewhat formal, relying predominantly on a traditional panel interview. There are similarities in the generic questions asked with all consultant interviews—communication skills, managing under pressure, personal strengths and weaknesses, etc. The main difference is that the clinicians in the laboratory are looking for evidence and facts that substantiate the answers, i.e. the answers must have substance, rather than opinion.

What else might I commonly need to do as part of the interview process?

The interview process will be highly reliant on the panel questions and candidate answers. It is unusual for there to be a presentation as part of the consultant interview.

Helpful hints

There is certainly homework to be done to be ready for this interview, including:

- Finding out about the Trust, department and team structure and priorities
- Ensuring familiarity with major initiatives, papers and directives that could be influencing the department, e.g. the various Carter Reports

To get the greatest depth of insight, try to see the site and relevant people before the interview, or at least have a fairly substantial conversation with them. Make sure you want the post and, remember, there are few jobs that are your perfect job but plenty of jobs your skills can be applied to.

Critical factors leading to success

- Confidence and being seen as composed
- Not only able to answer questions confidently but also able to put the replies into a personal context or illustrate with personal experience if possible
- Demonstrating a logical and considered thought process
- Looking the part—appropriate, professional appearance

Critical factors leading to people falling down at pathology and laboratory-based consultant interview

- Being unprepared and not sufficiently familiar with the post and person specifications
- Lack of knowledge about the Trust and/or department
- Unable to demonstrate the requisite competency
- Unable to demonstrate knowledge or understanding of management issues, e.g. staff issues, trainees in difficulty, and time and self-management

Key questions asked at pathology and laboratory-based specialty interviews

- How do you see yourself working in the specialty in 10 years time?
- With automated machines to carry out many laboratory functions, along with training of consultant BMS, is there a need for the laboratory clinician/consultant?
- If you are head of your pathology department and have been asked to make a 10% reduction in costs, what areas would you look at and why?
- Can the consultant BMS replace the laboratory clinician in the discipline?
- How important is pathology to the Trust as an income generator?

- How do you think the Darzi and Lord Carter reports will impact on how you deliver your service in the next 5–10 years?
- How do you think we need to change training for pathology trainees to make them the consultants of the future?
- Can you still have a clinical consultant who can be a laboratory doctor and physician as well?
- How important is it to maintain and measure the quality of the pathology services that we deliver?
- How would you manage the delivery of a 24-hour acute laboratory service within the Trust?

Common specialty-specific questions

- **Histopathology**: How would you deliver acute and specialist diagnostic services within the Trust?
- **Haematology**: Is the role of a laboratory doctor and physician feasible any more as a haematology consultant?
- **Chemical pathology and metabolic medicine**: How do you see your role in working with other specialities in the Trust?
- **Medical microbiology and virology and infectious diseases**: The specialty is changing in practice and training for the future—what impact will that have in the way you see yourself working on a daily basis?
- **Immunology**: You are already a rare breed of consultant/specialist—do you feel that the role of the immunology consultant is becoming redundant?

Typical ethical dilemmas

Haematology

- You are asked to see a Jehovah's Witness who is due to have an emergency laparotomy for a colonic obstruction and is already anaemic with an Hb of 9g/dl. How would you discuss options with this patient?
- You have been asked to deal with an SUI (serious untoward incident)—a patient has had extravasation of chemotherapy and has complained that she was not informed of this as a potential adverse event. How do you deal with this?

Histopathology

- How does the Human Tissue Act impact on the service and potential training using patient biopsy samples?
- You are concerned that one of your colleagues may not be reviewing all of her histology and indeed may be falsifying reports. What would you do?

Virology

- A junior member of staff has ordered a blood sample from a clinic patient for an HIV test without discussing it with the patient as the GP referral letter suggested this might be a possible differential diagnosis. The patient was unaware of this and the result is positive. How do you deal with this situation?

General

- You are concerned that one of your colleagues' reporting is not up to standard. What would you do?
- Your very-conscientious colleague is working up to 14 hours per day. You are concerned for her mental health. What would you do?

The radiology consultant interview

Dr Muaaze Ahmad, Consultant Musculoskeletal Radiologist, Barts and the London NHS Trust.

The interview panel

In addition to establishing competency in radiology practice, the interview panel often has two objectives.

Firstly, they want to identify if the candidate demonstrates an understanding of the role of radiology in the wider organization and that he/she understands the requirements. Prospective candidates need to be organized and meticulous, and be able to manage their time well. Problems such as staff shortages and large waiting lists need to be tackled. Innovative thinkers willing to lead changes to improve patient care and reduce waiting times will therefore stand out in the current climate.

Secondly, candidates are often required to demonstrate an interest in teaching and research. Opportunities in radiology research are extensive with emerging technologies. The ability to perform research and write is often explored by the panel. The increasing changes and requirements placed upon trainers supervising registrar trainees leads to focused questions to establish a prospective applicant's understanding and potential contribution to these aspects.

Psychology of the specialty

In common with many analytical or diagnostic specialties, radiology draws many individuals from the Island of Intellect. Methodical work requiring attention to detail defines the environment and the work can feel quite individual. However, radiologists are increasingly part of MDTs and have an input to many departments within a typical Trust. Finally interventional radiology attracts many Island of Opportunity individuals who previously have followed a career in surgery.

What does the panel want to see from a radiology consultant colleague?

Radiology has evolved over the last 30 years. It now plays a central role in the management of most patients across all specialties. This is in both elective and emergency settings, especially with the increasing role of interventional radiology in the management of patients. In addition, a number of clinical radiology meetings take place. Consequently, a clear communicator who is able to work closely with different teams to help deliver pathways for streamlined patient care is crucial.

The interview panel will also be very keen to establish if an applicant is able to demonstrate a clear understanding of their role. It is important for the successful candidate to be able to work as part of a team to deliver the Trust objectives in terms of managing lists and waiting times.

What is a consultant radiology interview like and how does it differ from other specialty interviews?

Radiology interviews do not usually test clinical knowledge. There is usually a review of training, to establish that the candidate is clinically able to take up the post. Following this, the majority of questions are to do with service management, teaching, research and ethical dilemmas.

What else might I commonly need to do as part of the interview process?

Increasingly at consultant interviews, candidates are asked to make a presentation lasting about 10 minutes. The topics can usually be divided into the following two broad areas:

- The future of radiology in the next 5 or 10 years
- How you will develop the specialty/subspecialty over the next 5 or 10 years

Helpful hints

It is important to visit the department and hospital and meet as many people in the department as possible. In researching a job, you need to know and understand how the department and wider hospital is performing, along with the hospital vision and aims. You need to understand, and at interview explain, how you can contribute to the departmental and/or wider hospital vision and objectives. This demonstrates a clear value and allows the interview panel to develop confidence that you are prepared to work for the achievement of these and other goals.

Critical factors leading to success

Preparation for the interview is vital for success. This includes an appropriate application and CV, as well as visiting the department and staff in the department prior to interview. This enables you to prepare for the interview and demonstrate an insight into the department and wider hospital.

A wider understanding of radiology in terms of outsourcing, teleradiology and private providers in the NHS is important to convey that you understand how you would shape services with the advent of changes around you.

Critical factors leading to people falling down at radiology consultant interview

Lack of knowledge about the job itself or lack of enthusiasm or interest in the department is likely to result in failure!

Key questions asked at radiology interviews

- Tell me about the strengths and weaknesses of your training so far
- What research have you done that has had the most impact on patients?
- How would you teach a group of medical students assigned to you for a week?
- What do you think about the extended role for radiographers?
- Describe your ideal radiology department
- What service, if any, would you consider introducing to the department?
- How do you ensure quality in the patient journey in radiology?
- How would you go about setting up a new service in the department?
- What would you like to change or improve about this department?
- Can you describe your experience of audit?

Common specialty-specific questions

- How will you keep up-to-date with general radiology?
- You find out that there are about 10 reports (not reported by you) that are incorrectly reported. What would you do?
- How do you measure quality in radiology?
- Do you see a role for outsourcing radiology in the NHS?
- What do you think of the NCEPOD (National Confidential Enquiry into Patient Outcome and Death) review of emergency admissions in relation to availability of radiology out of hours?

Typical ethical dilemmas

- You discover one of your colleagues has a screening time much longer in fluoroscopy than the average. What do you do?
- A follow-up radiological examination reveals a previously missed lesion. Do you tell the patient about the missed lesion?
- Do you accept hospitality from a manufacturer who is negotiating a contract to supply contrast agent or equipment to your Trust?

The surgical consultant interview

Mr Hiro Tanaka, Consultant Orthopaedic Surgeon, Royal Gwent Hospital.

The interview panel

'A physician does nothing and knows everything, a surgeon does everything and knows nothing.'

The single most important key to success in a surgical consultant interview is to establish rapport with the interview panel. A typical AAC panel consists of members who tend to be of an opportunistic personality type and includes the Chief Executive, Medical Director, Clinical Director and the Royal College assessor. Luckily most surgeons tend to fall into this category. Opportunistic individuals favour confident, determined, goal-orientated leaders.

Most successful candidates remember their interview as a series of conversations as opposed to an interrogation. Prior to entering the room, see the interview in your 'mind's eye' as a pleasant chat and this will be reflected positively in how you answer your questions.

In order to succeed you must understand what these individuals look for in a consultant surgeon. This can be broken down into three domains:

- Can you do the job? (competency)
- Will you do the job? (motivation)
- Will you fit into the department? (character)

Questions regarding these areas will be predictably asked by certain members, and whilst the question itself may vary, the focus will be the same.

Psychology of the specialty

When you consider the nature of the specialty it involves a high degree of very practical work in a pragmatic environment where there is an element of risk. That risk is mitigated by clear and decisive communication that is sometimes devoid of the sensibilities in favour of the pragmatism. Surgery is often a competitive environment and there is often a strong sense of professional rivalry between other services in the same specialty. All of this adds up to an environment that tends to draw more people from the Island of Opportunity than from other islands. This needs considering when answering questions. See Chapter 4.

What do the panel want to see from a consultant surgical colleague?

The best analogy to the strengths a panel looks for in a consultant surgeon is that of a submarine captain. They are consummate leaders of a team with the understanding that they cannot run the ship on their own. They impart confidence to the team by always knowing what to do even if they are not sure. They bear the burden of command and the responsibility to deliver upon a single goal. They are charismatic, likeable, respected and yet feared. Use this picture in your mind to guide your answers and behaviour during the interview.

The prerequisite characteristic of a surgeon is the ability to cope with stressful circumstances and maintain calm. Even though it may seem unforgiving, displays of nervousness during the interview reflect poorly. Practice is the key to avoiding this pitfall.

It is vital that you have a consolidated logbook of cases that you have performed and you have a broad idea of the number of cases you have performed in key index procedures. This will be the strongest evidence that the College Assessor will rely upon to make his or her judgement. The College Assessor may ask a clinical question relating to a complex emergency case. You must be mindful that the question is designed to determine whether you are aware of your clinical limitations. A newly appointed consultant must first and foremost be safe. Do not say you will take on everything.

What is a surgery consultant interview like and how does it differ from other specialty interviews?

The surgery consultant interview is fast-paced and dynamic. It should feel like a conversation between equals where that conversation might at times be perceived, by others, as challenging.

It is unusual in a surgical consultant interview to be asked direct clinical questions, though it is not unknown, especially by the College Assessor. These questions will probably relate directly to the specific area of surgery that the candidate has applied for and often encompass areas where there is significant debate as to the preferred management approach or where there are new innovative approaches to management.

What else might I commonly need to do as part of the interview process?

It is increasingly common for the interview process to start with a 10- to 15-minute presentation, candidates having been given the topic in advance. First impressions tend to last and the presentation is one of the most important aspects of your interview process and a poorly presented or prepared talk will not hold you in good stead. The presentation is an excellent reflection of your motivation, preparation and confidence. The panel members are more interested in your manner (body language, poise, delivery) than the content. Prepare for the talk well and follow instructions to the letter. Practise the talk in front of an audience multiple times until you can concentrate on the delivery rather than the content (I would strongly recommend around 10 times). Look each panel member in the eye whilst you are giving the talk and try not to rely on cue cards or notes. Learn how to use hand gestures, as this demonstrates confidence. The key to a successful presentation is style.

Helpful hints

Surgery is often the income powerhouse of a Trust and the panel will want to know how you will enhance their business, income and reputation. This can mean multiple things. Firstly, how will you enhance their ability to deliver on their business agenda? Secondly, what do you bring to the table that they don't already have but want? What makes you valuable to them? Think about how you will impress or excite them. If this is consistent with their service strategy then you are half way there. It's important to find out what you can in advance.

The Clinical Director's questions are critical and will focus on whether your expertise is in keeping with the needs of the department. Be mindful that you do not oversell yourself. The department will have a predetermined clinical need and it is essential you know this in advance and demonstrate how you fulfil that need. You may have fellowship training in a highly specialized procedure, but one of the common failures is to suggest that you will be expecting to develop a new and expensive service when the department has no need for it. The key is to explore the department's needs in advance and use this as a guide as to what best sells you as the candidate of choice. If you are expected to set up a new service, then you will be asked how you will achieve this. If you know this, it is important to have a confident answer as to how you would establish this.

Critical factors leading to success

- Dress smartly but conservatively
- Practise your interview technique and presentation
- Concentrate on maximizing your body language to reflect your clinical answers
- Keep nerves under control and establish rapport with all the panel members
- Smile and look each panel member in the eye
- Be clear what type of colleague the service or Trust is looking for

Critical factors leading to people falling down at the consultant surgeon interview

- Not understanding what type of surgeon the department is looking for clinically
- Insisting on offering a service that is not needed by the department
- Criticizing the Trust or department (in a non-constructive manner)
- Not answering the questions directly or refusing to give an opinion
- Excessive display of nerves

Key questions asked at surgical interviews

- How do you know you have been fully trained?
- Why did you apply for this job? What is your special interest in this department?
- What are your greatest strengths?
- What will you bring to the hospital?
- If appointed, how will we know in a year's time that we have made the correct decision?
- What are your plans for professional development over the next year?
- How will you set up your service?
- What strategies would you employ to address the current waiting list problem?
- Give an example of evidence-based medicine and how you have applied it to your practice
- How would you improve the quality of training/research of the junior staff in the department?
- What is the purpose of 'payment by results'?

Common specialty-specific questions

- What are your views of specialty training in the independent sector?
- Do you think surgical trainees should be part of hospital-at-night?
- Should we offer surgery to smokers?
- Should we operate on overweight and obese patients?
- Does Darzi have anything to offer surgeons?
- How would you instruct established consultants when operating using new surgery/ techniques?

- What is your niche surgical interest?
- What are your views on centralization for small-volume complex surgery?
- What are your views on the demise of the general surgeon?
- What do you know about 18-week targets?
- What are the problems and conflicts within the 18-week targets for surgical specialities/patients?
- How would you go about improving theatre efficiency?
- Surgical activity is expensive. There are a lot of outgoings. What do you need to consider when 'balancing the books'?
- How would you go about improving surgical throughput?
- What are your views on treatment centres?
- What are the pros and cons of trauma centres?
- What are your views on EWTD and surgical training?
- How do you maintain surgical training within the confines of EWTD?
- Do you agree with the Royal College of Surgeons lobbying for an increase in the number of hours for surgical trainees within EWTD? Why?
- What are your views on specialty training in the independent sector?
- What will your surgical practice be like in 10 years time?
- How would you counsel a patient asking for surgery in x?
- My mother needs an operation on her x. In the current climate of 'league tables' how do you show the general population that you are the best person for the job?
- Are mortality rates a good way of comparing one surgeon with another?
- How should we measure surgical outcomes?
- What aspects of clinical governance are particularly important in surgery? Why? How would you go about addressing them? What support can the Trust provide for you?
- What is your worst surgical nightmare and how did you deal with it?
- What is your complication rate? How do you assess it?
- How would you develop laparoscopic services in x?
- Do we have everything required to run a good x service?
- What is your opinion on procedure x? (This sort of question is usually asked where there may be a range of opinions.)

Urology

- How would you develop laparoscopic services?
- Do we have everything required to run a good 'stone' service?
- What sort of 'beast' will urology be in 10 years time? What will urology be like in this hospital in 10 years time?

Vascular surgery

- What is your opinion on carotid artery stenting?
- Do you think that EVAR (endovascular aneurysm repair) is a safe procedure? Should we be doing it to patients over open AAA (abdominal aortic aneurysm) repair?

- How would you tackle a carotid endarterectomy with a high bifurcation?
- Should we offer vascular surgery to smokers?

Ethical dilemmas in surgery

- Tell me about an occasion where you conformed to a policy with which you did not agree. What did you do to address your concerns?
- You have concerns about the clinical performance of a colleague (his hip dislocation rate is 10%). What will you do?
- You wish to cancel a patient from your elective list for an urgent trauma case, but all the patients are 'breachers'. What will you do?
- A 22-year-girl has been involved in an RTA. There is significant blood loss and she needs a transfusion. Her boyfriend tells you she is a Jehovah's Witness. What would you do?

Chapter 11
Presentations in interviews

Introduction

It is increasingly common at consultant interviews to be asked to make a presentation. Presentations enable others to observe a variety of skills deemed necessary to be an effective consultant, including:

- Clear communications skills
- Teaching skills
- Ability to confer potentially complex information in a clear and succinct way
- Ability to engage, influence and persuade
- Ability to organize your thoughts and to develop:
  - rapport
  - a cohesive argument
  - conclusions
- Your ability to inspire others
- Ability to remain calm and relaxed in a stressful situation

It is important from the outset to understand that it is these attributes that are being examined, not the panel's burning desire to increase their knowledge in your chosen subject. Consequently, the enabling question you need to ask yourself is *not* 'What content would be interesting?' but 'How can I demonstrate the above attributes most successfully through the presentation I have been asked to give?' This latter question should direct the content, style and approach you take.

Format of presentations

Presentations at consultant interview can take a variety of formats:

- PowerPoint presentation to a larger audience prior to the interview
- PowerPoint presentation to the interview panel immediately before the interview
- Presentation without visual aids to the interview panel immediately before the interview
- Rarely interviewees are given a short period of time (e.g. 30 minutes) to prepare a presentation, usually to the interview committee only, immediately prior to their interview

The format does not alter the primary purpose—which is to assess those 'consultant attributes or qualities' that we mention above in the Introduction—but will affect how you go about your preparation and delivery.

Key topics

Topics are not always easy to predict but will often relate to something that is currently troubling the consultant body or Trust, i.e. is topical and relevant. Examples include:

- With cuts to training numbers how would you ensure this department meets the EWTD requirements?
- What will be the effects of the government White Paper on this service?

- How can service x work more effectively across primary and secondary care?
- How could our services be delivered in a community setting?
- How would you ensure the survival of our service?
- What is the role of clinical networks in x?
- Should NICE influence how we treat our patients?

Sometimes, interview panels ask for presentation on you personally, i.e. they provide you with a direct opportunity to really sell yourself. Typical questions or topics for this include:

- What difference will you make to this hospital?
- Why should we give you this job?
- What added value will you bring to the Trust?

It is these latter questions that are often given just before the interview and, consequently, it is vital that you undertake a thorough, prior preparation, as suggested in Chapter 5, focusing on how to match your best attributes to the goals or needs of the Trust you are applying to.

How do presentations influence the interview process?

Much depends on whether the presentation is a formal part of the interview process or held separately, prior to the interview. We'll consider each in turn.

If the presentations are held as a separate event prior to the interview, they are unlikely to have a significant and direct impact on selection at the interview itself. However, they are used as a way of getting a broader opinion on your overall suitability and to gain a wider perspective on a candidate's 'fit' with the service, and so they do contribute to the overall 'feeling' of whether you are the right person or not. Often the Chair of the selection committee will ask the members of the audience whether they have any specific concerns about a candidate as a result of their presentation. Additionally, they may ask members of the audience whether they think specific questions should be asked at interview to further explore any particular issues.

If the presentation is done as part of the interview then it will definitely count as part of the selection process. The usual format is for the presentation to be done at the start of the interview. Usually, you will then be asked questions on your presentation before the panel moves into the interview itself. In this sequence, it is important to remember that the quality of your presentation and the manner in which you answer the questions will all provide an initial impression that will influence the panel further on. For instance, if you have been particularly impressive, subconsciously the panel will be now predisposed to seeing you as impressive and will consequently look for evidence to support that viewpoint. The flip side of this is that if you have not performed well, they may well be looking for evidence that you won't perform well in other scenarios too. The impact of this early event means that interview presentations do require very careful attention to preparation and delivery.

Developing an effective presentation

It would be nice to be provided with the title and some guidance with weeks to spare in which you can fully research and prepare. However, the ideal and life rarely match up and this is no exception. Typically, you may only be given a week's notice of your topic title and so, once you have it, you do need to get on and prepare swiftly. Consequently, this means it is essential that you are well ahead with the rest of your interview preparation so that when you get the presentation title you can then devote all of your efforts to it.

There are three key stages to the development of highly effective presentations. These are described in Box 11.1.

Phase 1—Planning and research

This is the most important phase as everything else follows and relies on the work done here. The planning and research phase is characterized by clearly defining your objectives in a distinct form and analysing your audience. By being explicitly clear on your objectives, you can ensure that everything in your presentation is pertinent and valuable. By gaining a thorough understanding of your audience, you can ensure that you tailor, word and deliver your presentation so that it has maximum impact for the right people. At this stage, from a practical standpoint, it is also worth reviewing the details you have been sent about your presentation, including:

- Presentation timings (usually 5 or 10 minutes)
- Guidance on the use of slides, e.g. how many slides, format/version information
- Anything they have told you about the audience (who)
- Specific information on the purpose of the presentation (it's rare to get this)

> **Box 11.1 Key stages in the development of effective presentations**
>
> - Phase 1—Planning and research
>   - Clarify your objectives
>   - Understand your audience
>   - Research your topic
> - Phase 2—Building
>   - Structure your message
>   - Decide on your key points
>   - Put an opening and closing statement together
>   - Decide on supplementary material
> - Phase 3—Delivery
>   - Prepare yourself as a speaker
>   - Practise your delivery
>   - Get yourself into a confident state to present

Objectives

Your primary objectives are just that—the objective of your presentation. They are rarely about educating someone in the topic they have given you! They are more closely related to what you want the audience to do as a result of the presentation or what you are trying to achieve by delivering the presentation. To better understand this we use an influencing model known as:

- THINK
- FEEL
- DO

Starting with the 'do', consider what it is that you want to happen as a result of your presentation. In most cases, the purpose of your presentation is to ensure that your audience wants to appoint you as their consultant colleague. This is a little simplified and you could provide more specificity to this by adding a presentation-specific element to it. For instance, this might sound like 'to hold me as the candidate of choice because of my articulate reasoning'. Clearly the key is to know what is likely to make the audience appoint you. We want you to think very carefully about this and consider whether they are likely to appoint simply because of your knowledge in the presentation subject—unlikely!

Once you have defined *exactly* what you want your audience to do, you need to consider what they need to 'think' and 'feel' that will make them 'do' the automatic course of action. To answer this question correctly, you will need to consider:

- The audience
- The type of job you are applying for, e.g. academic vs teaching hospital vs DGH
- Key words used in the job description to describe the type of colleague wanted, areas of expertise, etc.

The objective or objectives should be a natural extension of the goal, coupled to the audience and the job. Let's say that you are applying for an academic post and your future professor will be in the audience. You should approach this as follows:

- What do I want my future professor to *do*?
  - Believe that I would contribute much to the academic success of the department and therefore be the best choice
- What must they *think* and *feel* to automatically do this?
  - That I am highly productive and can conduct excellent quality, high-value research
  - That I am competitive, seeking out high-impact-factor journals
  - That I bring something else to the department that is additive to what's already there
  - That I am a goal-driven, results-orientated individual but with a sense of perfection too

You can then test this out by putting yourself in their shoes and asking yourself 'If I thought and felt those things, would I appoint this person?' When you can answer 'definitely' then you have your objectives!

Armed with these objectives, you can now work out what to put into the presentation and what to leave out. If it helps deliver on the primary objectives then it goes in and if it doesn't then it's 'baggage' and can only act as a distraction. This helps keep you focused and adds specificity to the content of your presentation.

Audience

It is vital that you find out who will be in the audience for your presentation. If you have not been provided with this information, contact the Medical Staffing officer to find out who will be in attendance. Frequently, presentations are to mixed groups of people who might include executive directors, non-executive directors, staff at all levels within your speciality and even individuals from related specialities. However, the audience could easily consist of entirely nursing staff or the specific team you would work with if you were appointed, including administrative staff and secretaries. It is not uncommon to have an audience made up of patients or user groups. This will, of course, significantly alter your presentation focus and style. Once you have a clear picture of who will be in attendance, break them down into key players and other significant individuals, and consider their roles and context, their psychological group or island and any specific interests or purpose they are likely to have. It's critical to think about what this means to your presentation.

When you come to write your presentation you will need to put yourself firmly in the shoes of your audience and think about what they specifically would need to 'think' and 'feel' to appoint you to the consultant post. Building on this, you might want to consider the answers to the following questions, each of which will give you a greater understanding of how you need to pitch your presentation:

- Why are they attending my presentation (what's their role)?
- What do they hope to gain or what are they looking for?
- What are their natural feelings, concerns, issues and needs likely to be?
- Why should this audience listen to and appoint me?
- How will or could they personally benefit from what I have to say?

USEFUL TIP: A presentation that does not connect with your audience's world will never be a good presentation—you must diagnose your audience and tailor your presentation accordingly.

Researching the presentation topic

When researching the presentation topic do not forget to ask your present departmental lead and consultant for their thoughts and ideas. They may well be able to give you a perspective on why this topic has been set. If the topic is controversial, brainstorm the various debates with your registrar colleagues or meet with your current consultant to discuss the issues and arguments. Specifically, consider what flashpoints or areas of disagreement exist so that you may be extra careful when dealing with them. When you have completed your research stage take time to decide what message you want your audience to take from your presentation and how this delivers on your primary objectives.

Take-home message

The take-home message is the essence of your talk captured in a few words and primarily used as the closing statement. It is different from the summary in that its purpose is to leave the presentation on a high and the audience firmly thinking along the lines of your primary objective. A good way to think about this is:

- If you only had 30 seconds in which to deliver your whole presentation what would you say?
- What is the essence of your whole presentation in a single sentence?
- What message, above all else, do you want the audience to take away?

Another useful way of thinking about this is as the 'elevator pitch' of your presentation. This is often described as being shut in a lift with somebody rich and famous. You have just seven floors to get your message across and cause them to act in a certain way. What would you say? It's a really useful discipline for ensuring that you can succinctly deliver messages that have impact.

Phase 2—Building

Before you begin to build your presentation effectively you need to be clear on both your primary objectives (think, feel, do) and your take-home message, otherwise you risk filling your presentation with information that not only is not valuable but also may in fact distract from what you need to be demonstrating. As you construct the presentation keep asking yourself:

- Does what I am saying contribute to either my primary objective or my take-home message?
- If you cannot see the link then ask yourself whether you should be including that item

Take the relevant information and fit it into an appropriate structure for the presentation.

Structure of a presentation

When writing your presentation, remember that all formal presentations, whatever their duration, should have the same overall structure, as follows:

- Opening
- Overview
- Key idea 1
- Transition
- Further key ideas
- Recap or summary
- Close (take-home message)

It is best not to depart from this too much. If you try to make it too different or clever, you are leaving yourself open to very variable opinions on whether it works or not. Equally, you don't really want to be remembered for the quirkiness of your presentation. It's what you say and deliver that counts.

> **USEFUL TIP:** Concentrate on the beginning and end of your presentation. It is what your audience will remember most.

Opening

When constructing your presentation, leave writing your opening to last, as you will benefit from knowing what has gone into it and why. It is important to recognize that the beginning of a presentation is not so much about opening the presentation itself but more about opening up your audience so that they want to become engaged in your presentation and subject matter.

It is often said that you have around 5 seconds to get an audience's attention and then just 30 seconds to develop their interest and curiosity sufficiently that they will remain with you for the duration. That's quite a challenge and therefore your opening must focus on getting your audience engaged as quickly as possible. By leaving the writing of this to the end you will have a much clearer idea of where you want to start people so that they are hooked into your topic from the outset. When you have decided on your opening, analyse it carefully:

- Is it relevant to the audience?
- Is it relevant to the presentation?
- Does it fit with your objectives?

A bad way to open a presentation

Good morning, I am Dr Peter Jones. I am a final-year registrar in paediatrics with a special interest in paediatric gastroenterology. I am presently working at St Elsewhere's with Drs Smith and Williams.

Better ways to open a presentation

You may want to try one of these ways (but not all of them at once):

- Ask a provocative question
- Stress the benefits to the audience of listening to your talk
- Tell a story (preferably a human-interest one), but only if it is aligned with your objectives and take-home message
- Start with an interesting or unusual fact
- Arouse curiosity by asking a rhetorical question
- Use a prop, e.g. a newspaper (this gives your audience something to look at, which is a very good way of gaining attention, as it is likely to contribute to them recalling your presentation each time they see a newspaper!)
- Use a topical reference from the media, but only if it is relevant to your presentation

Do not worry about formally introducing yourself, as someone else will already have done this and you don't want to waste precious seconds telling the audience something they already know.

Overview

Briefly outline your talk, giving an insight into the theme and structure of your presentation. This lets the audience know what to expect during the presentation, demonstrates you have thought carefully and enhances your credibility as a speaker. In your overview, it is important to reinforce the benefits of your presentation rather than simply delivering a factual agenda, e.g. 'I will cover the psychology of presenting so that you can tailor your presentations more accurately for individuals'.

Key ideas

A generally successful formula for short presentations is to have at least one but not more than three key ideas. Most people can only remember around three key points from a presentation and anything beyond this could be overload. If you include too many ideas the important messages may not be remembered or could be hidden in the volume of information delivered to your audience. In this situation, your presentation may fail to deliver the impact you intended.

It is very important when presenting to start with the big picture and to get your key messages across up front. This is counter to most people's training in presentations, but we advocate this because a proportion of your audience (often those in senior leadership and management roles—the decision-makers) will, by nature, only have a short attention span and may miss your key ideas and messages if you leave them until later on. If you get the key messages in early, even if they switch off thereafter, they have got the crux of the matter.

Once you have presented a key message, you will need to substantiate it with the evidence, anecdotes and other information elicited during your preparation. Try to create your argument in digestible bits by identifying key segments within your idea. Consider using examples, metaphors, quotations, statistical data, props, visual aids, anecdotes and critical commentary to further reinforce your message. Always remember to ask yourself 'Do they really need to know this to think and feel what I need them to?'

Transitions

Top-notch presenters make the transitions between points virtually seamless. Ideally, you need to move from one key point to another without people being aware of the join in between. A good way of doing this is to:

- Recap on the previous segment (thus reinforcing your message)
- Include/create a reason for moving on

An example might be '. . . and in conclusion we now see the importance of prior planning, whose stages we will now examine in more detail'.

Recap or summary

In just the same way you would when answering interview questions, it is important to summarize the key points of your presentation, as this repetition aids recall later on.

The best presenters find ways of telling their audience what they have heard but explaining it in a different way. This keeps things fresh and interesting whilst giving two perspectives towards a single goal. It can be useful at this stage to reinforce the benefits of the presentation for the audience.

Closing

The close of your presentation should be brief, catchy and memorable to ensure you stand out from the other interviewees. Effective closing statements are powerful and influencing. Consider both your primary objective (think, feel, do) and your take-home message when constructing this. You want your audience to be left in a positive mood, feeling good, wanting to know more and wanting to appoint you.

Key tips on developing your presentation can be found in Box 11.2 and on using PowerPoint in Box 11.3.

Phase 3—Delivery

You do not want to be turning up on the day of your presentation with the delivery left to chance and so it is vital that you have an opportunity to practise. Ideally, you need to have your presentation ready for a run-through 2–3 days prior to the interview or presentation day. Aim to practise it in front of your present consultant colleagues and

---

Box 11.2 Key tips for developing your presentation

- Sixty percent of the UK population process information in a visual way. Use pictures, diagrams and schemata to reinforce your messages
- Repetition is important if you want your message to be heard so find novel ways of repeating it without appearing to!
- Your audience's concentration will be highest at the beginning and end of your presentation. Make sure you get your key messages across at these points
- Do not overload people with too much information—the brain is limited in capacity to process and store information
- Every great presentation contains:
  - At least one, but not more than three, key ideas
  - Each key idea has around three supporting points
    - Metaphors and anecdotes
    - Hard evidence, data and statistics
    - Stories and examples
- Beware of your own knowledge. It is quite rare for someone to complain that a presentation was too short but very common for people to complain there was too much information. Only tell your audience what they need to know not everything you know
- Do not underestimate how long your presentation will take. Most interview panels will hold you strictly to time. If you get stopped early, you will have missed your opportunity to close effectively

Box 11.3 Key PowerPoint tips

- Limit the number of slides—no more than one a minute
- Keep it simple—avoid PowerPoint overload. The purpose of a presentation at interview is never to demonstrate you know how to use the 'build' function
- Use a single, commonly used font, e.g. Arial or Times Roman
  - If not, the presentation which looks excellent on your home computer may look poorly formatted on the hospital computer which does not carry your font
  - Although you could load any special fonts onto the seminar room computer when you load your presentation, it's one more thing to worry about and many hospital computers will not always allow you to do this. This is too big a risk to take
- A smaller font size with increased line spacing will often look much better than a large font size
- No more than 6 lines of the same font size per slide
- No more than 8 words per line
- Consider a simple background—white is very effective
- Create a visual path, use arrows, justify or centre text
- Use punchy phrases rather than whole sentences. Do not write down everything you are going to present
- Use pictures, simple diagrams and schemata where possible
  - Remember, the majority of your audience will process information in a visual way
- Save your presentation as a PowerPoint 97-2003 version rather than a more modern version of PowerPoint (we can't express how catastrophic it is to find your presentation won't play)
  - This way you will be able to guarantee being able to open it on the day

ask them about its impact and effect. However, rather than asking your audience 'How good was it?' it is important to get feedback on what it did and what they took away from it. For example, ask 'What do you remember from my presentation?' or 'What key messages will you take away from my presentation?' This will give you a much clearer idea on whether you are getting your message across.

Do not over-practise your presentation or you will rapidly learn it by heart. This can come across as being 'read' on the day, which is likely to be boring rather than dynamic. It could also suggest to people that you find presenting fearful.

> **USEFUL TIP**: When practising your presentation, rather than asking your audience 'Was my presentation OK?' ask them:
> - 'What key message did you take away from my presentation?'
> - 'What opinion did you make of me as a result of my presentation?'

Box 11.4 looks at key audiovisual considerations when practising your presentation which, if not considered in advance, can cause candidates to stumble on the day.

Should you use notes?

Not everyone is a natural presenter and presenting as part of the consultant interview can be particularly nerve-racking. Many very experienced presenters use notes and it will not be held against you if you decide to do the same. However, it is important that your notes do not become a script which you just read or a distraction from you the presenter.

To help prevent this and to make your notes practical and easy to use, utilize A5 or smaller key cards. Avoid using A4 paper, which will accentuate any shaking in your hands that you have from nerves (the paper will rustle). Only write key phrases or headings on your key cards (see Box 11.5, second example) and do not fall into the trap of writing down the whole presentation, as this becomes a script that you might read. More importantly, you will not be able to access the important information easily when you need to and this can contribute to greater nerves, rather than fewer.

Making delivery professional

Moving professionally around the presentation equipment will enhance your standing as a presenter and consequently as a consultant. Make sure you fully understand how to get back to where you were, if you should happen to accidentally move off your intended slide (nerves can make this a common accident).

If you are going to speak for a few minutes without using a slide or you wish particularly that the audience concentrates on what you are saying, use the 'B' key in full presentation mode to black the screen. Pressing 'B' again brings back the presentation. Calmly and smoothly integrated into your presentation, it firmly delivers the message that presenting is second nature to you.

Box 11.6 highlights additional important recommendations when delivering your presentation.

On the day

Key to reducing nerves is having nothing to worry about beyond actually delivering the presentation. Being a bit over-prepared in this regard is actually helpful. Always carry multiple copies of your presentation in multiple formats, for instance:

- On a memory stick (or even two)
- On a CD/DVD
- On your laptop
- Hard copies for the audience
- Consider emailing a copy of your presentation to the person organizing the presentations or even to yourself to download if necessary

When you name your presentation, avoid calling it 'Interview Presentation' or the title you have been given. If there are four candidates, you may find yourself fishing

Box 11.4 Key points when practising your presentations

- Try doing it both with your laptop in front of you and without it
  - Many presenters are dysfunctioned by not being able to see their computer screen, thus having to rely on the projected image for prompting
  - When you do not have a computer screen to rely on make sure you do not
    - Block the projection
    - Turn your back on your audience
    - Read your slides
- If possible, practise in front of a mirror
  - Ensure you make eye contact with yourself
  - Assess whether your manner is engaging
- Try recording or videoing yourself
  - Use your laptop camera or microphone
  - If you have a video camera and a tripod, use this
  - Your phone probably records video
  - Critically appraise how you came across

through the presentations to work out which one is yours. A good discipline, which helps demonstrate you think, is to name it using the following convention:

Your Name—Time—Date—Short Title

This might look like:

John Smith—1430—21 January 20XX—White Paper

Box 11.5 Presentation notes

Poor set of notes

Good morning, ladies and gentlemen. I am Dr Smith. I have been asked to talk on my views of the Coalition Government's White Paper for the NHS which was published on 12th June 2010 by Andrew Lansley, the Secretary of State for Health. I am going to look at the paper from three perspectives; the opportunities I believe it offers, the problems I see, and what this means for paediatrics.

Good set of notes

- **Opening** *Daily Mail* 13th June
- **Primary objectives** Effect of White Paper on paediatrics at St Elsewhere's
- **3 Key opportunities and threats**
- **What this means** Baby Jones's story
- **Take-home messages**
  - Whilst some will fight internally about this being wrong, others will gain momentum and make it work for their patients and their service
  - We must not allow ourselves to be left behind

> **Box 11.6 Key points when presenting**
>
> - Remember your open and close
> - Do not read either the slides or your notes
> - If you wish to use a pointer:
>   - Take your own, with new batteries in it
>   - Practise using it in advance (remember, if you are nervous a pointer will accentuate this)
>   - Do not assume you will be able to use the mouse on the computer to point things out
> - Take your time
>   - Reinforce your key messages by slowing down when presenting them
> - Make good eye contact with the audience, especially the key people
> - Speak with conviction and confidence

If somebody else is loading the presentations then it makes their job a cinch. Nothing like being helpful to engender the right feelings from the start!

Additional tips for being prepared

- Make sure you arrive early for the presentation—there's nothing worse than being sat in traffic worrying about being late
- If it is being done outside of the interview process, e.g. in a separate location, ask to see the room and the equipment in advance
- If you do not know how to use the audiovisuals, ask for a demonstration
- Load your presentation onto the desktop and make sure it opens correctly
- Consider where you will stand to deliver your presentation
- Consider where you will put your notes if you have them

Presentation nerves

Public speaking features in the top three greatest fears of the population. It is therefore quite natural to feel a little nervous before your presentation. Make sure you have some water with you to drink and follow the advice in Chapter 6 for calming your nerves. In particular, the following methods are great for both interview questions and presentations:

- Visualization—a mental run-through of the presentation going brilliantly
- Diaphragmatic breathing just before you start
- Asking enabling questions, e.g. how can I best help this audience understand my key points?

The more you can relax because you are well prepared and have controlled for the typical problems people face, the more confident you will sound (and feel) and the better it will go. Good luck (not that you'll need it if you follow the advice!).

Chapter 12
Psychometric testing in interviews

Introduction

Psychometric testing is widely used outside medicine as part of an employee selection process, although its use has attracted a great deal of criticism too. In the NHS, psychometric tests are often used for selection of mangers and a growing number of Trusts are now using psychometric testing as part of the consultant interview process. This chapter looks at the implications of this and at some of the more commonly known tools.

Psychometric tests include personality tests, e.g. Myers—Briggs and Insights, as well as aptitude tests designed to assess an individual's general logical ability, and verbal, numerical and technical reasoning. Aptitude tests are thought to be more accurate in predicting job performance than personality tests but have not been widely used in medicine. The tools used within medicine tend to look at a person's personality, how they behave within teams and how they respond to conflict.

Some of the more commonly used tools are:

- Myers—Briggs Type Indicator® (MBTI®)
- 16 Personality Factor (16PF®)
- Insights Discovery® Personality Profile (Insights)
- Fundamental Interpersonal Relations Orientation (FIRO-B®)
- Thomas—Kilmann Conflict Mode Instrument (TKI)
- Strength Deployment Inventory® (SDI®)

Two of these tools, MBTI and SDI, explicitly state that they should not be used as part of a selection process. However, they are increasingly being used, driven by the advice of unqualified or unscrupulous behavioural consultants!

What should I do if asked to sit a test?

You are who you are. Do not panic and do not try to work out what the panel want when answering questions about your personality. In general you will only get it wrong! The outcome of your assessment will not be you and the person you appear to be may be less suited for the job than the real you. Equally, this is not something you can practise—you can't really 'get good' at something that is designed to simply show the real you!

It's also worth remembering that if the panel members are determined to employ someone you are not, ask yourself whether you would be happy in the role. You should be seeing your consultant post as a long-term appointment, and although it is possible to manipulate the answers, if the result is being stuck in a job you hate because it was designed for someone different then this is not really a win.

Myers—Briggs Type Indicator (MBTI)

Most doctors have heard of Myers—Briggs and many have been through the Myers—Briggs process to identify their personality 'Type'. MBTI can be very useful in many areas of behaviour, including career counselling and guidance, as well as developing greater insight into your own behaviour to improve your interaction with others. However, it is not designed to help decide who should be appointed to a specific post and, indeed, trained MBTI facilitators are taught explicitly that it should not be used as part of selection processes. This does not mean that this does not happen!

The MBTI assessment is a psychometric questionnaire designed to measure psychological preferences in how people perceive the world and make decisions. If you have not been through a formal Myers—Briggs process it is important to be aware that your 'Best-Fit Type' is only identified as a result of both completing the Myers—Briggs questionnaire and by self-reflection with the support of a trained facilitator. This self-reflection is unlikely to be offered as part of a selection process and it is very common for the self-reflection element to amend your 'final' type.

> **USEFUL TIP:** You should not be asked to do Myers—Briggs as part of a selection process. If you are, you may want to gently probe whether you will get the opportunity to agree your Best-Fit Type and how the information will be used.

MBTI is based on Jungian psychology and identifies your personality type based on your preference for each of four dichotomies (see Box 12.1).

It is important to be aware that the definition of some of these dichotomies, e.g. extrovert and introvert, are somewhat different to the normal English-language definition. As a result there are 16 distinct types of personality, each of which comes with natural strengths or affinities and each of which has elements that an individual needs to be aware of.

MBTI does not predict behaviour reliably, as people have a choice of how to use their preferences, and it does not predict competence. A person may have his or her inborn or emerged preferences, but the behaviour he/she utilizes is situational. It is because of this fact that it should not be used to select candidates for a specific job. At best it will give an indication of someone's general preference for a working environment and how they might naturally fit in with others, but as having a whole department of like-wired people is a poor strategic choice anyway, it is more likely to lead to inappropriate choices than appropriate ones.

Practicalities

The MBTI questionnaire takes 15–20 minutes to complete, although there is no time limit for completing it. It can be done as both a paper and an online questionnaire. Done properly, with self-reflection to reach a Best-Fit Type, it takes an additional hour with a trained facilitator.

16 Personality Factors (16PF)

Unlike MBTI, 16PF has been designed to play a major role in selection and recruitment. Derived by psychologist Raymond Cattell, the 16PF personality questionnaire

> **Box 12.1 Myers—Briggs dichotomies**
>
> | | | | |
> |---|---|---|---|
> | **E-I**: Where you prefer to get and focus your 'energy' or attention | **Extraversion (E)** Prefers to draw energy from the outer world of activity, people and things | OR | **Introversion (I)** Prefers to draw energy from the inner world of reflections, feelings and ideas |
> | **S-N**: The kind of information you prefer to gather and trust | **Sensing (S)** Prefers to focus on information gained from the five senses and on practical applications | OR | **iNtuition (N)** Prefers to focus on patterns, connections and possible meanings |
> | **T-F**: The process you prefer to use in evaluating information and coming to decisions | **Thinking (T)** Prefers to base decisions on logic and objective analysis of cause and effect | OR | **Feeling (F)** Prefers to base decisions on a valuing process, considering what is important to people |
> | **J-P**: How you prefer to deal with the world around you, your 'lifestyle' | **Judging (J)** Likes a planned, organized approach to life, and prefers to have things decided | OR | **Perceiving (P)** Likes a flexible, spontaneous approach and prefers to keep options open |

measures a set of 16 traits that describe and predict a person's behaviour in a variety of contexts. 16PF provides comprehensive information about a candidate's:

- Personality
- Potential
- Capacity to sustain performance in a larger role

Additionally it helps identify individual development needs and so could provide guidance on how to support individuals on entry to new posts.

Over 70 years of research has gone into 16PF. This research has shown it to be useful in predicting behaviour in a range of settings. Used properly as part of a selection process 16PF should point an interview panel to where they should focus their questioning and probing of each individual candidate.

16PF consists of 185 multiple-choice items which ask about actual behavioural situations to determine scores against 16 key normal adult personality dimensions. These scores range between two extremes of each trait. For example, for the personality trait of Privateness, scores may range anywhere from 0 (Forthright/Candid) to

> **Box 12.2 Personality traits measured by 16PF**
>
> - Warmth
> - Reasoning
> - Emotional stability
> - Dominance
> - Liveliness
> - Rule-consciousness
> - Social boldness
> - Sensitivity
> - Vigilance
> - Abstractedness
> - Privateness
> - Apprehensiveness
> - Openness to change
> - Self-reliance
> - Perfectionism
> - Tension

10 (Discreet/Private). In addition, scores for five Global Factors are computed. The traits measured by the 16PF document are shown in Box 12.2.

Five Global Factors can be revealed from the 16PF questionnaire. These describe personality at a broader level. These Global Factors, which help to show the degree of relationships among the 16 primary scales, are:

- Extraversion
- Anxiety
- Tough-mindedness
- Independence
- Self-control

Practicalities

The test itself consists of 185 multiple-choice items and usually takes 30–50 minutes to perform.

Insights Discovery Personality Profile (Insights)

Correctly known as Insights Discovery Personality Profile, Insights is a personality tool that helps individuals and teams understand more about themselves and others. In particular, individuals gain understanding of how their personality affects themselves and their relationships, both at home and professionally. It gives greater understanding of your natural strengths, weaknesses and communication style. It helps you understand the contribution you make to a team and your natural leadership and management style.

Insights is marketed to be used within the selection process. Like 16PF, the findings of the assessment should point a selection panel to where they should focus their questioning. Indeed, the Insights report done in the context of selection provides the panel with a list of questions to be explored with the candidate to 'probe and stretch' in distinct areas.

Practicalities

Candidates complete a 25-frame online evaluator. This usually takes 15–20 minutes. Based on this the panel receive a 20–40 page report, including a page on what should be specifically raised within the interview process.

Fundamental Interpersonal Relations Orientation (FIRO-B)

The Fundamental Interpersonal Relations Orientation (FIRO-B) instrument is a personality questionnaire focusing on how individuals behave towards others, and how they expect others to behave towards them, especially within the context of a small group. It can reveal mismatches between wanted and expressed behaviour.

The tool, which was developed to assess how teams behaved in the US Navy, looks at individuals' preferences in satisfying three basic social needs:

- **Inclusion**
  - The degree to which one belongs to a group, team or community
- **Control**
  - The extent to which one prefers to have structure, hierarchy and influence
- **Affection**
  - One's preference for warmth, disclosure and intimacy

For each preference, individuals are scored on how much they want this need from others and how much they express this need towards others.

FIRO-B is marketed for use in the selection process. However, as a tool it is particularly useful in exploring the reasons behind difficult and complex relations when other psychometric tools have failed to reveal this.

Scores are graded from 0–9 in scales of expressed and wanted behaviour for each need.

Practicalities

FIRO-B is both an online and a paper-based tool where individuals are presented with 54 statements which they either agree or disagree with. For each need area the individual statements in the questionnaire appear very similar. By agreeing or disagreeing with each statement the individual develops a score out of 9 for each social need from both an expressed and a wanted perspective.

Thomas—Kilmann Conflict Mode Instrument

This tool measures an individual's response to conflict situations. Conflict situations are described as those in which the concerns of two people appear to be incompatible. An individual's behaviour in conflict is described along two dimensions:

- **Assertiveness**
  - The extent to which the person attempts to satisfy his or her own concerns
- **Cooperativeness**
  - The extent to which the person attempts to satisfy the other person's concerns

These two basic dimensions allow the definition of five different types of behaviour in response to a conflict situation (see Box 12.3).

Box 12.3 Thomas—Kilmann Conflict Mode Instrument

- **Competing** is assertive and uncooperative—an individual pursues his own concerns at the other person's expense
- **Accommodating** is unassertive and cooperative—the complete opposite of competing. When accommodating, an individual neglects his own concerns to satisfy the concerns of the other person, i.e. there is an element of self-sacrifice
- **Avoiding** is unassertive and uncooperative—the person pursues neither his own concerns nor those of the other individual, i.e. he does not deal with the conflict
- **Collaborating** is both assertive and cooperative—the complete opposite of avoiding. Collaborating involves working with others to find some solution that fully satisfies their concerns by looking at the underlying needs driving their and your behaviour
- **Compromising** is moderate in both assertiveness and cooperativeness. The objective is to find some expedient, mutually acceptable solution that partially satisfies both parties. It falls intermediately between competing and accommodating

The tool recognizes that individuals are capable of using all five conflict-handling modes and that rarely does someone have a single style of dealing with conflict. However, an individual will use some modes more than others either because of his/her personality or practice.

Practicalities

The tool takes 15 minutes to complete and, unlike many other psychometric tools, can be self-scored.

Strength Deployment Inventory (SDI)

This psychometric tool explores individuals' underlying motivational values, giving them greater insight into their own natural behaviour as well as their relationships with others. It is based upon Relationship Awareness Theory and can help individuals gain a deeper understanding of the impact of their interactions with others, along with their likely natural leadership and management style. This is obviously beneficial in helping them adapt their behaviour or develop better behavioural flexibility in order to improve relationships, by more proactively managing communication with others who are not like them, as well as both personal and interpersonal conflict. Again, this is not a tool that should be used in a selection process as it does not give any information about competence, ability or aptitude. In common with MBTI, the emerging behavioural preferences are subject to whether an individual chooses to stick with them or depart from them and so it is not a terribly reliable predictor of behaviour, only a general indicator.

SDI clusters individuals into one of seven different areas of behavioural motivation, based on three distinct dimensions—the degree of:

- Assertive—directing motivation
- Analytical—autonomizing motivation
- Altruistic—nurturing motivation

The combination of propensity towards each triangulates an individual's position amongst the seven broad areas, providing a picture of typical behaviours that this person might exhibit or have preference for.

Practicalities

Individuals access 20 stem questions each with three branches. For each stem a total of 10 points have to be distributed across the three stem responses. Ten stem questions are about when the individual is happy and ten when they are unhappy or in conflict. Remember, like MBTI, you should not be asked to do the SDI as part of a selection process.

Chapter 13

New ways of interviewing

Introduction

Over recent years there has been a significant move away from the traditional interview format for junior doctor appointments with the increasing use of either competency-based interviews (also known as criteria-based interviewing, behavioural interviewing and situational interviews) or assessment centres. Both of these approaches are labour intensive but are felt to ensure a more objective, rather than subjective, approach to choosing the right candidate. Additionally, assessment centres give candidates an opportunity to reinvent themselves between 'stations' and a new set of assessors. Assessment centres also give those candidates who naturally struggle with the interview format more opportunities to shine, and for the assessment team to get to the underlying person in more ways.

These two approaches are now being explored and utilized in some consultant interviews. Behavioural or competency-based interviews are often being done back-to-back with a traditional interview. Assessment centres are being used more and more for senior appointments, e.g. Medical Director posts, advertised externally.

Finally, it is even possible today to find yourself subject to Objective Structured Clinical Examination (OSCE) in an interview situation. However, this is rare but may become more prominent as different colleges take differing approaches to exit exams and final CCT attainment. However, preparation for this, besides what has already been covered in preparing yourself, developing confidence, etc., is beyond the scope of this book. If you find yourself in the unusual position of undertaking an OSCE, then it must be considered in the same light as any other clinical exam, with preparation accordingly.

It is likely that new techniques and combinations will be adopted in interviews, as the requirements of consultants evolve and so too do the methods of assessing them. It is important to always find out exactly what will happen to you so that you can be appropriately prepared.

Competency-based interviews

These are also known as criteria-based interviewing, behavioural interviewing and situational interviews. They are increasingly used in StR interviews and there have been some trials at consultant interview level. In essence, they work on the premise used throughout this book that past behaviour is the best predictor of likely future behaviour, although in this type of interview it is being overtly looked for rather than covertly given by the interviewee. This type of interview is thought to be more objective than traditional interviews, which often ask very generic questions inviting someone to give what they think is the answer the interviewer wants to hear, i.e. they are not an accurate reflection of what the candidate might do so much as what he or she thinks the interview panel would want them to do. These semantic questions are poor predictors of behaviour as they are highly subjective.

Is competency-based assessment fairer?

Theoretically, competency-based assessment is fairer than traditional interviewing as it provides a more objective assessment of a candidate's suitability. However, this approach does not stop an interviewer giving one candidate significantly more prompting than another to get the right answers, and so everything we have covered on rapport, first impressions, etc. remains valid here too.

What competencies are assessed?

The purpose of the competency-based interview is to ensure you have the right qualities, skills and behaviours to do the job. To understand the competencies that will be assessed, carefully reread the following:

- Job advert
- Job description
- Essential and desirable criteria

Underline any key words or phrases as it will be these things that the interviewers will be looking specifically at in the interview process. Additionally, think about the discussions you had in your pre-interview visit. What did they highlight they particularly wanted their new colleague to do? What problems have they faced, e.g. conflict between consultants? What islands are they from and therefore what issues or problems might you be able to predict?

How do I prepare?

Once you have your list of competencies, qualities and skills, take time to ensure you have good examples to use to demonstrate these competences. It is important to recognize that competency-based questions often address situations where there may be emotions attached or where things did not necessarily go according to plan, for example:

- Tell me about a time when a patient or his relatives upset you
- Tell me about an occasion where you failed to communicate clearly to the patient

Consequently, the examples you identify need the factual information to validate them as much as the behaviour that was exhibited at the time. Typically, the factual information includes:

- The event
- The date or point in time
- Where it happened
- Who was involved

An example of how this unfolds could be 'Last June, whilst I was working in St Elsewhere's, I was in clinic and an elderly lady came in with her daughter . . .'. This is known as describing the 'situation' as the set-up for the story and it is important because it helps to give the panel a feeling that they are hearing a real response, not a semantic, invented ideal answer.

How are competency-based questions assessed?

If competency-based interviews are being done correctly, key members of the panel will meet in advance of the interview to reach consensus on what skills and qualities need to be assessed for and the questions or assessment stations necessary to draw these out. Competency-based questions will usually involve asking candidates for an example of a previous behaviour. A structured scoring system is agreed, with both positive and negative indicators. The panel will then be looking for evidence of either the positive or negative indicators in the story you tell.

Box 13.1 gives an example of a competency-based question and its scoring.

> **Box 13.1 Example of a competency-based question and its scoring**
>
> Tell me about a time when you and a colleague disagreed on a course of action for a patient.
>
> - What was the cause?
> - What did you do?
> - What was the outcome?
>
> **Indicators**
>
> | Positive indicators | Negative indicators |
> |---|---|
> | Remained calm | Insisted their view was right |
> | Listened to the other's point of view | Defensive |
> | Tried to establish the reason behind this point of view | Allowed other person to overrule decision without discussion and negotiation |
> | Asserted their own view and the reasons underlying it | Did not satisfactorily resolve the situation |
> | Worked with the colleague to achieve the right action for the patient | Attempted unsuccessfully to deal with the situation alone when clear it was not easily resolvable |

Marking system

0	No evidence	No evidence reported
1	Poor	Little evidence of positive indicators
		Mostly negative indicators, mainly decisive
2	Areas for concern	Limited number of positive indicators
		Many negative indictors, one or more decisive
3	Satisfactory	Satisfactory display of positive indicators
		Some negative indicators but none decisive
4	Excellent	Strong display of positive indicators
		Few negative indicators and all minor

A decisive negative indicator is one for which the panel will not forgive you. In the context of medicine this might be not asking for help when it was needed—even the best consultants sometimes need help!

Typical competency-based questions

The following are a selection of competency- or behavioural-based questions. Interviewers are not always perfect at asking them in the right way. The key is to understand that they are looking for an actual example of something you did, so that they can look for the evidence of how you behave in that situation.

- Tell me about a time when you worked hard and felt a great sense of achievement
- Describe a time when pressure at work has led to you feeling angry
- Tell me about a difficult clinical decision you have had to make
- Tell me about a time you solved a problem that others were struggling with
- Tell me about how you lead the clinical team at night
- Tell me about a time when you had to break bad news to a patient
- Tell me about a time when you had to explain a complex situation to a patient
- Tell me about a time when relatives or a patient was cross with you
- Tell me about a time when you failed to communicate effectively
- Tell me about the last audit you did
- Tell me about how you managed a risk that you spotted
- Tell me how you have involved patients in your specialty
- Tell me how you teach the medical students
- How do you cope with having time off work for annual or study leave?
- Tell me about a recent episode when you had to delegate an unpleasant task to a junior doctor

- Tell me about a time when you had decided you were not going to do something and then changed your mind
- Tell me about how you decided on a course of action when you were struggling to make a definitive decision
- Tell me about an occasion when you were proud about the way you led the team
- Tell me about a time when you had to persuade your colleague about your point of view
- Tell me how you approached a critical incident you were involved in

Answering competency-based questions

A useful and well-recognized approach for answering competency-based questions is the STAR approach. The acronym STAR unfolds as:

- Situation
- Task
- Action
- Result

Using this approach enables you to answer questions in a meaningful, structured manner, providing you with ample opportunities to reinforce your strength as a candidate and the benefits to the service and organization, without having to overtly state them.

> **USEFUL TIP**: Use the STAR approach to answer competency-based questions.

Situation or task

Briefly describe either

- The situation or
- The task that needed to be accomplished

Remember, you are not being accessed on your ability to tell a story and it is important to keep this section relatively short and factual. Only include information if it helps you in the rest of your answer (see Chapter 5 for more details). The right level of information in this segment of the answer is determined by pitching it so that:

- The interviewers have enough information to understand the situation, i.e. the context of the story
- They have enough points of reference to feel confident that the story is real, i.e. it is a reflection of what actually happened

Action

This is the most important section in the STAR approach, as this is where you need to demonstrate the qualities, skills and behaviours that you believe the panel will be looking for. The important differentiator between a great candidate and the pack is that the great candidate understands that you must not just say what you did, but how you did it and why you did it so that the panel can easily spot the positive indicators in your thought process and behaviour. If you do not talk about how and why, the panel will need to make many assumptions from your answers and you may score relatively few points.

Important points when describing your actions

- Talk about what you personally did. Practise using the word 'I'. Avoid the word 'we' or 'the team'. The interviewers are keen to assess your specific role
- Aim to clearly demonstrate three key skills, qualities or behaviours. These will need spelling out. Do not expect the panel to jump to the right conclusions just from the actions you took

For example, rather than saying 'I listened to what the patient said and then apologized' say 'I am aware how easy it is to jump to conclusions and not properly answer patients' concerns. I sat Mr Smith down in a quiet room and actively listened to what he had to say; this helped him to slowly calm down. I then very gently probed him as to why these things were important for him. I did this because I am very aware through experience that not all complaints are real complaints and that complaints are often a way of expressing worry or fear. Indeed, it became clear that Mr Smith's main concern was a fear that we were hiding something from him. I apologized for the anxiety this was clearly causing him and reassured him that as soon as the results were available we would share them with him and his wife'.

(In the fuller answer you demonstrate why active listening is important and an understanding that not all complaints are really complaints, that you can apologize without admitting you have done anything wrong and that you clearly develop empathy with patients.)

- Remember to tell the panel
  - WHAT you did
  - HOW you did it
  - WHY you did it
- Even if you have been asked about a time when something went badly, avoid making the answer come across as completely negative. Are there things that went well that you can also highlight during your What, How, Why description of your actions? Again, if you have been asked to describe something that went wrong, end with the fact that you reflected after the event or organized an 'after-event review' with the team
- Avoid using jargon. Talk naturally as you would in a normal conversation, e.g. don't say 'I used a transformational leadership approach' but rather 'I spent time with my team developing a vision of what we could achieve together and motivated and inspired them so that together we were capable of achieving the goal'

Result

This is where you describe what happened in the end. If this was a positive result, it is important to summarize what you personally accomplished, what personal qualities and skills you used to enable the result and the specific benefits these attributes brought.

This section must, if appropriate, include what you learned from the episode and what you now do differently as a result. It is therefore a further opportunity to reinforce new skills or behaviours learned and demonstrate that you are open to feedback and reflect on events to improve what you do.

Assessment centres

Assessment centres build on competency-based interviews. In an assessment centre there may be a whole selection of different tools used to choose the appropriate candidate. These might include:

- A formal presentation
- Psychometric testing
- A behavioural interview
- A normal interview
- A group task to assess how you work within a team of senior people
- A group discussion to enable a wider team to be involved in the interview process
- A scenario exercise relevant to your area of practice, often based around communication skills

Within the context of the consultant interview, it remains somewhat unlikely that there will be a pure clinical skills station, as this should have been assessed through workplace-based assessments (WPBA) and Royal College exit exams. At present, assessment centres are most likely to be used for senior consultant interviews, e.g. for Medical Director positions, but it is likely that we will see them used ever more frequently for all consultant posts. The typical assessment centre is a collection of approaches that we have already described, and so the generic strategy is to adopt our guidance relevant to that particular aspect. For instance, if an assessment centre contains a competency-based interview, then use the STAR approach for answering the questions.

Preparation for assessment centres

Preparation for assessment centres is no different to any other interview scenario. Without repeating ourselves, it is important to undertake the sort of preparation you would for a standard interview, as covered comprehensively in earlier sections of this book.

Once you know that you will undertake an assessment centre, it is important to ask for the format, who will be at the assessment centre and what roles they will be playing. This will allow you to more specifically prepare and tailor your answers most closely to the relevant people.

Chapter 14
If you do not get the job

Introduction

If you do not get the job you are bound to feel disappointed, particularly if you have worked really hard in preparation. Remember, there can only be one appointment and it is possible you did everything right on the day and it sadly came down to something tiny. Interview panels can deliberate for hours, but the answer you get is still either 'yes' or 'no' and, if it's the latter, it hurts. However, it is important to both learn from the experience through feedback and reflection and pick yourself up and start again, positively and proactively. This chapter looks at:

- Getting effective feedback
- Reflecting on that feedback
- Common feedback
- Picking yourself up and starting again

Getting feedback

You should always be offered feedback if you are unsuccessful at interview and it is really important that you accept this, despite how hurt you may feel in the aftermath. Indeed, if you are not offered feedback, always ask for it because it is an essential component of either improving next time or perhaps even not changing your approach at all. If someone else had a skill you just didn't have, you can't easily change that in short order and so if everything else was spot on, don't break the formula!

> **USEFUL TIP:** If you are unsuccessful at consultant interview always ask for feedback. Ideally get this several days after your interview when you will be more receptive towards what is said.

The best time to have feedback is some days after the event but close enough that you can remember what happened. Having feedback immediately after being told you were unsuccessful is likely to be less productive, as you are carrying the pain of rejection and normal defence mechanisms make it more likely that you will reject the feedback. Remember, feedback on a failure to be appointed is much like receiving bad news in medicine and, as we were taught in medical school, when given bad news most of us will not hear beyond those first few words, in our case 'Sorry you have been unsuccessful'. By letting the dust settle and then approaching it with a mindset that says 'This will help me learn, improve and be successful next time', we can utilize the feedback to hone our approach to the next level.

When people do give feedback, it is often somewhat vague or indeed vaguely reassuring but without giving you anything to action. It is therefore useful to have some questions ready to ask that will help you identify the key learning points from your interview experience. These might include:

- Which areas or questions did I answer particularly well?
- Which areas or questions could I have answered better? What would have improved them?

- How did I come over to the panel?
- Was there anything that particularly concerned you or the panel about my CV or interview?
- If I were to do the interview again, what would you advise me to do differently?
- Was there any experience missing from my CV?

When being given feedback, the key is to listen but not respond. Do not try to justify why you did something, or worse, tell the person giving you feedback why he/she is wrong. If you do this, the feedback session will rapidly dry up and you will start to develop a reputation as being someone who does not listen. Get used to using the phrase 'Thank you, that's very helpful'.

It can be helpful to write yourself notes as you get your feedback. It is amazing how easy it is for you to change your opinion on what was actually fed back to you, if you do not do this.

> **USEFUL TIP:** It is also important to remember that feedback is a gift. Always take time to genuinely thank the person who gave you feedback from the interview, even if that feedback has hurt or caused distress. It still allows you to learn and improve.

Reflection

Having received feedback, much as you may want to ignore it, take the time to reflect on what was said. Many people have a natural tendency when given feedback they do not want to hear to initially reject it. Only later, if they take the time to revisit the feedback, do they start to accept that it may have some truth and therefore offer an opportunity for them to develop and learn. We recommend that, having got your feedback, you do not immediately reject it or accept it, but give yourself several days to reflect on it. When you do reflect, remember this is what this particular interview committee thought. A different interview committee, in a different hospital, with different values and ideas about a consultant colleague, may have viewed you in a very different way.

A good discipline to develop is that of formally deconstructing the feedback. This involves breaking it into chunks and then interrogating it (and you). It works as follows:
- Isolate individual statements in the feedback, e.g. 'The other candidate demonstrated more passion for this job', and then test it with questioning
  - What did the other candidate do that led to this?
  - What did I do or not do that undermined my apparent passion?
  - Which panel members would 'passion' most likely have resonated with? Why?
  - What could I have done to demonstrate more passion?
  - Which episodes in my history would be good examples of passion?

The good news with this technique is that you don't have to admit you were wrong, only that you might not have matched your approach most effectively to this panel, and therefore it is important to work out how and why, so that you can improve it further next time.

Picking yourself up and starting again

When you have had time to reflect on your feedback and given yourself a few days to mourn the loss of this particular job, it is important to move forward and take action. This isn't unlike grieving. Nobody is saying you shouldn't mourn, but there comes a point when it is time to get on with life! That means working out why you weren't appointed and possibly fixing things that need fixing.

The commonest reasons given to candidates about why they were not appointed are:

- Not coming over as passionate and interested
- Not appearing to have the right experience or expertise
- Not appearing enthusiastic about the post

Appearing dispassionate

Appearing dispassionate is the commonest reason given to candidates who are persistently unsuccessful at the consultant interview. Why is this? Unfortunately for these individuals, consultant interview panels tend to be dominated by enthusiastic, action-orientated, goal-driven people from the Island of Opportunity (see Rupert in Chapter 4). As discussed in this chapter, these characters like people who are dynamic and enthusiastic and who appear passionate about what they do. This is particularly a problem for those individuals who are wired to behave in the opposite way—the people who stand on the bridge between the Island of Team Spirit and the Island of Intellect. These individuals, who are highly numerous in medicine, tend to believe that it is wrong, or even rude, to oversell themselves and consequently they can down-play their achievements, and assume panels will recognize and remember these achievements, or even that panels will infer them from their CV. People on this bridge tend to naturally speak in a somewhat dispassionate, relatively slow, considered manner compared to Island of Opportunity dwellers, which can be translated as being generally dispassionate about the job or location, as well as calling into question their ability, even though they may well be superb high achievers.

The key to resolving this is to get used to, for the short term at least, talking confidently about your achievements. As you are likely to feel uncomfortable with this, the earlier you can start the better. Review everything you were taught in Chapter 5 about getting to know yourself, but also think about what is important to you in your specialty. Once you are clear on your selling points and achievements, share with a partner or close colleague (preferably an Island of Opportunity person) that you are trying to practise confidently selling yourself and then spend time telling them about all of your excellent achievements. You could even give them a series of interview questions to ask you and then ask them to score your answers out of 10 according to how much you really sold yourself. When you know what your default score is, set yourself a distinct goal to achieve, e.g. to move from my present 6 to a 9+ by the next interview.

> **USEFUL TIP:** Find someone prepared to listen to you trying to 'sell' yourself and ask them to score you out of 10 on how convincing and passionate you came across as.

If you find yourself talking about problems, difficulties or weaknesses or downplaying your achievements, stop and take time out. Ask yourself why you are doing this and then challenge the beliefs around this. For instance, some people believe that it is *wrong* to boast. That makes them uncomfortable 'selling' themselves. We encourage them to think of it not as boasting but as actively selecting the words and manner that help another individual understand something he/she might miss, i.e. it is the appropriate thing to do to help the other individual develop a clear picture.

When you are talking about what is important to you, make sure you speed up your voice, increase the volume slightly and put passion in your tone. Practise smiling and maintaining good eye contact with the person helping you. When talking about your key achievements, slow down your voice to really emphasize their importance.

Didn't have enough expertise

The first thing to consider is whether this comment is true or not. In other words, did you truly not have enough expertise or did you simply not sell or present your expertise comprehensively?

Not enough expertise

Take time to consider what actions you could take to improve your expertise. Could you utilize skills you already have to demonstrate this better, e.g. management skills by managing a project, audit skills by undertaking an audit that fully follows the audit cycle? Could you go on a course? Could you spend 6 months in a different unit? Would you benefit from doing a locum consultant post or acting up as a consultant within your own organization? For clinical or surgical skills, see if you can do a disproportionately high amount of this type of work to really boost your experience.

Did not sell your expertise

There are two reasons why this may have occurred:

- You did not properly prepare using the guidance in Chapter 5
- You did not sufficiently consider the personalities of the members of the interview panel and how to develop natural rapport with them (see Chapter 4)

Firstly, take time out to really understand what your expertise is by using your CV and the 'getting to know you' exercise (Chapter 5) as a guide. Really build up examples that demonstrate your strengths, qualities, skills and attributes. As you go through this exercise, constantly ask yourself why are these strengths, skills, qualities and attributes important for the type of consultant post I am looking for. Once you have built this toolbox of examples, practise talking about them to a trusted partner or friend.

Didn't behave as if you wanted the job

If the panel don't get a feeling of certainty that you really want the job, they are unlikely to offer you it. Consequently, this feedback often comes as a result of a less than confident response to 'If we offered you the job, would you take it?'. Not only is there always just one answer to this question (YES!) but also it needs to be said without thinking and with confidence and conviction. An alternative to the somewhat short 'YES!' is something along the lines of 'Definitely, I've wanted to come here for the last x years'. If you cannot answer this question in that manner truthfully, then you should not have been at the interview! Before your next interview, ask yourself whether you definitely want the job. If definitely yes, practise answering this question out loud in front of a mirror. Make sure your body language and tone of voice match your words. Again, practise with a friend and ask them to give you an honest opinion of whether they were convinced.

Chapter 15

Getting the job—what next?

Introduction

Congratulations. You were successful at your consultant interview and you are now looking forward to the next phase of your career. So what happens next? It's easy to think of the journey as being essentially complete at this point, but we strongly advocate using this period—between acceptance and starting—productively to ensure that your interview success turns into a fulfilling consultant career. This chapter outlines some of the key things to consider during the period leading up to starting as a consultant and in those very first few days and weeks in your new post.

The chapter starts by looking at some of the immediate considerations:

- When should you resign?
- When should you start?
- Should you take a break?

It then moves on to think about how you start to establish yourself in the first 90 days as a new consultant—probably the most important period you have to face yet!

When to resign

It is very tempting, having been offered a consultant post, to immediately resign your StR or SAS post—don't! Your offer of a post no doubt came with some conditions. These might include:

- Subject to references
- Subject to a satisfactory health check
- Subject to confirmation of your qualifications

Until you have confirmation that all of the conditions have been satisfied, hold back from handing in your notice. We're not being pessimistic and you are probably reasonably certain that everything will be fine, but until you actually hand in notice, you have full employment rights with your present employer, even if they know that you intend to leave. Until you have the security of employment confirmation without conditions, it is just safer to be cautious.

> **USEFUL TIP:** Do not resign until you have a formal job offer and all conditions within it have been satisfied.

Starting date

Depending on factors such as the remaining length of your post, etc., it is usual to have to give 3 months' notice if you are resigning from an StR or SAS post. If you are in a locum consultant position, check your contract and if necessary seek advice from Medical Staffing. Before deciding on your resignation date consider what this might mean for your starting date. Starting on call on 1 January, or indeed on any other

Bank Holiday, may not be such a good idea! In some hospitals you are not allowed to formally commence clinical work until having completed a corporate induction programme. When do these corporate inductions take place?

Most organizations, once an appointment has been made, are keen for the appointment to commence as soon as possible. There are instances when some coordination is necessary, such as where a locum is already in that post. They may have some notice that must be worked too. Ultimately, the actual start date needs to be an intelligent choice that suits you, your new employer, your new colleagues and any practical constraints. Don't just leap, simply to be helpful.

Taking a break

There are few opportunities for most of us in medicine to take a career break to do something significant. Why not consider taking one now? It may be another 30 years before you get a further chance! The opportunity to re-evaluate your life and set yourself clear goals for your consultant post and your life outside work will be invaluable. Equally, appreciate that your plans to do a month-long tour of New Zealand will never be easier than now. Once in post, juggling rotas, being on-call and colleague's work commitments makes finding these larger gaps really difficult.

If you are moving to a consultant post within the same hospital then taking a break is a *must*. It is almost impossible to move smoothly from being the StR on Friday to being the consultant on Monday. You may know the difference, but it might not feel different and everybody else might not treat you differently. At the very least, have a 2-week holiday and consider how you will re-invent yourself in your new role. More on this as we examine the first 90 days.

Re-inventing yourself

If you are moving to a new hospital to take up your consultant post you have the perfect excuse to re-invent yourself as the type of consultant you would like to be. We are not suggesting there is anything wrong with the old you. After all, it got you to this precise point. However, this is a significant transition, if not *the* most significant career transition there is in medicine. You are now in charge, responsible and more independent. It's worth taking a step back and considering the following:

- How would you like to be addressed?
- How do you want people to see you, e.g. approachable, firmly in charge?
- What ground rules do you want to apply?
- What do you want to be known for?

You will only have one *easy* chance at this, so getting it right from the start is essential. As we have said before, you never get a second chance to make a first impression, but you can spend many years trying to repair the consequences of the wrong impression.

If you are staying in the same hospital, you will already be addressed by staff in a certain way and will already have a known or perceived 'personality'. How are you going to help others understand you are no longer an StR? How will you help them see you in a new light? You might consider the following:

- Go out and buy a new wardrobe of clothes. Make sure you look like the sort of consultant you'd like to be seen as
- Take a holiday—a gap is important for establishing your new identity and psychologically sets up others for other changes when you return
- Consider carefully what practical steps you will need to take to leave the StR role behind, e.g. not being too available, not saying 'yes' when asked to do jobs that aren't usually down to a consultant. We will discuss this in more depth below

The first 90 days

In industry, professionals often talk about the first 90 days (sometimes 100 days, just to give a new author a different book title!) of a new job. In essence, in a new job you have around 90 days to establish yourself in the role, build your team and move from being a net detractor from to a net contributor to the service. In the early period, beyond basic tasks, people understand that you are learning, finding your feet and generally not that productive. The more you move through this period, the less accepting they become of anything less than a full contribution. So, your initial goals need to be around getting up-to-speed and fully operational across this period of time, without accepting things left, right and centre, simply to demonstrate a contribution.

If you are to maximize your chances of being successful in this period, adopt the following rules or strategy as a framework for getting it right.

Key rules for a new consultant

- Develop a new purpose
- Take time to have a proper induction
- Meet your key stakeholders (internally and externally)
- Develop your team or get to know them well
- Don't take on too much
- Don't take on too little
- Leave the StR/SAS role behind
- Learn to say 'no'
- Remember, you don't know everything
- Get a mentor
- Ensure you establish a healthly work—life balance

These rules are both a guide to getting this period right and a warning about typical traps new consultants fall into. Just like for the interview that got you here, prepare well and enjoy the positive benefits that come from the adoption of the above.

Develop a new purpose

The biggest mistake that new consultants make is not to establish a new purpose. What does this really mean? Most juniors have spent 10+ years focused on their career, learning, CCT, etc., with a perfectly sensible final goal of achieving consultant status. Consciously or subconsciously, you have been moving towards the day when you are successful at the consultant interview and now, having made it, it is very easy to heave a sigh of relief, relax and allow life to gently float by for a little while. The longer-term consequences of this can be catastrophic and we spend a great deal of time counselling senior consultants who have done just that and are now 'lost' about what to do next and where to go, only knowing for sure that their current situation isn't it. By not being purposeful, you submit to be driven by your environment and circumstances, rather than being master of your own destiny—strong words, but then we see the results every week.

Start by considering what you wish to be associated with going forward for at least the next 2–3 years. This is best done prior to commencing the post so that you have a clear vision right from the start. Consider what your 'special' interests will be:

- Will it be teaching?
- What will your clinical special interest be?
- Will it be a sub-speciality clinical interest?
- Will it be audit or risk management?

Being clear about what you want to do and how you'd like to be seen has many benefits:

- It will help you be seen as a consultant in your own right (not just within the department but outside it too)
- It will give you clear purpose and indeed a sense of purpose (this helps steer decisions and provides drive)
- It will help you manage your time more effectively by ensuring that you focus on the right things, not just anything
- It will allow you to say 'no' when all your new colleagues ask you to take on the bits of the job they no longer want to do (trust us, they've been storing this stuff up, just for you!)

Humans are designed to be purposeful. When we do not have a sense of purpose, we feel lethargic, meandering and even bored.

Induction

> **USEFUL TIP:** You only get one chance to be inducted. You are never too busy to do this. Make it a priority.

Corporate induction

Even if you have worked in the department or hospital for a number of years, it is important that you have an induction. Most organizations run corporate inductions at regular intervals, many of them now running to several days. It may seem easy to delay doing this, but the longer you leave it, the more unlikely it is that you will ever do it. There is no doubt that much of these inductions can be tedious and boring, but hidden within them are key pieces of information about the organization that could take years of osmosis otherwise. Equally, it might actually take longer to formally learn about this information if you have to go and find it all for yourself.

It's worth remembering that those dull topics like fire lectures and major incident plans are much more important to know about when you are in charge. If there is an incident, people will be looking to you for leadership. Although you rarely hear of a hospital burning down, hardly a week goes past when the fire brigade isn't called for something. With toast the staple diet of almost every doctor on a rota, the potential for toaster fires is immense and you'll look pretty daft as a leader if you don't know what to do when they evacuate your department. Also, people look to their leaders to lead by example. It is difficult to do this well when you do not know how the Trust works or what is expected of you.

In addition to the formal corporate induction, consider who you want to meet at a senior level as part of your induction process. Who could help you understand how things work and how to tread the right political steps? At this point their doors are probably open, ready to welcome a new colleague, but in a few months' time it might take you 6 months to get an appointment to see the Chief Executive, unless he thinks your meeting is important. Many departments will formally set up key meetings for their new consultants with the Chief Executive, Medical Director, Operations Director and Finance Director. If your department has not, think about why you would want to meet these people. Part of meeting at this stage is to build early rapport with the key players in the organization. It is also an opportunity to discuss ideas for service development in more detail.

Local induction and meeting your key stakeholders

Again, this may have been organized for you in advance. However, take the opportunity before starting in post to decide what you need to know to make your future consultant post as successful as possible. For example:

- If the department uses equipment you are unfamiliar with, how will you learn about it?
- Does the department have specific guidelines and policies?
- Who are the stakeholders to your post, i.e. anyone who influences how you do your job? For instance, for a surgeon this might include:
  - Clinical Service Lead
  - Business Manager
  - Anaesthetists
  - Theatre manager

- Other key theatre staff
- Ward sister
- Other surgeons in the same speciality
- Medics in a similar field
- Histopathologists
- Radiologists
- Booking clerk

How are you going to ensure you meet with all the important people as early as possible after starting the post? (See 'Meeting key stakeholders' below.)

- How are you going to make time to and ensure that you get to know your team well?
- How will you ensure you know about all key meetings, educational opportunities, etc?

Meeting key stakeholders

It can be extremely bewildering when starting a new job to decide who you need to go and see formally and who you can meet on a more informal basis over the first few months. A tool you can use to help you make this decision is stakeholder mapping.

Essentially, draw a circle with your name in it in the middle of a sheet of paper. Around this write the name of any individual or groups of people that might have an influence on the way you perform your job or on the future service you would like to develop. Think as widely as possible at this stage. As much as possible, try to name individuals, e.g. in the previous example of who a surgeon might want to meet, rather than writing down 'Anaesthetists' it is better putting down Dr Jones who you do three sessions with each week.

Once you have your stakeholder map you need to prioritize which are the most important relationships, as this is where you will start. Asking yourself the following two questions can help clarify this for you:

- What would be the advantage of an enhanced relationship with this individual?
- What would be the downside of no or a poor relationship with this individual?

Then, make appointments as soon as possible to meet with the key or most important players. Remember, at these early meetings the aim is to develop rapport rather than to try to gain something. Taking time to listen to the other person's point of view can be very powerful and far more productive than simply telling them about you and your wish list. Their insight and what you read between the lines can be incredibly valuable in avoiding the political traps that are rife in every big organization. Everyone you meet will have their likes, dislikes and allegiances.

Advantages of listening

- The more you listen at this stage the more you will understand what is important to other individuals, knowledge that will be vital if you are to influence them with your ideas in the future
- The more you listen, the more they are likely to listen to you and want to help you in the future

- The more you listen, the more you will understand how to step into their shoes and develop natural rapport (see Chapter 4)

Overall, the goal for your early stakeholder meetings is to set the relationship up in the right way, build rapport and gain a full picture of who, what, where, how and whether their views support or differ from your own.

Develop your team relationships

As a consultant, you will have a team of people who work with you. This may be a shared team or your own team, depending on your service circumstances. Recognize that your team is much more than a collection of clinical individuals. It's easy to focus too much on medical staff and forget that the nurses and PAMs (professions allied to medicine) may be with you for many years to come too. In your early weeks, actively and consciously make time to get to know your team, finding out what is important to them as individuals, working out which island they are from and the strengths they bring to the table. Listen to their ideas for developing the service and doing things differently. Investing this time now will reap massive benefits for you personally in the future.

Just like for your stakeholders, this is a period of rapport and learning, which we term 'integration'. Your goal is to become a valued team member, not an outsider who is simply in charge.

Don't take on too much

When you start as a new consultant, it is very easy to find, very quickly, that you have taken on too many things. When any department appoints a new consultant, almost invariably every other consultant makes a decision that they are going to give something up and the new consultant is just the right person to take on this task. If you were to take on all these tasks, you would rapidly become completely overloaded. Unfortunately many new consultants do just that out of a sense of duty or flattery. Their consultant colleagues ask them in a very flattering way and because they are not sure what it is they want to do as a consultant (i.e. they have no clear purpose), they find it very easy to say 'yes' and very difficult to say 'no'.

The key is to decide in advance of starting the job what your purpose is and set clear goals for achieving this. This allows you to not only have the confidence to say 'no' to something that isn't in your game plan but also provide the reasoning behind it, making the actual conversation easier. For instance, you can feel good and contributory about saying 'I'd really like to help, but I want to make my early priority establishing a range of respiratory management protocols'.

Don't take on too little

It is equally important not to take on too little. Remember, you have 90 days to make your mark and become a net contributor. Decide on your purpose and start taking action towards it so that others can see the visible difference you are making. If you do nothing other than your basic clinical work, you will be bored, your performance will fall and you will not make your mark within your team or the wider organization.

Leave the StR/SAS role behind

It is very easy as a new consultant not to leave your previous role behind, especially if you become a consultant in the same unit. For many new consultants, resorting back to the StR role feels both safe and busy. It also makes you feel needed. However, you need to remember that if every time you are asked to do a job that should be done by a junior you do it:

- The nurses will continue to ask you
- You will always be too busy to establish the new things you want to do as a consultant
- The people who are supposed to do these jobs will never learn to do them

As a new consultant, you do need to be visible, as it is an important way of getting to know your team, but this does make you more clinically available. However, establish the ground rules early, firmly and politely, remembering you are being asked to do these jobs primarily because you happen to be there, the other person wants the job done and they do not really care who does it. A polite 'That's a job for the registrar' helps to ensure they know and respect the role you now have.

Learn to say 'no'

If you do not want to become overloaded you have to learn to say 'no' in a way that is comfortable for you. It will be easier to say 'no' when you have a clear purpose and a definite game plan. It is also worth remembering that saying 'yes' and then not achieving is, for many others, a worse crime than saying 'no' at the outset. When saying 'no', consider which island (Chapter 4) this person is from. Ask yourself how you can say 'no' to the different islands without offending them and in a way they hear and understand:

- Directly to the Island of Opportunity: 'Sorry, I can't do it in that timescale'
- Empathetically to the Island of Team Spirit: 'I'm really sorry but I've got so much on that I don't want to risk letting you down'
- With justification to the Island of Intellect: 'I can't take this on because I want to make my early priority establishing a range of respiratory management protocols'

Remember, you don't know everything

This is perhaps the most important rule to remember as a new consultant. There is no doubt there will be lots of organizational things that you need to ask questions about and you are unlikely to feel embarrassed doing so. Remember, it is much more embarrassing to ask these questions 3 years down the line, so better to get used to asking now.

You will also be surprised that things that were relatively easy to make decisions about as a junior suddenly seem a lot more difficult when the buck stops with you. If you observe your senior, more-experienced colleagues you will notice that, when they have to make difficult decisions, many of them will discuss their problems with others, including their juniors. This is not an act of weakness but an act of maturity, more heads being better than one to solve a problem. In addition, the act of speaking out loud about a problem often clarifies your thinking and is enough for you to be clear what the right decision is.

When you do ask your colleague for an opinion, the manner in which you ask will be important for your own self-esteem. Adopt the mindset that you are bouncing ideas because of your commitment to get the very best result for the patient. That might sound like 'Hey, Bob, can I just run a course of action past you to see if you can add anything?' It would be a pretty cold-hearted, arrogant colleague who developed a negative viewpoint based on one peer discussing the right thing to do with another peer.

Get a mentor

If you do not already have a mentor, get one! A mentor is someone who can help you achieve as a new consultant. Mentoring in new roles, especially the new consultant post, is thought to be so valuable that a number of Trusts organize specifically for all new consultants to be assigned a mentor and consequently train their interested, established consultants to take on this role. Some Trusts utilize their SAS doctors for this too.

Mentors come in all shapes and sizes in the NHS. Under the traditional NHS definition, they are the healthcare equivalent of 'coaches', utilized in the business world, i.e. they are someone who will help you reach your goals, who you can bounce ideas off, but who do not solve your problems for you. Rather, they ask intelligent, often reflective, questions that help you solve your problems for yourself whilst learning in the process. The principle here is that, as adults, we generally do not like being told what to do, but we do benefit from help and support in deciding for ourselves the right course of action. A mentor who works in this capacity does not have to work in the same specialty, as you, or even in the same organization (although it is generally beneficial). A lack of familiarity with your distinct context can make a mentor more predisposed to asking the sometimes critical, obvious question that someone else may assume you have answered already!

Many mentors do not behave in the way described above and act more as advisors, wise or otherwise. This can be useful when it comes to treading the political minefields that can exist in Trusts, as well as highly beneficial in simply learning how things work or how to get things done. The key is to decide what you want out of the mentoring and it is not unreasonable to consider having more than one mentor, each with a different role, skillset or knowledge base.

Ensure you establish a healthly work—life balance

Becoming a consultant is an ideal time to reassess your work—life balance and ensure you have a game plan for life that works for you. Indeed, the transition from a largely learning and delivery role to a largely leading, less-structured environment can be a killer for work—life balance, and so maintaining control from the start is critical. Starting off and then staying in the right place is much easier than trying to correct things 3 years down the line when life is out of control and work has taken over.

A tool that can be very beneficial in assessing work—life balance is the Wheel of Life, which we introduced in Chapter 1. Use the Wheel of Life firstly to decide how satisfied you are with your level of achievement or results in each facet of life, and then work out a range of critical success factors or things that you can do to ensure that this facet always remains on track. The goal is to define a list of critical things to keep doing and then build the rest of life around them. This keeps you on the straight and narrow. For example:

Family and friends

- As a consultant I leave work at 5 pm on Tuesdays and Thursdays to take Oliver swimming
- As a consultant, except when on call, I play tennis with all the family every Saturday morning

Health

- As a consultant I walk 2 miles to work on Mondays, Wednesdays and Fridays

You will note that these critical success factors are all written in the present tense, are possible and are positively worded. They are also SMART, i.e.

- Specific
- Measurable
- Agreed
- Realistic
- Time specific

By making the effort to write them in this way, they are much more likely to be achieved. Abstract goals are difficult for the brain to plan for, whereas highly specific ones, with boundaries, are much easier.

It is easy to find yourself always at work in your new job. This does not make you efficient or lead to people admiring you. Indeed, most people admire those who get the job done, who achieve at a high level, are approachable and calm and yet who clearly have a life outside work too. Start right and stay right.

The 'final' chapter

This final chapter is not only *not* final but in truth a new beginning. You've worked hard, you've achieved and this has been rewarded with a new consultant post and a new chapter in your life. Therefore, that just leaves us to say congratulations on the new position and we wish you success and prosperity from this point forward. Enjoy.

Index

16 Personality Factors (16PF) 245–7

active vs passive verbs 112
added value 117–18
adverbs 111
Advisory Appointments Committee (AAC) 10
anaesthesia, interview analysis 198–202
anxiety
  breathing 151–2
  building confidence 149–51
  centring energy 152–3
  the interview 146, 148–53
  positive questions 151
  visualization 150–1
application form 13, 19–21
  covering letter 34
  employer's/applicant's perspectives 13
  formatting in Word 20
  know your CV/application 91
  NHS Jobs application form 28–35
application process 9–35
  top tips 27
assessment centres, new ways of interviewing 258
audit, examples 18

behaviour and motivation 54–78
  case studies 55–6
  classification framework 57–8
  difference, relevance to interview 54–5, 59–60
  differing communication styles 63–5
  disagreements 126
  examples of questions asked 126
  failure to get job 263
  from stimulus to behaviour (think, feel, do) 72, 100
  golden rules 66
  habits and tics 114
  humbleness, down-playing 98
  interpersonal impact 61–3
  presentations 77–8, 118, 243–50
  qualities and skills 89, 92–5
  rapport 66, 77, 159, 160–1
  self-awareness 65, 66
  STAR 127
  strengths 118–19
  see also islander principles; language

behavioural interviewing 252–8
behavioural questions 125–7
  interview questions 179
benefits, vs products 16–17
break, taking, and new job 267
breathing, controlling anxiety 151–2
British Medical Association (BMA), membership 12
British Medical Journal 193
  BMJCareers website 11–12
  electronic newsletter 194
bullied junior 138

career break, and new job 267
CCT 115, 116, 177
centring energy 152–3
Chairperson 156
character strengths 118–19
character weaknesses 119–20
Chief Executive 156
choice of job 6
clinical dilemmas and ethics, interview questions 188
clinical governance
  interview questions 99, 135–6, 185–7
  questions on 99, 135–6
clinical questions 133
colleague, poorly performing 138–9
communication, interview questions 180
communication questions 131–2
communication skills 32
competency-based interviewing 252–8
  answering, STAR approach 256–8
  question and scoring 254–5
confidence-building 149–50, 157–8
conflict resolution 130–1
consultant interview courses 195
courses attended 116
  learning from, demonstration 17–18
criteria-based interviewing 252–8
CV strategy 14–28
  context purposefulness and application. 16
  covering letter 34
  criteria
    and compensating facets 26
    essential and desirable criteria 25
  formatting in Word 20, 24
  gaps in CV 121–2

CV strategy (cont.)
   gaps or weaknesses 92, 121–2
   job description 25–6
   key topic areas 94
   know your CV/application 91
   length of CV 21
   personal statement 27–8
   personalization 25
   presenting important facts 19
   professional preparation 20–1
   questions about 176–8
   referees 23, 33
   selling yourself 15–16
   structure of CV 21–4
   table of contents 24
   theme 17
   writing and structuring 19–21

'deletion' 15
Direcorate Business Manager 49
Doctors.net.uk 193
drunken colleague 138

eMedicus 194
emergency medicine, interview analysis 202–4
ethical questions 139–41
   see also specialty-specific interviews
examples, real 112
experiences, and their requirements 91
expertise, assessment 263
expertise assessment, failure to get job 263
eye contact 160

facts, presenting important facts 19
failure to get job 259–64
   behavioural assessment 263
   expertise assessment 263
   feedback 259–61
   reflection 261
   start again 262
feedback 259–61
first 90 days, new job 268
five-year plan 117
Fundamental Interpersonal Relations Orientation (FIRO-B) 248

gaps in CV 121–2
gaps in training 18
GMC Specialist Register 10

habits and tics 114
haematologist 220
head-hunting 172–3

Health Service Journal 193
histopathologist 220
humbleness, down-playing 98

induction
   corporate 270
   local 270
Insights Discovery Personality Profile 247
interview 95–6, 145–68
   accepting a job when you really want another one 167–8
   answer all questions 163
   anxiety 146, 148–53
   clarification 164
   difficult questions 163–4
   ensuring best chance of appointment 156–9
   feedback on responses 163
   first impression 158
   'Have you any other questions?' 165–6
   key points 158
   length and form 153–5
   locum consultant post 166–7
   new ways of interviewing 251–8
   pauses 164
   practical preparation 146–8
   specialty-specific 197–228
   see also presentations; specialty-specific interviews
interview candidates 169–74
   added value 117–18
   head-hunting 172–3
   internal candidates 99
      advice 170
      becoming an internal candidate 171–3
      must-dos and don'ts 171
      presence, and being an external candidate 10
interview panel 68–70, 155–8, 199
   angry or aggressive interviewer 161–2
   differing communication styles 63–5
   first impressions 71
   nervous interviewer 162–3
   pre-interview visit 70
   researching 69–70
   responding to each question 96–7
   role of individual panel members 156
   typical (Island) thoughts and feelings 74–5
   unprepared interviewer 162
   where do their questions come from? 96
   see also specialty-specific interviews
interview preparation and practice
   control of process 99
   conversation not a test 100

delivering answers 75–6
initial impressions 157–8
islander principles 57–63, 72–3
presentations 77–8, 229–42
purpose and definition xi-xii
self-awareness 65
understanding you and your interviewers 53–79
where do questions come from? 96
see also interview question practice; presentations
interview question practice 76–7, 95–100
 behavioural questions 125–6
 clinical governance 99, 135–6
 clinical questions 133
 clinical training and experience 115–16
 communication questions 131–2
 conflict resolution 130–1
 control of process 99
 dynamics 142–3
 ethical questions 139–40
 five-year plan 117
 key points 176
 leadership and management 129, 133–4
 meeting the needs of more than one interviewer 141–2
 negative questions 123–4
 opinion questions 128–9
 professional dilemmas 137–9
 research 124–5
 response to questions 73, 96–104
  2-minute rule 104
  3 three key points from each response 106–7
  interviewer concentration vs interviewee performance 105
  key rules for answering 100–2
  present tense 110
  use of "I" 109–10
 sources of questions 96
 structure and timing 102–4
  specific structures 107
 use of language 108–14
 use of video 95–6
interview questions 175–88
 about clinical governance 99, 135–6, 185–7
 about communication 180
 about CV 176–7
 about political/hot topics 187–8
 about post 178–9
 about research 186
 about self 177–8
 about teaching and training 180–1
 behavioural questions 179

clinical dilemmas and ethics 188
 general questions 181–2
 personality/skills 183–4
 professional dilemmas 182–3
 team player 184–5
Island of Intellect 58–9, 63, 68
Island of Opportunity 57–8, 62–3, 67, 71
Island of Team Spirit 58, 61–2, 67, 71
islander principles
 applying to interview situation 72–3
 presentations 78–9
 signs or behaviours 68, 71
 typical thoughts and feelings 75

job advertisements 10–11, 16–17
job applications 9–35
 top tips 27
job criteria, rheumatology 4
job description 17
 CV strategy 25–6

key rules
 2-minute rule 104
 answering/response to questions 100–2
 behaviour and motivation 66
 golden rules 66
 new consultant 268

language, use of 108–14
 active vs passive verbs 112
 adjectives 113
 adverbs 111
 body language 160
 conveying character strengths 118–19
 enthusiasm 113–14
 habits and tics 114
 listening 271
 numbers 112
 present tense 110
 smiling 114, 160
 speed and pitch of speech 113–14
 use of "I" 109–10
leadership and management 129, 133–4
locum consultant post 166–7
 registering interest in 172
locum positions 12–13

mantra 149
Medical Director 156
medicine/physician, interview analysis 204–7
mentor 274
'methodical' character strengths 119
motivation *see* behaviour and motivation
Myers—Briggs Type Indicator (MBTI) 244–5
 dichotomies 246

negative questions 123–4
neonatal medicine, interview analysis 214–17
networking 193–4
new consultant 265–75
  first 90 days 268
  induction
    corporate 270
    local 270
  key rules 268
  leave behind StR/SAS post 273
  mentor 274
  new purpose 269, 272
  resigning present StR/SAS post 266
  saying no 273
  start date 266
  taking a break 267
  team relationships 272–3
  work—life relationship 274–5
new purpose 269, 272
new ways of interviewing 251–8
  assessment centres 258
  competency-based 252–8
NHS
  DH website 194
  Jobs website (www.jobs.nhs.uk) 2, 11
  and political agenda 141–2
NHS Jobs application form 28–35
  communication skills 32
  formatting 31
  overcoming the presentation challenge 29–30
  saving as a Word document 28
  team working 32, 118
numbers 112

obstetrics/gynaecology, interview analysis 210–13
opinion questions 128–9

paediatric/neonatal medicine, interview analysis 214–17
Pareto Principle xii-xiii
pathology, interview analysis 217–20
patients, telling history 101
'people skills'
  behaviour and motivation 54–78
  disagreements 125–6
  humbleness, down-playing 98
  interview panel 68–70
  islander principles 68–79
  language, use of 108–14
  qualities and skills 89, 92–5
  self-awareness 65, 66

selling yourself 15–18
weaknesses 119–20
see also behaviour and motivation; language; qualities and skills; team working
personality/skills, interview questions 183–4
physician, interview analysis 204–7
political/hot topics, NHS 187–96
  how to/how not to prepare 195–6
  interview questions 187–8
  keeping up-to-date 193–4, 195
  political agenda 141–2
    importance 191–2
    time allocation 190
poorly performing colleague 138–9
positive questions 151
post, interview questions 178–9
PowerPoint, key tips 239
pre-interview visit 37–51, 70, 199–200
presentations in interviews 77–8, 229–42
  developing an effective presentation 232–40
    planning 232–5
    building 235–8
    delivery 238–40
  format 230
  influence on result of interview process 231
  islander principles 78–9
  key PowerPoint tips 239
  key topics 230–1
  notes 241
  opening 236
  structure 235–6
proactivity 92
  character strengths 119
  registering interest in locum consultant post 172
professional dilemmas 137–8, 182–3
  interview questions 182–3
psychiatry, interview analysis 207–9
psychometric testing 243–50

qualities and skills 89, 92–5
  character strengths/weaknesses 119–20
  courses attended 116
  examples/evidence 92
  key topic areas 94
  leadership and management 129, 133–4
  practising questions 95
  right person for the job 90
  use of video 95
  see also 'people skills'
questions see interview question practice

radiology, interview analysis 221–3
rapport 66, 77, 159, 160–1
referees 23, 33
registration 12
research
   interview question practice 124–5
   interview questions 186
resigning present StR/SAS post 266
revalidation 129, 196
Royal College Representative 156
   at interview 14
Royal College/Society websites 194
rules *see* key rules

self, interview questions 177–8
self-awareness 65, 66
   golden rules 66
   negative questions 123–4
selling yourself 15–18
   'how not to' and 'how to' 18
short-listing 34
signs or behaviours 68, 71
situational interviewing 252–8
skills *see* qualities and skills
smiling 114, 160
SPAs 181
Specialty Registrar (StR), last two years 2
specialty-specific interviews 197–228
   anaesthesia 198–202
   emergency medicine 202–4
   medicine/physician 204–7
   obstetrics/gynaecology 210–13
   paediatric/neonatal medicine 214–17
   pathology 217–20
   psychiatry 207–9
   radiology 221–3
   surgery 223–8
stakeholder mapping 49, 271
STAR (situation, task, actions, result) 127
   competency-based interviewing 256–8
start date, new job 266
strategic approach 1–8

Strength Deployment Inventory (SDI) 249–50
strengths and weaknesses 118–20
success 265–70
   offer of job 264
surgery, interview analysis 223–8

teaching 129
teaching experience 18
teaching and training, interview questions 180–1
team working
   character strengths 118–19
   the good team player 98, 118
   interview questions 184–5
   NHS Jobs application form 32
   see also 'people skills'
think, feel, do 72, 100, 233
Thomas—Kilmann Conflict Mode Instrument 248–9
thoughts and feelings 75

University Representative 156

verbs, active vs passive 112
virologist, interview analysis 220
visualization 150–1, 152–3

weaknesses 119–20
websites
   BMJ 193
   BMJCareers website 11–12
   DH 194
   Doctors.net.uk 193
   eMedicus.co.uk 194
   Jobs website (jobs.nhs.uk) 2, 11
   NHS Choices website 191
   Royal College/Society 194
Wheel of Life 6–7, 35
Word, formatting, and application form 20, 30

Lightning Source UK Ltd.
Milton Keynes UK
UKHW020047220421
382417UK00001B/2